A foremost authority on the history of religion and of esoteric practice, especially in eastern England, **Francis Young** gained a PhD in history from the University of Cambridge and is a Fellow of the Royal Historical Society. He is the author and editor of several previous books. These include *English Catholics and the Supernatural, 1553–1829* (2013), *The Gages of Hengrave and Suffolk Catholicism, 1640–1767* (2015), *The Abbey of Bury St Edmunds: History, Legacy and Discovery* (2016), *Catholic East Anglia: A History of the Catholic Faith in Norfolk, Suffolk, Cambridgeshire and Peterborough* (2016), *A History of Exorcism in Catholic Christianity* (2016), *Magic as a Political Crime in Medieval and Early Modern England* (I.B.Tauris, 2017) and *Edmund: In Search of England's Lost King* (I.B.Tauris, 2018). He broadcasts regularly for the BBC on historical and religious topics.

'Francis Young lucidly shows how the rich and varied theologies, liturgies and practices of the Church of England are reflected in the history of its complex attitudes to exorcism: from endorsement of the demonic to marginalisation to outright rejection as either Catholic superstition or evangelical surfeit. The author further demonstrates how the waxing and waning – and now contemporary resurgence – of demonic possession and exorcism within Anglicanism must be read not only against internal tensions between the Church's conservative and liberal wings, but also against a wider history of the esoteric, spiritualist and occult traditions of modern spirituality, on the one hand, and religious engagement with secular and scientific scepticism, on the other hand. Dr Young has written a fine contribution to the general study of exorcism while offering, too, the first complete history of the subject within the Anglican tradition. He has also issued a salutary and a sobering reminder of the enduring power of traditional demonology within an apparently secularised society. A fascinating book.'

– Philip C. Almond, Emeritus Professor of Religion,
University of Queensland, author of
*England's First Demonologist: Reginald Scot and
'The Discoverie of Witchcraft'* (I.B.Tauris, 2014)

A HISTORY OF ANGLICAN EXORCISM

Deliverance and Demonology in Church Ritual

Francis Young

LONDON · NEW YORK · OXFORD · NEW DELHI · SYDNEY

T&T CLARK
Bloomsbury Publishing Plc
50 Bedford Square, London, WC1B 3DP, UK
1385 Broadway, New York, NY 10018, USA

BLOOMSBURY, T&T CLARK and the T&T Clark logo
are trademarks of Bloomsbury Publishing Plc

First published in Great Britain in 2018 but I.B. Tauris & Co. Ltd.
Paperback edition first published by T&T Clark in 2020

A catalogue record for this book is available from the British Library.

A catalog record for this book is available from the Library of Congress.

ISBN: HB: 978-1-7883-1347-6
PB: 978-0-5676-9293-1
ePDF: 978-1-8386-0793-7
ePub: 978-1-8386-0792-0

Typeset by OKS Prepress Services, Chennai, India

To find out more about our authors and books visit
www.bloomsbury.com and sign up for our newsletters.

For Talitha

Contents

Preface

Exorcism, or 'deliverance ministry' (as the contemporary Church of England prefers to call it) is a significant element of the modern Church of England's pastoral provision for the nation under its care. Most dioceses have a specially trained team, appointed by the bishop, to advise on alleged paranormal phenomena and, if necessary, to exorcise a place or person. Many people in an increasingly secular contemporary Britain, including elements of the media, tend to regard exorcism as an eccentric (and perhaps harmful) hangover of 'medieval' Christianity. Ironically, however, the widespread and officially authorised practice of exorcism is a novelty in England's established church, dating back only to the 1970s. The revival of exorcism in late twentieth-century British Anglicanism contrasts with the strongly 'sceptical' stance towards alleged occult phenomena widely adopted in the established church for over 300 years. This book seeks to explain the Church of England's curious reversal of attitude with regard to the practice of exorcism, setting it in the context of the entire history of exorcism in the Church of England since the beginning of the English Reformation in the sixteenth century.

This book emerged from the process of writing *A History of Exorcism in Catholic Christianity* (2016), which was the first comprehensive history of the rite of exorcism in English, albeit confined to Roman Catholicism. During the course of my research for that book I encountered a number of interesting Anglican sources that I was forced to set aside owing to my exclusive focus on Roman Catholicism. However, since the religious history of England has always been the primary focus of my research, I intended to return to these sources later in order to do justice to the history of Anglican exorcism in a separate study dedicated to that subject. The same methodology I adopted in *A History of Exorcism in Catholic Christianity*, whose focus was on the clerical exorcists, on the liturgical development of the rite of exorcism, and on the canonical processes by which exorcism has been authorised, is applied here to the Church of England's historic and present practice of exorcism. Similarly, the earlier study's focus on sceptical responses to exorcism is continued here. However, this study differs in one important way from the earlier book by being confined (with a few exceptions) to England. This book is primarily a history of exorcism in the Church of England rather than in global Anglicanism.

I have incurred many debts of gratitude in the writing of this book. I am indebted to the staff of Lambeth Palace Library and the Manuscripts and Rare Books rooms of Cambridge University for their help and support. My wife Rachel and daughter Abigail have incurred my deepest gratitude by being my greatest supporters and wisest counsellors. I am especially grateful to Dr Jack Wheeler and Hayley Stevens for reading portions of the book and generously offering their expert advice, and to Deborah Aldridge for kindly proofreading the text. I thank Alex Wright of I.B.Tauris for being unfailingly supportive of this project and of all my research.

All dates in the text take the year to begin on 1 January, but no attempt has been made to convert dates occurring before 14 September 1752 to the Gregorian Calendar. Quotations from original sources retain their original spelling, and naturally I take responsibility for any errors in the text.

Chronology of Key Events

1922   Gilbert Shaw and Max Petitpierre perform exorcisms of places at Eynsham, Oxfordshire

1923   Students including Petitpierre exorcise a ghost at Magdalene College, Oxford

1926   Shaw and Petitpierre perform exorcisms of places at Burgh-le-Marsh, Lincolnshire

1943   Shaw and Petitpierre exorcise a woman in a Soho basement

1947   Shaw begins touring the country, lecturing clergy on exorcism

1952   Shaw and Petitpierre begin advising the Church of England's subcommittee on demonology

1953   Shaw advises Lambeth Palace on demonological matters

1956   Donald Omand begins his ministry as an exorcist in the diocese of Portsmouth

1958   Exorcism is mentioned for the first time in a report of the Church of England on healing

1960   The Convocations of Canterbury and York request greater episcopal oversight of exorcism

1962   Beginning of the charismatic revival in the Church of England

1964   The bishop of Exeter convenes a committee to prepare a report on exorcism

1969   Canon 72 abolished

1971   John Richards begins lecturing on exorcism at Queen's College, Birmingham

1972   Publication of the Exeter Report, which recommends the appointment of an exorcist for every diocese; Christian Exorcism Study Group (CESG) established

1974   Michael Taylor murders his wife following an exorcism by an Anglican priest

1975   Trevor Dearing begins a televised campaign of mass exorcism at Hainault, Essex; Geoffrey Lampe and Don Cupitt organise a campaign against exorcism in the Church of England; the House of Bishops issues guidelines on exorcism

1980   *The Alternative Service Book* reintroduces a form of pre-baptismal exorcism

Introduction

The practice of exorcism – understood as an attempt to cast out demons from a person by imperative command – is probably more widespread in contemporary England than at any other time in history. The Church of England is by no means the main provider of these exorcisms (most of which take place in independent churches), but every one of the 42 dioceses of the Church of England designates at least one member of the clergy to advise on exorcism. England's established church regulates the practice of exorcism at both a national and diocesan level, and 'deliverance ministry' (which may include exorcism) is accessible (at least in theory) to any parishioner. Yet the Church of England's practice of exorcism is an historical puzzle, because it virtually sprang into existence in the 1970s in a church that had spent centuries condemning exorcism as Catholic superstition or evangelical excess. This book tells the story of the Church of England's approach to exorcism since the Reformation in the sixteenth century, and aims to explain how and why such a remarkable transformation in the church's attitude to the rite of exorcism occurred in the twentieth century.

This study approaches exorcism from the perspective of church history as an ecclesiastical process, concentrating on exorcists and on the theological, canonical and liturgical development of their practices. It is not a history of demonic possession or of demoniacs, the people supposed to be under demonic influence. The history of possession and possession-phenomena is the proper realm of social history and the history of medicine (in particular, the history of psychiatry), rather than church history. Although manifestations of possession-phenomena vary to some extent across cultures, it would make no sense to study possession-phenomena as manifested in response to the exorcisms of a particular church, which is why most studies of these phenomena either range widely across denominations and religions or concentrate on specific local or national case studies. The process of exorcism, by contrast, is distinctive to each Christian denomination that practises it, and is embedded in a particular way in each church's ecclesiastical structures. The history of Christian exorcism, therefore – as opposed to the history of the phenomenon of possession – is first and foremost a subject for the church historian.

EXORCISM AND DEMONOLOGY

The English words 'exorcise' and 'exorcism' derive from the Latin word *exorcizo*, which was in turn borrowed from the Greek *exorkizō*. The Greek word's origins can be found in legal language; *exorkizō* literally meant 'to swear an oath', a *horkos*.[1] Swearing an oath in ancient Greece meant, by definition, invoking a deity to punish the oath-taker if he or she failed to keep the oath, and it is this meaning of 'exorcise' – the invocation of a deity by powerful oaths to perform a specific task – that lies at the root of the term's religious usage in Christianity. The Gospels portray Jesus casting out evil spirits by his own divine authority, meaning that these divine dispossessions were not exorcisms in the strict sense of the term (Jesus did not need to invoke himself). On the other hand, Jesus' disciples cast out demons by invoking the name of Jesus, and Luke reports that exorcisms in the name of Jesus were effective even when performed by non-disciples (Luke 9:49–50). The early Christians certainly did not invent exorcism, which was widely practised in the ancient Near East from the beginning of the historical record, but they made the distinctive claim that the name of Jesus was more powerful and effective for casting out demons than the name of any other deity. Early Christian exorcism took the form of an imperative command, such as the words spoken by Paul to a female slave in Acts 16:18: 'I command you in the name of Jesus Christ to come out of her'.[2]

Between the first and third centuries exorcism remained an entirely 'charismatic' practice, something done by those who believed they were the recipients of a particular gift from God. However, by the beginning of the third century some Christian churches, including the church of Rome, began to incorporate liturgical exorcisms into the rites of baptism.[3] The inclusion of exorcism in the liturgy meant that defined formulas of exorcism and individuals appointed to this specific task were required. Liturgical formulas of pre-baptismal exorcism became increasingly elaborate, and formulas for the exorcism of demoniacs (usually known at this time as energumens) mirrored the older baptismal exorcisms.[4] By the middle of the tenth century, fairly standard liturgies of exorcism for catechumens (candidates for baptism) and energumens had found their way into the Roman Pontifical, although significant local variations still remained.[5] These local variations in the practice of exorcism were so significant that in some territories the liturgical exorcism of demoniacs by imperative adjuration (commanding a spirit to depart) barely took place at all. In medieval England, for example, people generally pinned their hopes of dispossession on the shrines and relics of specific saints rather than on the clergy.[6]

During the course of the Middle Ages a number of other exorcistic practices grew up which differed from the original 'charismatic' form of exorcism and its role in baptism. These included the 'exorcism' of material substances such as water, oil and salt prior to blessing. The exorcised materials might then be used as an apotropaic protection against evil or even for a form of 'remote exorcism', drawing on the spiritual virtue of the original exorcism pronounced over the water, oil or salt. Just as the term 'exorcism' came to be applied to a rite performed on non-living substances, so it was also applied to the banishment of the ghosts of the dead from particular places. Clearly, neither the 'exorcism' of substances nor the 'exorcism' of ghosts is exorcism in the original biblical sense of a command to a spirit to leave a human person in the name of Jesus. However, since these activities were referred to as 'exorcism' at the time (as well as today), they must fall within the scope of any book on exorcism, although this study's primary focus remains the exorcism of living human beings.

The Reformation brought further complications, with many Protestants rejecting the idea that any spiritual being other than God should be addressed directly. The refusal of many Protestants to address demons or the devil followed logically from their rejection of direct addresses to the angels and saints in the form of prayers. Although some Protestants stopped exorcising in any way, others continued to do so, but 'reformed' their exorcisms. This meant turning the old imperative exorcisms into 'deprecative' prayers addressed only to God, asking him to release a person from the oppression of evil spirits. Protestants began to speak of 'dispossession' rather than 'exorcism', with its negative connotations of Roman Catholic ritualism. However, since the intention of a Protestant 'dispossession' was broadly the same as that of an exorcism, and the omission of imperative adjurations was a means of continuing to meet popular demand without compromising Protestant principles, it seems unreasonable to exclude activities of this nature from the broader category of exorcism. This in turn raises the question of whether an exorcism is defined primarily by its form (a command to a spirit) or by its function (the dispossession of a person).

Defining exorcism by its form is well nigh impossible, given the historic variety of the practice. Christian exorcism is and always has been a practice with a strong charismatic element to it, its form largely determined by the exorcist in any given instance. On the other hand, defining exorcism by its function raises the question of what actually happens in an exorcism. If exorcism is defined as whatever words and actions free a person from the influence of evil spirits, this seems to presume the reality of such spirits and the possibility that they might take control of a person. Beginning with Jean-Martin Charcot in the nineteenth century, many historians have developed alternative interpretations and explanations of 'demoniac' behaviour, ranging from the sociological and psychopathological to the 'communicative performative'.[7] However, other historians are critical of such attempts. Historians cannot accept exorcists' claims about the existence and activity of demons, because historians cannot and should not act as demonologists. On the other hand, however, the 'historical diagnosis' of demoniacs is all too often a dead end of historical reductivism, resulting in historians imposing 'pet theories' on the evidence that are all too easily challenged and discredited.

Possession behaviours are a complex cultural phenomenon, apparently universal to almost every human culture, and not fully understood. It is not necessary for the historian – especially in a book whose focus is the process of exorcism rather than possession itself – to speculate on the causes or 'reality' of such behaviours. What matters is that in most past societies (and in many present ones) people have *believed* in demonic possession, and such belief has informed their reactions to it. This book therefore speaks of demoniacs and possession *as if* real, simply because they were perceived as real by exorcists. This is not intended in any way to imply belief on the part of the author that any supernatural phenomena actually occurred; rather, it is intended to allow the book to be an unobstructed narrative of beliefs and behaviours without speculating on the psychological or spiritual 'realities' that may or may not lie behind them.

It is important to note that demonologists distinguish between a number of forms of demonic activity of which full-blown demonic possession is just one.[8] Exorcism is the church's traditional response to all of these phenomena, so to define exorcism solely as deliverance from possession is too limiting. Indeed, a complete definition of exorcism as practised today in any Christian church is frustratingly elusive. The term encompasses both imperative adjuration and deprecative prayer, both liturgical and charismatic practice, both direct interpersonal ministry and the indirect application of exorcised substances or objects, as well as rites designed to deliver people from everything from full-blown possession to mere 'infestation' (the presence of demonic phenomena in a place). The difficulty of adequately defining exorcism is one reason why many practitioners now prefer the term 'deliverance ministry', or even just 'spiritual warfare'. This book proceeds on the basis that any ritual act – such as adjuration, anointing, prayer and even Christian preaching – done with the direct intention of delivering someone from demonic influence is liable to be described as exorcism. In this way, the historic diversity of 'exorcism' within the Church of England is acknowledged.

A particular view of demonology, the branch of theology dedicated to the study of demons and their manifestation in the world, underpins every exorcism, whether the exorcist acknowledges this or not. Demonology is not the same as exorcism itself (it is possible to be committed to demonological beliefs without advocating the practice of exorcism), but 'practical demonology' may be defined as specific advice and guidance for the practice of exorcism. Most practical demonologists (but not all) have also been exorcists, and it is arguably impossible to be a practising exorcist without being a practical demonologist. Demonology is important to the history of exorcism because exorcists will behave differently depending on what they think they are dealing with in a particular instance. For example, in the sixteenth, seventeenth, eighteenth and nineteenth centuries many possessions in England were attributed to witchcraft, with the concept of possession becoming almost completely conflated with the concept of bewitchment by the seventeenth century. Likewise, whereas medieval exorcists thought they were exorcising the souls of the dead when they exorcised a place, after the Reformation 'ghosts' were often interpreted (especially by Protestants) as demons rather than disembodied souls. An exorcist who believes demons have physical properties is more likely to use violence towards a demoniac, while an exorcist who believes demons can be inherited across the generations may be especially prone to exorcising children. Even when they do not explicitly articulate their demonological preconceptions, exorcists often reveal them in their practice.

The historical literature on possession and exorcism is very extensive, although some periods (such as the early modern era, roughly between 1500 and 1700) are much better represented than others. Furthermore, most historians have tended to focus on possession phenomena rather than the development of the rite of exorcism.[9] Historians typically concentrate on a case study or series of case studies, or on exorcism in a particular country in a particular period. Some historians of early modern Britain have chosen to study beliefs in possession and exorcism from a denominational perspective, such as David Hempton and Owen Davies's studies of Methodism, Peter Elmer's work on Quakerism and my own research on English Roman Catholicism.[10] Hitherto missing has been any study of the Church of England's distinctive tradition of exorcism, perhaps because historians have been tempted to assume that the practice disappeared in the established church after 1604, or that it had only ever been an eccentricity of the 'puritan wing' of the church. It is an aim of this book to challenge the stereotype of exorcism as an exclusively 'puritan' preoccupation in the sixteenth- and seventeenth-century Church of England.

THE CHURCH OF ENGLAND

The adjective 'Anglican' used in the title of this book is not, strictly speaking, entirely interchangeable with 'Church of England', because the term 'Anglican church' can refer to other global churches whose theological and institutional roots lie in the Church of England (the churches of the Anglican Communion). The term 'Church of England' refers primarily to the church established by statute in 1559 which still exists today (apart from a period of suppression under Parliament and the Commonwealth between 1646 and 1660). A history of 'Anglican exorcism' in its widest sense would have to cover the practice of exorcism in every church worldwide that describes itself as Anglican – a very challenging task, since every province of the Anglican communion has its own rules governing exorcism. Although this study touches occasionally on the practice of exorcism by Anglicans outside England, it is primarily concerned with British exorcisms.

Use of the terms 'Anglican' and 'Anglicanism' when writing the history of any period before the middle of the nineteenth century is problematic, since the terms were not used by earlier adherents of the post-Reformation Church of England to describe themselves. 'Anglican*ism*' is an especially problematic word because it seems to ascribe a distinctive and unified ideology and theology to the established church. No such unity even remotely existed in the period 1559–1646 when the Church of England was racked by divisions between puritans and anti-puritans. This book does not seek to identify a distinctive 'Anglican' theology of exorcism, recognising instead that different exorcists at different periods have operated within very different theological frameworks. Rather, the book is concerned with any exorcisms (understood in the broad terms outlined above) performed by clergy of the established church (whether or not those clergy were acting with the approval of their bishops). In the sixteenth century many puritan-minded clergy were engaged in a ministry of exorcism without the knowledge or approval of their diocesan, but this does not make their activities any less a part of the history of exorcism in the Church of England.

Some laypeople who were adherents of the Church of England (in the sense that they attended services in their parish church) also performed exorcisms, most notably the cunning-folk who were the first port of call for many people who believed themselves to be possessed or bewitched in the seventeenth and eighteenth centuries. However, cunning-folk largely perpetuated a 'sub-Catholic' form of exorcism grounded in 'folk religion' strongly condemned by the clergy. Associating these practices with the established church is problematic, since they took place despite rather than because of the Church of England. Unlike the practices of the clergy, lay practices did not influence or inform the church's official thinking on exorcism and so they are not a focus of this book. By contrast, the practices of the clergy, even when not authorised by bishops, reveal how those clergy understood their role in the community and therefore something about the Church of England.

This book includes discussion of exorcism as practised by the Nonjurors and Methodists, groups closely related to and derived from the institutional Church of England. The Nonjurors were clergy of the Church of England who refused to take oaths to William and Mary in 1689 (and later George I in 1714) and therefore ministered outside of the church's institutions, but still considered themselves to be members of the Church of England even if the official church regarded them as schismatics. The term 'Methodist' was used from the 1730s onwards for a movement of devout evangelicals within the Church of England that gradually evolved into an entirely separate church over several decades. The history of Methodist exorcisms before the two churches went their separate ways is as much part of the history of the Church of England as of the Methodist Church. The Nonjurors and Methodists cannot be omitted from a history of

Anglican exorcism because their approaches strongly influenced later Anglo-Catholic and evangelical theologies. Similarly, this book considers the exorcistic practice of contemporary charismatic evangelical Anglicans, whose practice is still part of the history of the Church of England even if their methods and demonology are largely inspired by other Christian denominations.

THE CHURCH OF ENGLAND AND EXORCISM

This book is the first to be devoted to the history of exorcism in the Church of England, which has been little studied apart from one brief period: the Elizabethan crisis of exorcism of the 1580s and 1590s. The controversial literature produced during this period, when the Church of England was divided on the subject of exorcism, has been studied extensively by Frank Brownlow, Philip Almond, Marion Gibson, Thomas Freeman, Andrew Cambers, Marcus Harmes and others.[11] The evidence has attracted the attention of historians of witchcraft and of medicine as well as scholars interested in the development of the Elizabethan church. However, the scholarship on the period after 1604, when a canon prohibited exorcism without an episcopal licence, is very meagre indeed, and there are no studies of exorcism in the Church of England in the seventeenth and eighteenth centuries. This is perhaps because an assumption has long prevailed among historians of early modern England that the clergy of the established church were all opposed to exorcism, and that no exorcisms of any kind took place during this period. However, scholars of witchcraft such as Owen Davies and Jonathan Barry have shown that the clergy were involved in 'unbewitching', exorcism of ghosts and even the occasional exorcism of demoniacs during this period,[12] something that has been largely overlooked by church historians. Similarly, Thomas Waters has uncovered evidence of the clergy's involvement in unbewitching in the nineteenth century.[13]

The history of the development of the Church of England's current attitudes towards exorcism is to be found as much in the development of its broader demonology as in actual instances of exorcism, which were exceptionally few and far between until the

1920s. Studies by Janet Oppenheim and Georgina Byrne have traced the evolution of the Church of England's response to Spiritualism,[14] which would have such a profound effect on the church's attitudes to demonology and, thereafter, exorcism. The Anglican exorcists of the twentieth century remain largely unexplored by historians, with the exception of an informative biography of Gilbert Shaw by R. D. Hacking,[15] a brief treatment of prominent Anglican exorcists in a broader study of exorcism by J. M. Collins,[16] and a detailed study of the development of Anglican charismatic approaches to 'spiritual warfare' (including deliverance ministry) by Graham Smith.[17] However, a rich published primary literature exists written by the exorcists themselves, and important unpublished primary sources are accessible in a number of archives. Newspapers and magazines are likewise useful sources for attitudes to exorcism both inside and outside the church. Furthermore, the historical material on exorcism is complemented by a small number of studies of Anglican clergy conducted by sociologists of religion and psychologists.[18]

The Church of England's approach to exorcism is shaped by a number of factors, only one of which is confident belief in an unseen world of malevolent spirits. Although some Anglican exorcists are completely committed to the traditional belief that evil spirits take possession of people's bodies, there is a wide and colourful range of demonological views among exorcists, with some believing someone can be literally possessed by Satan himself, others arguing that only lesser demons can possess a person, and still others choosing to speak more generally of a 'spirit of evil' dominating rather than literally possessing a person. Others may be entirely agnostic about the possibility of possession, and even the existence of a personal devil, yet believe the rite of exorcism has psychological benefits. Furthermore, exorcists may be as much interested in paranormal phenomena as in demonology. This may include the belief that exorcists can clear 'haunted houses' of 'place-memories' by means of prayer or by celebrating the eucharist. Characteristically, exorcists who believe in paranormal phenomena often believe they possess psychic abilities, and many (perhaps most) contemporary exorcists in the Church of England do not regard the paranormal as demonic or evil per se.

Some exorcists may be motivated not primarily by an interest in demonology or the paranormal but by pastoral concern for people who are suffering as a result of the belief they are under a malign spiritual influence. Exorcism, on this reading, is a spiritual 'therapy' that is a response to popular demand, and many clergy seem to believe they can provide reassurance for people distressed by their own perception of events while maintaining an open mind regarding the objectivity or reality of supposedly demonic phenomena. Some clergy may opt to use simple prayers rather than full-blown imperative exorcisms, or they may use an ambiguous form of words that leaves it open to interpretation whether a genuine demonic personality is involved.

The contemporary Church of England emphasises the healing dimension of exorcism, portraying it as just one form of healing among many bequeathed to the church by Jesus Christ. Some exorcists may advocate the use of other forms of healing prayer before exorcism is attempted. The practice of exorcism as a form of healing is also characteristic of charismatic evangelical practice, and in this tradition it may even extend to attempts to exorcise physical illnesses from the body of a sufferer. Furthermore, the evangelistic potential of exorcism should not be overlooked as a reason why the church continues to practise it. Although the public exorcisms of the sixteenth century are unthinkable in today's church, exorcism continues to be one of the few services offered by the church that seems to be in equal demand from Christians and non-Christians alike. Today, clergy are more likely to see exorcism as an opportunity to demonstrate the church's loving concern rather than its power, but the possibility remains that a 'successful' exorcism might draw someone into active membership of the church.

Finally, the continued existence of exorcism within the Church of England can be attributed partly to a kind of liturgical antiquarianism that values ancient Christian rites for their own sake. There is no evidence that the eighteenth-century Nonjurors who revived rites of exorcism ever used them on demoniacs. Indeed, they do not seem to have worried about demoniacs at all, and their revival of the rites was simply an effort to imitate the early church. Similar motives and concerns seem to have brought about the revival of a form of baptismal exorcism in the *Alternative Service Book* (1980), perpetuated in *Common Worship* (2000). Furthermore, the insistence of some contemporary exorcists that exorcism is still a possible ministry, even if there are virtually no circumstances in which it might be justified, reflects a desire for 'theological authenticity' by advocating the continued existence of rites of exorcism even if exorcism is never practised. Many clergy may support exorcism not because they worry about demons but because they are reluctant to be perceived as theologically liberal or 'inauthentic'.

RESEARCHING EXORCISM

The historian researching the Church of England's attitudes to exorcism between the sixteenth and nineteenth centuries is reliant on primary printed sources such as books and newspapers as well as manuscript sources such as letters in ecclesiastical archives. In this respect, the study of exorcism in this period is much like the study of any aspect of church life, with the difference that sources relating to exorcism are especially sparse. When it comes to the twentieth century, however, the historian encounters the challenge that the Church of England's records of exorcisms are confidential and kept in sealed diocesan archives. It is therefore necessary to rely on the published or unpublished testimony of exorcists themselves, which severely limits the possibility of hearing the voices of those exorcised and their interpretations of what took place. That possibility is also limited by ethical concerns; in the course of my research I encountered a few documents from the 1970s describing exorcisms of persons who may still be alive. I considered that it would be unethical to incorporate these accounts into the book, even with names changed or omitted. Although these documents are technically in the public domain because they exist in a public archive, it would be my decision to publicise them – in contrast to accounts of exorcisms in existing published works, which I consider to be open to historical analysis since another author made them public.

This book is dependent entirely on written sources, whether published or in public archives. As such, it is intended to serve as an introduction to the history of exorcism in the Church of England rather than a comprehensive study of the subject. There are many more archives to be explored, and much scope for further studies by both historians and anthropologists of religion that draw on interviews with both exorcists and people who have been exorcised. Such studies will allow the 'official' views on exorcism espoused by documents of the Church of England to be compared with exorcism as experienced by practitioners and 'clients' (as the contemporary Church of England calls people who are exorcised), as well as giving a chance to finally hear the voices of those 'clients', whose stories are usually told exclusively by exorcists. Furthermore, some people who were involved in the Church of England's transformation into a provider of exorcism in the 1970s are still alive at the time of writing. However, it is important to note that the Church of England's rules of confidentiality mean that exorcists are not supposed to reveal the details of specific cases (even when names are changed or omitted), and can therefore speak about their practice of exorcism only in general terms (although some exorcists do not seem to adhere to this recommended best practice in their published works).

STRUCTURE OF THE BOOK

The book follows a chronological approach, beginning in the sixteenth century. Chapter 1 will explain how the Protestant Reformation introduced clerical exorcism of demoniacs to England (something absent from medieval England) and traces contrasting episcopal attitudes towards exorcism. Bishops were always divided on the practice, with Archbishop Matthew Parker opposing exorcisms from the early 1570s but other bishops authorising them as late as the early 1600s. The chapter describes the development of dispossession by prayer and fasting as a 'reformed' style of exorcism among the clergy of the established church, arguing that exorcism cannot be characterised purely as a sectarian practice of 'puritans' within the Tudor Church of England. Finally, the chapter addresses Bishop Richard Bancroft's determined campaign against exorcism in the 1590s and 1600s which established a new anti-exorcistic orthodoxy at senior levels of the church.

Chapter 2 gives an account of the enactment and consequences of Canon 72 in 1604, which forbade any exorcism without a specific licence from a bishop. There is no evidence that any such licence was ever granted by any English bishop, but the existence of the Canon implicitly legitimised exorcism as theoretically possible. This ensured that cessationism (the view that the gift of miracles – including exorcism – ceased on the death of the last apostle) never completely dominated the theology of the Church of England, and the chapter unearths evidence for sporadic unauthorised exorcisms performed by clergy of the established church in the seventeenth and eighteenth centuries. Furthermore, Nonjurors who refused to take the Oath of Allegiance to William and Mary created their own liturgies in which they revived forms of exorcism, while Methodists enthusiastically embraced the practice of exorcism in the years before their secession from the Church of England.

Chapter 3 takes the arrival of Spiritualism in England in 1852 as a watershed in the Church of England's attitude to demonology. The anti-Spiritualist movement within the church revived the use of demonological language, and the widespread belief that Spiritualists really were in contact with a spirit world began to undermine the clergy's traditional scepticism. As early as 1877 the archbishop of Canterbury authorised an exorcism in Barbados, although it was not until the early 1920s that an Anglican priest in England, Gilbert Shaw, began experimenting with exorcisms of places. During the 1930s a number of priests became interested in the possibility of exorcising haunted houses, but exorcism of persons remained unknown.

Chapter 4 charts the careers of the prominent Anglican exorcists of the twentieth century, most notably Gilbert Shaw, who was the first Anglican priest in England to exorcise a person in modern times (in 1943). After World War II Shaw began a campaign to educate clergy about exorcism and was recognised by the church as an authority on the subject. Shaw was largely responsible for the section on exorcism in a report on healing produced by the church in 1958, and acted as an advisor to the archbishop of Canterbury on paranormal matters throughout the 1950s. Shaw's protégé Max (Robert) Petitpierre continued his work, editing a report prepared for the bishop of Exeter in 1972 (the Exeter Report) which set the pattern for the future development of deliverance ministry in the Church of England, since it advocated control of exorcism at the diocesan level and the appointment of diocesan exorcists.

Chapter 5 begins with the momentous year 1975, when the position of exorcism in the Church of England was thrown into doubt by the media storm surrounding the Ossett murder case, in which a man returned from a late night exorcism to brutally murder his wife. A leading Anglican theologian, Geoffrey Lampe, mounted a determined campaign to persuade the bishops to outlaw the practice of exorcism in the church, and received much support. However, the archbishop of Canterbury, Donald Coggan, decided that exorcism should be controlled at the diocesan level and issued very brief guidance on exorcism in General Synod in July 1975. That guidance remains in place today, and Coggan's decision legitimated and normalised exorcism as part of the church's pastoral practice, resulting in the implementation of most of the recommendations of the Exeter Report. In the 1980s, the Church of England adopted the euphemism 'deliverance ministry' to refer to exorcism, but the rise of charismatic evangelical Anglicanism ensured that enthusiasm for adjuring demons remained undimmed.

The book's final chapter examines the development of the Church of England's stance on exorcism since the turn of the millennium, which has largely involved the publication of more detailed guidance aimed at ensuring deliverance ministry complies with other church policies, such as child protection and safeguarding. However, the chapter argues that the church's failure to debate exorcism openly has created a situation in which the practice of exorcism is entrusted to clergy in each diocese who often operate in a closed and self-sustaining worldview where scepticism about paranormal phenomena has little role to play. The chapter explains the current canonical and liturgical status of exorcism and assesses the extent to which an established 'tradition' of exorcism can be said to exist within the Church of England, as well as providing a critique of the extent to which the practice of exorcism is compatible with the church's commitment to safeguarding.

The contemporary Church of England advocates a close working relationship with psychiatrists and other medical professionals where deliverance ministry is concerned, yet many exorcists seem to operate in a 'historical vacuum', unaware of the history of their own ministry. History is replete with examples of how exorcism can go wrong and the pitfalls of reinforcing belief in demonic possession. Furthermore, there is now an extensive academic literature interpreting cases of possession and exorcism from the perspectives of social history, the history of medicine and gender studies. Contemporary exorcists need to be aware of this history and historiography, as this knowledge might cause them to re-evaluate their practice. Exorcism in its present form has not always existed in the Church of England, and contemporary exorcists ought to be aware of its origins. Whether the historical evidence should lead the Church of England to change its approach to exorcism – or even abandon the practice altogether – is for the church to debate and decide and not for the historian to judge. However, this book is intended as an honest assessment of the 'tradition' of exorcism in the Church of England and the process by which exorcism has become an accepted form of ministry.

CHAPTER 1

The Church of England and the Reformation of Exorcism, 1549–1603

The sixteenth-century Church of England enjoyed a paradoxical relationship with exorcism of the demonically possessed. England had no medieval tradition of clerical exorcism, which was introduced for the first time by ministers of the Elizabethan established church in the 1560s. By the 1590s, however, most bishops had turned decisively against the practice of dispossession by prayer and fasting. Bishops made strenuous efforts to suppress godly exorcists such as John Darrell and the controversy over exorcism became intense in the last five years of the reign of Elizabeth I (1598–1603). The controversy resulted in the enactment of Canon 72 by the Convocation of Canterbury in 1604, which prohibited any dispossession by prayer and fasting without a licence from the bishop. Although the Canon did not entirely end the practice of exorcism (as will be shown in Chapter 2), it ensured that an anti-exorcistic tradition would dominate the Church of England until the twentieth century.

Thomas Freeman, in his influential study of the Protestant exorcist John Darrell, has argued that the bishops suppressed exorcism 'because it magnified those aspects of puritan worship which the ecclesiastical authorities most feared – its anti-hierarchical tendencies, its strong sense of communal solidarity and its potential as a vehicle for protest'.[1] Keith Thomas claimed that most demoniacs belonged (or had belonged) to the 'godly' minority,[2] and historians usually describe those Elizabethan clergy who performed exorcisms as puritans, or even 'presbyterians'.[3] Without denying that exorcism mattered to puritans, this chapter challenges the labelling of all Protestant exorcisms in England as puritan per se, since this overlooks the fact that some exorcisms were episcopally authorised. Furthermore, exorcisms often involved whole communities and included people of a variety of theological hues.[4] It is important to avoid the circular error of defining exorcists as puritans because exorcism by prayer and fasting was a puritan practice.

Exorcism cannot be written off as a sectarian activity of a puritan 'church within a church' inside the Church of England, since the practice enjoyed the support and toleration of senior clergy in the 1560s and 1570s, and sometimes even later. 'Puritanism' was not a Christian denomination in the modern sense; indeed, it was not even a coherent movement with a single agreed-upon theology within the Tudor church.[5] Not all Protestant exorcists were puritans, and very many puritans opposed exorcism. It is equally misguided to see Richard Bancroft, Samuel Harsnett and their supporters as an 'Anglican party'[6] of sceptics whose views foreshadowed the Enlightenment scepticism that dominated the eighteenth-century Church of England.[7] History must not be read backwards, and if the likes of Bancroft and Harsnett were disbelievers in possession and exorcism it was for religious and political (rather than 'scientific' or 'rational') reasons.

Bishops such as Bancroft defined exorcists and demoniacs as theological deviants, but this does not necessarily mean that exorcism lay outside the mainstream of Elizabethan conformist Protestantism, or that exorcists themselves thought their ministry was subversive. Marcus Harmes's characterisation of exorcisms as 'sites of religious contestation between different religious factions vying for power' is not altogether helpful.[8] It is not possible to identify all exorcists and participants in exorcisms as members of a definable 'faction', and there is little evidence to suggest that exorcists acted with political motives or wished to seize power from bishops. Rather, in many cases the exorcists simply desired a space within which to continue their ministry.

The place of exorcism in the Elizabethan Church of England was contested from the very beginning, but neither the exorcists nor their opponents could claim a completely decisive victory in either affirming or eliminating exorcism as a legitimate ministry of the church. This chapter advances the argument that, until the late 1590s, exorcism was a mainstream rather than a sectarian phenomenon within the Elizabethan Church of England. Exorcists were interested in bringing the bishops around to their way of thinking rather than wilfully defying them, and exorcisms were a response to popular demand as well as an opportunity for puritans to advance their theological agenda. Indeed, given the prevailing scepticism of Calvinists throughout Europe towards miracles, exorcism by prayer and fasting represented a significant compromise that can be set alongside other Elizabethan compromises with popular religion that, together, created the Church of England's characteristic *via media*.

However, as Nathan Johnstone has argued, cultural compromise with an ongoing demand for dispossession is not enough to explain the 'enthusiasm of many Protestants for exorcism by prayer and fasting'. Dispossession provided an opportunity for a dramatic confrontation with the devil that showcased the resistance to temptation expected of the Calvinist Protestant,[9] which was enshrined in the language of the Elizabethan Prayer Book. Exorcism 'contributed to the rebuilding of the kudos of the ministry on Protestantism's own terms', and was much more than just a reaction to the competing challenge of Catholic exorcists.[10] The historical puzzle of the last two decades of Elizabeth I's reign is not why exorcism was so popular and significant to the Church of England, but why the practice was so vehemently opposed by bishops that it did not, in the end, become part of the Church of England's *via media*.

THE MEDIEVAL BACKGROUND

No established tradition of clerical exorcism of demoniacs existed in medieval England,[11] a fact that makes the flourishing of the practice in post-Reformation England especially remarkable. England experienced for much longer than many other European countries what

André Goddu called the 'crisis of exorcism', whereby clergy lost confidence in their ability to expel evil spirits from the bodies of the possessed.[12] Belief in demonic possession was as strong in England as anywhere else in Christendom, but medieval English demoniacs did not go to priests for liturgical help. Instead, they made pilgrimages to the shrines of saints particularly associated with dispossession or sought access to their relics.

By the end of the fifteenth century the two most popular locations of pilgrimage for demoniacs were St Bartholomew's Hospital in Smithfield (where pilgrims would sleep at the shrine in the hope of receiving a healing vision of St Bartholomew in their sleep) and the shrine of King Henry VI at Windsor, whom Henry VII made strenuous efforts to have canonised after 1485.[13] Several saints were also famous for their supposed exploits as exorcists in their lifetimes, such as St Dunstan and Sir John Schorne, the Buckinghamshire folk-saint who was reputed to have confined the devil in a boot.[14] When Jane Wentworth displayed symptoms of possession at the shrine of Our Lady of Grace in Ipswich in 1516, the ecclesiastical dignitaries who visited her made no attempt to exorcise her, and Wentworth eventually claimed to have been freed by the Virgin Mary herself.[15]

The late medieval church tolerated demoniacs carrying stones and herbs on them as a means of relief,[16] and although the rite for the exorcism of a demoniac continued to be copied dutifully into English pontificals throughout the Middle Ages, there is no evidence that it was used. When liturgical exorcisms were deployed they were therapeutic and directed against physical illness, and often involved exorcisms of individual afflicted body parts, a tradition that derived from the Anglo-Saxon church.[17] The clergy continued to exorcise infants at baptism, of course, and to exorcise salt, oil and water, but by the late Middle Ages the terms 'exorcism' and 'blessing' had become virtually synonymous – so much so that when the Lollards attacked the practice of exorcism in the fourteenth century they referred only to the exorcism of things.[18] Similarly, the Protestant exile Nicholas Nicastor attacked Catholic exorcism of water and salt in 1554 but made no mention of exorcisms of the possessed.[19] In 1547 the physician Andrew Boorde classed the 'Demoniacus' with lunatics and maniacs and prescribed no remedy for demoniacs, advising only 'kepe them in a sure custody'.[20]

While medieval England had no substantial tradition of clerical exorcism of the possessed, it did have a longstanding tradition of 'ghost-laying' by priests, which was a kind of exorcism. Ghost-laying was intimately tied to belief in purgatory and the need to pray for the dead, although early instances were more 'hands on' and involved the gruesome physical mutilation of reanimated corpses (revenants).[21] Protestant controversialists were persistently puzzled as to why the Reformation failed to eradicate belief in ghosts, which they invariably connected to belief in purgatory.[22] Yet a preoccupation with ghosts would remain (and remains) an abiding feature of English popular culture and would go on to have a significant impact on the development of the Church of England's approach to exorcism.

The almost complete absence of clerical exorcism of the possessed from medieval England meant that there was no tradition of exorcism for sixteenth-century reformers to reject, other than exorcism of objects and dispossession by the power of shrines and relics. Ironically, the end of pilgrimages led to an increased focus on the clergy (as well as other practitioners such as cunning-folk) as a source of deliverance. The Elizabethan clergy enjoyed a prestige as exorcists that their medieval predecessors could only have dreamed of, at a time when the Protestant clergy was seeking a new professional *raison d'être*.[23] The same was also true of Roman Catholic missionary priests in England after the Reformation, who were in high demand as exorcists outside the Roman Catholic community until the late seventeenth century (and in some cases even later).[24]

In 1585–6 the Jesuit William Weston led the first major campaign of Counter-Reformation-style Roman Catholic exorcisms in the Thames Valley, working with a team of priests to free demoniacs in Catholic recusant households.[25] Weston worked with the deliberate intention of proselytising by exorcism until he was captured by the authorities, and the Church of England's response to exorcism from 1586 onwards must be seen against the background of a perceived threat from Catholic priests prepared to make use of exorcism to prove the superiority of their church. Protestants were forced to choose between playing the Catholics at their own game and rejecting exorcism altogether. However, the dominant anti-Catholic strategy of the established church was to expose Catholic 'superstition' as fraud,[26] so it was an uphill struggle for Protestant exorcists to convince the bishops they had a place in the church.

EXORCISM AT BAPTISM

Perhaps because it was so marginal in the pre-Reformation church, dealing with exorcism was a low priority for English reformers. This is most clearly evident in the survival of 'a striking and full-blooded' baptismal exorcism in the first English prayer book of 1549:[27]

> I commau[n]de thee, uncleane spirite, in the name of the father, of the sonne, and of the holy ghost, that thou come out, and departe from these infantes, whom our Lord Jesus Christe hath vouchsaued, to call to his holy Baptisme, to be made membres of his body, and of his holy congregacion. Therfore thou cursed spirite, remember thy sentence, remember thy iudgemente, remember the daye to be at hande, wherin thou shalt burne in fyre euerlasting, prepared for the and thy Angels. And presume not hereafter to exercise any tyrannye towarde these infantes, whom Christe hathe bought with his precious bloud, and by this his holy Baptisme calleth to be of his flocke.[28]

In addition to this verbal exorcism, the infant was to be signed with a cross on the forehead and the breast prior to baptism, accompanied by these words:

> Receyue the signe of the holy Crosse, both in thy forehead, and in thy breste, in token that thou shalt not be ashamed to confesse thy fayth in Christe crucifyed, and manfully to fyght under his banner against synne, the worlde, and the deuill, and to be continewe his faythfull soldiour and seruaunt unto thy lyfes ende.[29]

This pre-baptismal signing with the cross was distinct from the post-baptismal 'confirmation' signing with oil on the forehead, which clearly had no exorcistic significance because it was subsequent to baptism.[30] For David Holeton, as for Eamon Duffy, the 1549 rite was essentially an adaptation of the Sarum rite, with 'only the most obvious of the "dark and dumb" ceremonies' removed. Some exorcistic rites, such as the *ephphatha* or *effeta* (in which the priest blew in the catechumen's face) disappeared, but the baptismal rite of 1549 was essentially 'a cosmetic reform'.[31]

In contrast to Duffy and Holeton, Nathan Johnstone sees more discontinuity between the 1549 rite and its medieval predecessor, owing to 'a fundamental shift in the demonological rationale of Christian initiation'.[32] Whereas the exorcisms of the Sarum rite were expected to free a child definitively from the devil's influence, the baptismal liturgies of 1549 and 1552 initiated the infant into 'a constant struggle with the demonic'.[33] The 1549 exorcism was 'far less imposing than its predecessor', and the words accompanying the signing of the catechumen before baptism were re-drafted to deny its exorcistic efficacy (albeit it was probably still perceived as exorcistic by parishioners familiar with its purpose in the Sarum rite). The cross was now no more than a symbol indicating that the child should grow up to profess the Christian faith.[34]

Furthermore, Johnstone argues, 'removing the adjurations and prayers on either side of the formal exorcism took away the focus of attention from the rite itself'. The removal of the anticipatory prayers robbed the exorcism of its impact, and 'The Devil was now dispatched with such speed and ease that it is likely the exorcism was no longer satisfying to those onlookers who retained a profound sense of its spiritual and emotional importance'. The 'expedition' of the 1549 exorcism would have been 'confusing and unsettling' to parishioners.[35]

In the event, the exorcism of the 1549 Prayer Book was short-lived, and the 1552 Prayer Book removed baptismal exorcism altogether. Although the 1552 Prayer Book was soon suppressed under Mary I (who restored the Sarum rite), it was highly significant because it was revived in the 1559 Prayer Book of Elizabeth I and, later, formed the foundation of the rite of baptism in the 1662 *Book of Common Prayer*. The 1552 baptismal rite was influenced by the Strasbourg reformer Martin Bucer's *Censura* of 1551, which pointed out those parts of Cranmer's 1549 Prayer Book that Bucer believed required further 'reformation'. Bucer opposed the exorcism because such words were only appropriate to demoniacs and they wrongly implied that unbaptised infants were possessed.[36] Accordingly, exorcism disappeared entirely from the 1552 rite and was replaced by two prayers for regeneration whose only reference to the devil was to ask that the catechumens 'maye haue power and strength to haue victorie and to triumphe agaynste the deuyll, the worlde, and the fleshe'.[37]

The pre-baptismal signing with the cross was abolished in the 1552 liturgy, as was the 'confirmation' anointing after baptism, but as a compromise a single post-baptismal signing without oil was introduced, accompanied by the words of the prayer that had accompanied the pre-baptismal signing in the 1549 rite.[38] The signing 'thereby lost the exorcizing function implicit in its original place in the ceremony'.[39] Just as importantly, the disappearance of exorcism implicitly denied the minister's 'power of command over the Devil' and the placing of the signing with the cross after baptism ensured it was seen as a purely symbolic act.[40] As Darren Oldridge has noted, the reformed rite placed the baptised Christian in the traditional role of the exorcist, having been initiated into a lifelong struggle against Satan.[41]

It is not 'obvious', as Keith Thomas claimed, that early modern English people believed that unbaptised children were possessed by the devil.[42] Bucer was right that the words of the 1549 exorcism appeared to imply this, although before they were translated into English few parishioners would have understood the exact words being spoken. It was never the official position of the medieval church that unbaptised children were possessed. In the thirteenth century Archbishop John Pecham was concerned that the exorcisms had not been pronounced over children baptised by laypeople when in danger of death. Pecham ordered the exorcisms to be read over the children, but this was in order to complete the rite and assert the authority of the church to control the rite of baptism rather than because he thought the children might be possessed.[43]

The evidence suggests that baptismal exorcism may have originated as a rite analogous to the exorcism of water, salt and oil; no one actually thought these substances were always infested with demons, but exorcising them returned them to their pristine state as God's creatures so they could then be blessed and used in his service.[44] Rather than a dispossession, baptismal exorcism involved banishing and binding the devil, ensuring he had no further influence over the catechumens. Early baptismal liturgies envisaged the devil as 'a tempter lurking in the vicinity' of the unbaptised rather than as a possessing entity.[45] It is in the context of this banishing function that folklore associated with baptism, such as the so-called 'devil's door' located close to the font, should be understood. Other folklore, however, such as the belief that a child that cried at its christening was letting out the devil,[46] suggests a more literal belief in the demonic possession of the unbaptised.

The persistence of such popular beliefs into the seventeenth century was one reason why puritans so vociferously opposed signing with the cross in baptism as a 'charm'.[47] Although the signing now took place after baptism, the words that accompanied it were still those for the pre-baptismal signing in the 1549 rite, which had directly replaced signings in the Sarum rite that were clearly exorcistic. The lineage of baptismal signing was exorcistic, whatever its official justification, and it remains the last surviving vestige of baptismal exorcism in the *Book of Common Prayer*.

EARLY ELIZABETHAN EXORCISMS

There is no evidence of Catholic exorcisms of demoniacs during the reign of Mary I, apart from one report by John Foxe that a priest was sent for from Rome by Bishop Edmund Bonner of London in an unsuccessful attempt to exorcise the Protestant martyr John Mills.[48] If this story is true, it only serves to confirm the inexperience of the English clergy when it came to liturgical dispossession of the possessed. The experience of English Protestant exiles in Europe seems to have been crucial in introducing exorcism of demoniacs to England, and some of the earliest exorcisms either took place within communities of European Protestants in England or were conducted by exorcists who may have been influenced by European practices.

As Brian Levack has shown, exorcisms were common in Lutheran territories, where they were often given an apocalyptic interpretation, but less frequent in territories dominated by Calvinism.[49] One reason for this was that, while Lutherans accepted the continuation of miracles into the present age, Calvinists were generally cessationists, believing that miracles had ceased at the death of the last apostle.

Cessationism did not necessarily make it impossible to believe in demonic possession, but it did pose difficulties for believing in exorcism. The dispossessions performed by Jesus and his disciples were clearly of the nature of miracles, and Calvinists were therefore faced with a choice between denying the possibility of dispossession altogether and finding a way to argue that a dispossession could be performed in such a way that it did not count as a miracle. Alternatively, they could challenge cessationism altogether.

The Swiss reformer Benedikt Marti (known as Aretius) formulated an influential critique of exorcism, arguing from the original meaning of the Greek words *ekballō* ('cast out') and *exorkizō* ('bind by oath') that Jesus' dispossessions had not been exorcisms at all but rather expulsions of spirits by virtue of his status as the Son of God. The New Testament used the word *ekballō* to refer to these dispossessions – not *exorkizō*, which implied the use of a form of words by which a spirit was commanded and conjured to leave a person or thing.[50] This latter practice of exorcism was, in the view of Marti and many other Protestants, no better than magic, an impression heightened by the fact that, in English, 'conjurer' meant both an exorcist and a necromancer. Protestant exorcisms were, properly speaking, not exorcisms at all but dispossessions, and Protestant exorcists were often at pains to distance themselves from Roman Catholic 'conjuring priests'.

During the reign of Edward VI, Bishop John Hooper argued in favour of cessationism, writing in 1550 that there was no more need for miracles to confirm the truth of the Gospel.[51] However, the experience of Protestant martyrdom and foreign exile under Mary I led to a more diverse range of views on miracles and exorcism among English Protestants. Nevertheless, the theology of Elizabeth I's Church of England was influenced more heavily by Calvinism than by other strands of reformed theological thought. Oldridge has noted that English possessions and exorcisms did not conform to the standard Calvinist pattern of a heavily internalised and spiritualised combat with Satan. Instead, English possessions continued to be described in 'grossly material' terms, just as before the Reformation,[52] testifying to an enduring cultural tradition which English Protestantism chose to accommodate rather than reject.

The leading apologist of the Elizabethan reformation, John Jewel, bishop of Salisbury (1522–71) did not deny the efficacy of exorcism; he rejected the continued existence of the office of exorcist not because exorcism was impossible or wrong, but because those appointed to the office did not actually drive out devils.[53] In other words, Jewel was critical of Roman Catholics for not truly exorcising. Elsewhere, Jewel attacked the use of biblical verses as amulets to drive away demons, asking 'Wherein resteth the power of the psalms, wherewith the devil is vanquished? in the bare sound of the words, or in the sense and meaning of the same?'.[54] At no point did Jewel suggest that the reading of scripture did *not* have the power to drive out devils if done rightly.

The earliest recorded Protestant exorcism in England took place in Chester in February 1564. On 18 October 1563, 18-year-old Ann Mylner was returning from bringing her father's cows into pasture, but as she came close to Chester she 'was sodaynlye taken wyth great feare, and thoughte that she saw a whyte thing compassing her round about'. The account contains no suggestion that Mylner was either bewitched or punished for her sins – she was just the unlucky victim of an evil spirit. On arriving home Mylner found herself sore all over her body and began to go into trances and fits. In December, at the end of a sermon in Chester Cathedral, one of the canons knelt down and offered 'speciall prayers vnto God, for her deliuera[n]ce'. In January 1564 John Lane (d. 1580), rector of Aldford (and later a canon of Chester Cathedral) heard about Ann Mylner when two Chester men asked him 'whether ther were not some possessed wyth spirits as in times past'. The men asked Lane to come to Chester and visit Ann, 'hauing hearde howe it is well knowen to diuers credible persons in these partes, what rare and syngular remedye god hath wrought by M. Lane, to some that sustained of late no smal decay of minde and memory, or els being of that religion, as in theese dayes seeke myracles to confirme Gods woorde'. Lane clearly had a pre-existing reputation for healing mental illness at the time he was called in.

Lane visited Ann Mylner's home on the afternoon of 16 February, and witnessed one of her fits, in which Mylner arched her back off the bed and could not be held down. Lane first of all tested whether

Mylner was really possessed by attempting to hold her down, without success. Lane instructed the bystanders to pray for Mylner,

> And when she was in the veheme[n]t panges the beholders called upon god for her, maister Lane secretly sayd the fifty Psalm, & ofte[n] desired God, through the bloud of his so[n]ne Jesus Christ, to ease the Maiden, not doubting of his mercye in that behalfe. And when he had thus striued with her the space of two houres, that the drope trickled downe hys face, he had thought to haue commended her unto God: but then againe it came to mynde to tary the end, and so began a freshe to striue with her, euer secretly praying & calling upo[n] the bloud of Christ.

Lane then called for vinegar, which he put in his mouth and blew into Mylner's nostrils; this had been tried before, but to no effect. Mylner cried out 'a Lady, Lady' ('Our Lady'), but Lane 'willed her to cal upo[n] God, and the bloud of Christ', and the exorcism was successful. The next day Lane preached a sermon in St Mary's church, where Mylner was present, and on 4 March the archdeacon of Chester, Robert Rogers (d. 1595), preached in Chester Cathedral on Mylner's deliverance in the presence of the mayor, the bishop of Chester (William Downham) and the bishop of St Asaph (Thomas Davies).[55]

It is unclear exactly what words Lane used when he called upon the blood of Christ, but it seems unlikely that he adjured the evil spirit directly. In this sense, the exorcism was a distinctively Protestant one, especially since Lane appeared to encourage Mylner to call upon the blood of Christ instead of Mary. However, Lane's use of vinegar suggests a more 'Catholic' willingness to make use of physical objects to cast out demons, although this act might also be interpreted as a quasi-medical attempt to startle Mylner out of her trance state. Lane's recitation of a psalm under his breath is also reminiscent of Catholic practice; such 'secret' prayers were rejected in Protestant liturgies. Thomas described both Lane and Rogers as 'Puritan clergy',[56] but Lane had a licence to preach throughout the diocese and Rogers was an archdeacon.[57] Both men were establishment figures, and Rogers's approbation of the exorcism in a sermon preached before two bishops implied that those bishops approved of the exorcism too.

In January 1572 a 23-year-old man who was a member of the congregation of Dutch Protestant exiles in Maidstone, Kent, was dispossessed by another Dutchman, John Stikelbow, at the instigation of the minister of the Dutch church, Nicasius van der Schuere.[58] Although an English pamphlet was published about this exorcism, the events themselves seem to have been contained within Maidstone's Dutch expatriate community. However, in 1573 a widely publicised exorcism occurred in an English parish community at Herringswell, Suffolk. Edward Nyndge, a recent graduate of Cambridge University, identified his brother Alexander as possessed. The entire community gathered to witness the possession, and Edward conjured the spirit possessing his brother to speak.[59]

Edward Nyndge did not formally exorcise the spirit himself but called on the local curate, Peter Bencham, 'to conjure and charge him in the name of Jesus the Son of the Almighty that the spirit should declare to them whence he came, whither he would go, and what was his name'.[60] The actual ejection of the spirit was accomplished by reading passages of the New Testament (Matthew 5 and Luke 8), at which point Edward opened the window for the spirit to exit the building.[61] Alexander was re-possessed the next morning and his left ear 'was suddenly wrinkled like a clung walnut which falls from the tree before it is ripe'. Edward Nyndge sent for Bencham again, 'and desired him to take the Bible and turn to the place of Scripture where Christ gave authority to his ministers, and willed him to read and use that authority for the loosing of the ... ear'. This time Bencham attempted a direct, traditional imperative exorcism: 'We conjure you in the name of Jesus Christ our Saviour, the Son of the almighty God, that you depart and no longer torment the said Alexander'.[62]

By contrast, Edward Nyndge's vocabulary throughout the exorcism was thoroughly Protestant, and at one point he rebuked one participant for mentioning the Virgin Mary,[63] an incident that shows that even crypto-Catholic members of the community of Herringswell were involved in the exorcism. The reliance on communal prayers and extempore scripture readings were likewise Protestant innovations. In other ways, however, the Nyndge exorcism harked back to the Catholic past. There was no fasting and no suspicion of witchcraft; the implication was that Alexander had been possessed on account of his sins. Edward insisted that Peter Bencham perform the actual exorcism, owing to the special power inherent in ministers, a belief that echoed Catholic confidence in the powers of the priesthood. Edward's willingness to engage the spirit directly in dialogue was thoroughly Catholic, as was Bencham's eventual use of an imperative conjuration. The final exorcism differed from a Catholic one only in Bencham's use of a plural pronoun, 'We conjure you ...' The collective pronoun underlined the nature of a Protestant exorcism as a communal act rather than an exercise of individual sacerdotal power.[64]

Another 'hybrid exorcism' containing both Protestant and Catholic elements was performed by the martyrologist John Foxe in the Temple Church, London on a lawyer named Robert Briggs on 24 April 1574. Briggs was beset by feelings of despair after misinterpreting a Calvinist sermon. Foxe made use of a traditional imperative conjuration, 'Thou most wretched serpent ... O thou foul devil, I command thee to depart', and argued with Satan (who accused Foxe of being a witch) but the exorcism was ultimately successful, and several accounts of it circulated in manuscript.[65] Shortly afterwards Foxe became embroiled in a second exorcism when Elizabeth Pinder visited Foxe's house with her 11-year-old daughter Rachel, whom she hoped Foxe would exorcise. Instead, Rachel Pinder 'infected' Foxe's servant Agnes Briggs who also began displaying symptoms of possession.[66]

On 16 July Rachel Pinder was exorcised by two ministers, William Long and William Turner, who engaged in dialogue with the spirit and eventually 'commanded Satan in the blood of Jesus to depart'.[67] Before they did so, however, the spirit threatened to 'tear Foxe in pieces', thereby testifying to the significance of the celebrated exorcist.[68] The exorcism of Rachel Pinder was the first to attract significant adverse attention from a bishop, in this case Archbishop Matthew Parker, largely because the exorcism was publicised in a pamphlet. Parker had both Rachel Pinder and Agnes Briggs examined. Under questioning they confessed to fraud and performed public penance at Paul's Cross on 25 August.[69]

Freeman has argued that Archbishop Parker's intervention in the Pinder and Briggs case was partly motivated by his concern that the exorcising activities of Foxe, a figure who enjoyed an ambiguous relationship with the Elizabethan ecclesiastical settlement, had the potential to undermine episcopal authority. On one level, Foxe's martyrological work on the *Actes and Monuments* was the mainstay of the Elizabethan reformation because it furnished the English Protestant church with a powerful foundation myth. On the other hand, Foxe chose not to integrate himself into the hierarchical structure of the Elizabethan settlement. Although he was ordained and held a prebend in the diocese of Salisbury, he petitioned to be exempted from the requirement to wear the surplice and was not entirely happy with the compromises of the religious settlement of 1559. A book published under Parker's authority, *The Disclosing of a Late Counterfeyted Possession* (1574) included an indirect attack on Foxe, and Parker was one of the first figures in the Elizabethan church to deny the reality of possession altogether, setting a pattern for Archbishops Whitgift and Bancroft to follow.[70]

The exorcism of Rachel Pinder also set the pattern for future exorcisms by tying possession to accusations of witchcraft. The spirit possessing Pinder told William Long that it had been sent by 'Joan Thornton, dwelling on the Key', who had given the spirit a drop of her blood.[71] Although the exorcism did not lead to a formal accusation of witchcraft (because it was exposed by Parker as fraud soon afterwards), exorcism as witchfinding would soon become the norm, and the expectation that possession was the result of bewitchment became standard. The same expectations prevailed for Catholic exorcists, and the line between exorcism and 'unbewitchment' (the removal of a witch's curse) was often far from clear.[72] The use of exorcism as a remedy for witchcraft was a distinctively early modern phenomenon, since medieval demonologists had downplayed the usefulness of exorcism against witches.[73]

Another 'hybrid exorcism' of 1574 involved 17-year-old Alice Norrington of Westwell, Kent. Norrington was questioned thoroughly by Roger Newman, vicar of Westwell and John Brainford, vicar of Kinington. Like Rachel Pinder, Norrington accused 'Old Alice' of bewitching her, who turned out to be a servant in John Brainford's household. Like John Foxe, the Westwell exorcists had no qualms about directly addressing the demoniac, reporting that 'we did command him many times, in the name of God, and of his Son Jesus Christ, and in his mighty power to speak'.[74]

The earliest instance in England of fasting as a means of dispossession also occurred in 1574.[75] On 29 June 1574 Bishop John Parkhurst of Norwich wrote to the Swiss reformer Heinrich Bullinger,

> A certain young Dutch woman about seventeen or eighteen years of age, a servant of the preacher of the church at Norwich, was during a whole year miserably vexed by Satan. In all her temptations, however, and dilacerations, she continued stedfast in the faith, and withstood the adversary with more than manly fortitude. At last, by God's help, the devil being overcome left her, and almost at the same instant attacked the son of a certain senator, whom he also tormented in a most incredible manner for some weeks together. Public prayers were offered in the city by my direction, and a fast proclaimed until evening. The Lord had mercy also on the boy, and overcame the enemy.[76]

Parkhurst's account does not make clear whether it was solely public fasting that dispossessed the two Norwich demoniacs or whether an exorcist was involved as well. However, a bishop was one of the few people with the authority to declare a public fast for a whole city, so it is not altogether surprising that Parkhurst exercised his power in this way; indeed, it would be more surprising had a bishop deigned to personally perform an exorcism.

Like the Maidstone case a few years earlier, the Norwich possessions originated in the community of 'strangers', Protestant exiles from the war-torn Low Countries who were allowed their own churches and their own form of Calvinist worship in their native language.[77] Parkhurst, who had spent Mary I's reign in exile at Zurich, did not hesitate to accept the authenticity of the Dutch woman's possession and the power of fasting to deliver her. Nevertheless, Parkhurst's overt support for dispossession was unusual within the episcopacy, and it is impossible to generalise about the experience of exiles making them more sympathetic to exorcism. However, it may be no accident that the widely publicised dispossession of Alexander Nyndge occurred in Parkhurst's diocese, and it is possible that the exorcists in that case, Edward Nyndge and Peter Bencham, knew of Parkhurst's belief.

Fasting was regarded as a powerful means of obtaining divine favour by both Catholics and Protestants. In 1538 Mabel Brigge had been executed for fasting against Henry VIII,[78] and the right to proclaim fasts was a privilege of the highest authorities of church and state. Patrick Collinson noted that Canon 72 was directed primarily against unlicensed fasting and only secondarily against attempts to cast out devils.[79] Public fasts, whether or not they were exorcistic in intent, were a usurpation of episcopal authority, and any gathering of people and ministers outside church and outside the time of divine service ran the risk of being classed as a 'conventicle', outlawed by Canon 73.[80] On this interpretation, the bishops' campaign against exorcism as fraud was just an elaborate tactic for attacking their real targets, unlicensed fasts and gatherings. Glyn Parry has argued that Whitgift, Bancroft and Harsnett felt freed to go on the offensive against exorcists by the death of the earl of Leicester in 1588, since Leicester had been the protector of puritan interests.[81]

JOHN DEE THE EXORCIST

One exorcist who certainly did not conform to the 'puritan' pattern was the mathematician, astrologer and royal adviser John Dee (1527–1609). Dee was a 'conjurer' in both senses of the word, privately summoning spirits into a crystal with his medium Edward Kelley as well as getting involved in exorcism of the possessed. In August 1578 Dee was summoned to Norfolk, where Elizabeth I was on progress, in order to perform mysterious 'proceedings' (probably some sort of counter-magic) to protect the queen against harmful magic. Earlier that month three wax images, thought to represent the queen and two of her councillors, had been found in a barn at Islington.[82]

By 1590, Dee was in possession of Girolamo Menghi's *Flagellum daemonum* ('Scourge of demons'),[83] a defining text of Franciscan Counter-Reformation exorcism, and unlike other Protestant exorcists Dee remained interested in Catholic spirituality.[84] He did not share the then standard Protestant view that Catholicism was the faith of antichrist, and was prepared to receive communion from the Jesuits during his stay in Bohemia in 1584.[85] In 1596, when Dee was consulted on the possessions in the household of Nicholas Starkie, he borrowed other Catholic works including the sequel to Menghi's *Flagellum*, his *Fustis daemonum* ('Cudgel of demons').[86]

Dee was drawn into personally performing an exorcism in his own household in July 1590. On 22 July he wrote in his diary that his children's nurse, Ann Frank, 'had long been tempted by a wicked spirit: but this day it was evident, how she was possessed of him'. On 26 July Dee 'anointed (in the name of Jesus) Ann Frank her breast, with the holy oil'.[87] The rite of anointing of the sick had been removed from the Prayer Book in 1552, and even the rite that had been allowed to remain in the 1549 Prayer Book made clear that the anointing was purely symbolic and omitted any prayer of consecration for the oil.[88] Dee's use of the term 'holy oil' suggests he consecrated it in the old Catholic fashion (Dee had been ordained priest in Mary I's reign), and his decision to anoint Ann would indicate that Dee initially considered an anointing intended for the sick sufficient.

Dee's anointing, however, did not have the desired effect, and on 30 July Ann Frank requested a second anointing. It was at this point that Dee prepared himself for 'blessing of the oil to the expulsion of the wicked'. He was probably referring to the exorcism of oil in the Sarum ritual, which he may have believed imbued the oil with the power to exorcise demoniacs. This time, his anointing of the nurse produced symptoms he interpreted as those of demonic possession: 'And then coming to be anointed, the wicked one did resist a while'.[89] Dee made no reference, however, to words of imperative exorcism.

Dee's exorcism of Ann Frank was not a success. On 24 August he rescued her from an attempt to drown herself in a well, and on 29 August, in spite of being watched, she crept downstairs and cut her throat with a knife behind a door – an event that so shook Dee that he did not return to his diary for a month.[90] Almond has noted that early modern demoniacs rarely killed themselves, and suggested that Dee diagnosed Frank as possessed because she displayed the symptoms of depression rather than those typically associated with demonic possession.[91] However, in spite of its failure, Dee's exorcism of Ann Frank is significant. It was a private, 'therapeutic' exorcism rooted in medieval practices of healing by anointing rather than a public, evangelistic exorcism of the kind conducted by godly exorcists. Dee gave no indication that he tried to interrogate the possessing spirit, or even that he used any words at all. Furthermore, Dee's use of consecrated oil showed that he considered the provisions of the Elizabethan Prayer Book inadequate to deal with a case of this kind. In spite of his deep commitment to the Elizabethan religious settlement, Dee was prepared to draw on a Catholic rite when it was needed.[92] This may not have been Dee's last exorcism, since it was rumoured in 1602 that he exorcised Lady Sandes.[93]

THE CAREER OF JOHN DARRELL

John Darrell (*c*.1562–*c*.1607) was the most famous (or infamous) of Elizabethan Protestant exorcists, whose exploits would turn most bishops decisively against exorcism by the end of the 1590s. Darrell, who was born and lived in or near Mansfield in Nottinghamshire, was drawn into exorcism when a possessed teenager, Katherine Wright, was brought to him for healing in 1586. Much later, his arch-opponent Samuel Harsnett attempted to embarrass Darrell by accusing him of interrogating the devil during the dispossession of Wright, when he later disavowed the practice: 'for when he dealt with Katherine Wright, he had one or two pretie Dialogues with the Deuill'.[94] In other ways, however, the Wright case set the pattern for Darrell's future career because it led to a witchcraft accusation.[95] Darrell was instrumental in making 'exorcism as witchfinding' the expected norm.

Darrell rose to national prominence with the exorcism of 13-year-old Thomas Darling, 'the boy of Burton', at Burton-on-Trent in May 1596. Darling first of all had the scriptures read over him by a relative, Jesse Bee.[96] On 3 May Darling was visited by the vicar of Ashby-de-la-Zouch, Arthur Hildersham, who explained his stance on exorcism:

> Master Hildersham said openly that, howsoever the Papists boasted much of the power their priests had to cast out devils, and the simple everywhere noted it a great discredit to the ministers of the Gospel that they do lack this power, yet did he profess that there was no such gift in them, and that though the Lord oft in these days, by the prayers of the faithful, cast out devils, yet could he not assure them to cure him. To hold this faith of miracles to remain still in the church is an opinion dangerous. That seeing to be possessed is but a temporal correction ... it can not without sin be absolutely prayed against. All which notwithstanding, he said that there is a good use of prayer in such a

case, and of fasting also, to procure that the judgement may be sanctified to the beholders, and the possessed himself, yea to obtain also that he may be delivered also from it, if the Lord see it be best for his own glory.[97]

Hildersham's paradoxical stance was, in other words, that exorcism was wrong, that miracles were ceased, and that it might be sinful even to pray for deliverance from possession; but that prayer and fasting should nevertheless be tried as long as there was no automatic expectation of relief.

Accordingly, Hildersham led the community in prayer and preached, until Darrell came to visit Darling on 27 May. Darrell would not stay, however, and told Darling's family 'his assistance in prayer and fasting they should have, but not his presence, as well as to avoid note of vainglory, as also that he saw no such necessity by reason of the child's stern faith'.[98] Ironically, the perception that Darrell had the power to exorcise even from a distance only served to enhance his reputation. The dispossession of Thomas Darling was a textbook Calvinist exorcism, insofar as most of the exorcising was done by the demoniac himself,[99] with Darling engaging in continuous dialogue and argument with the devil. This may be why Darrell did not feel the need to stay; Darling was stage-managing the exorcism perfectly by himself.

Darrell left a book entitled *The Enemy of Security* and the community began a determined 'exercise' of prayer, fasting and scripture reading that finally led to Darling's dispossession the next day. Darrell then visited and exhorted Darling to a holy life in case he became possessed again, which occurred when Darling was at school on 5 June. He was taken home and successfully dispossessed by Hildersham.[100] The exorcism would have led to the trial of a local woman, Alice Gooderige, for witchcraft, but she died in prison awaiting trial. Darling accused Gooderige of causing his possession by bewitching him in a wood, and the Darling case seems to be one of the first in which possession was adduced as evidence of witchcraft in legal proceedings. Given the courts' growing preoccupation with witchcraft in the 1590s, the fact that possession began to be accepted as a form of evidence was a major boost to the exorcists.

In March 1597 Darrell was called in to exorcise seven demoniacs in the house of Nicholas Starkie at Cleworth in Lancashire. Starkie had already consulted John Dee, by then warden of the collegiate church at Manchester. According to one account, Dee did not want to get involved in the exorcism himself but advised Starkie to seek out godly ministers to replace the cunning-man Edmond Hartley, whom Starkie suspected of being the cause rather than the cure of the possession.[101] However, another account claimed that Dee lent a number of books on demonology to the magistrate Edmund Hopwood, who was dealing with the Starkie case,[102] while Bancroft later claimed that Dee's butler told Starkie about Darrell and caused him to invite the famous exorcist to Lancashire.[103] Eventually, Darrell admitted that Dee himself had written to invite him, although Darrell's supporters made strenuous efforts to distance themselves from Dee on account of his reputation as a conjurer.[104] Darrell's fellow exorcist George More, who wrote a detailed account of the case to rebut allegations later made against Darrell by the Commissioners for Ecclesiastical Causes, was at pains to emphasise that Darrell did not have 'some special gift that way above other men', and had in fact only given advice to the dispossessors of the Lancashire demoniacs, just as in the case of Thomas Darling.[105]

The irony of More's refutation of any notion that Darrell was like a conventional Catholic exorcist was that, in defending the reality of the Lancashire possessions, he produced a demonological treatise that strongly resembled Catholic models. More presented a list of 19 symptoms of possession that he believed only the devil could produce,[106] and reported that the demoniacs were 'tested' by being asked questions in Latin.[107] This sort of 'diagnostic demonology' was certainly not compatible with the wary approach to dispossession articulated by Hildersham in the case of Thomas Darling. David Frankfurter has noted the tendency of exorcists to become demonologists, shaping people's experience of possession as well as responding to it.[108]

On 5 November 1597 Darrell arrived in Nottingham in order to exorcise a young apprentice, William Sommers, a process which took two days. Once again, Darrell's procedure was more like that of a conventional exorcist than he would have cared to admit. According to an anonymous account of the dispossession published in 1598, Darrell's preaching exacerbated the torments of Sommers: 'And the said John Darrell, speaking at length on this text, "He came out of him," the said W. Sommers made as though he would have vomited'.[109] This was 'performative preaching', an oblique form of exorcism apparently directed at the assembled witnesses but in reality directed as an imperative command to the demoniac himself. Oldridge has argued that exorcisms served much the same function as sermons for Elizabethan Protestants.[110]

The Sommers exorcism proved to be the beginning of Darrell's downfall, since although the exorcist was appointed preacher at St Mary's church in Nottingham as a result, the accusations of witchcraft he stirred up ruffled feathers because they touched the relatives of leaders of local government. In March 1598 a commission was convened by Archbishop Matthew Hutton of York to examine Darrell's proceedings, which found no fault in the exorcist.[111] However, although Darrell was cleared of wrongdoing the commission drew national attention to the exorcist, who was summoned to London with George More by Archbishop John Whitgift and imprisoned, pending a trial before the Commissioners for Ecclesiastical Causes. The author of *A Brief Narration of the Possession, Dispossession and Repossession of William Sommers* (1598) denounced the trial as an unjust proceeding, and reported that numerous attempts were made to induce all of the demoniacs dispossessed by Darrell to confess to fraud.[112]

Darrell and More were found guilty of fraud in May 1599 and deprived of their livings as ministers. They were released from prison soon afterwards but their careers as exorcists were over.[113] Although Whitgift nominally presided over the process that ended Darrell's exorcisms, the campaign against the exorcists was really led by the bishop of London, Richard Bancroft, and his chaplain Samuel Harsnett, who published *A Discovery of the Fraudulent Practices of John Darrell* (1599). Darrell and More replied with their own pamphlets but Bancroft sponsored John Deacon and John Walker to write a two-volume work denouncing possession and exorcism, *Dialogical Discourses of Spirits and Devils* (1601–2). Harsnett's monumental denunciation of the Catholic exorcisms of William Weston,

A Declaration of Egregious Popish Impostures (1603) was also aimed obliquely against the godly exorcists, whom he attacked as 'devil-puffers, or devil-prayers'.[114]

THE EXORCISM OF THOMAS HARRISON

With the exception of the public fast proclaimed in Norwich in 1574 by Bishop Parkhurst, the only example of episcopally authorised prayer and fasting for dispossession occurred in the diocese of Chester in 1601–2. Richard Vaughan (*c.*1550–1607), bishop of Chester, granted a licence for the dispossession of Thomas Harrison, the 'Boy of Northwich'.[115] The exorcism of Thomas Harrison seems to have provided the real-world pattern for the potential episcopal involvement later envisaged by Canon 72. Vaughan appointed a commission to assist him and summoned Harrison to Chester, apparently with the intention of detecting fraud, since William Hinde noted that 'they could not find him a counterfeat, as some imagined'. Instead, 'this Rev. Bish[op] being moved with compassion towards the boy, did grant a Licence himselfe, together with the High Commissioners, for a private Fast in his fathers house, for his better help and release, according to Gods good pleasure'. The licence read,

> Having seen the bodily affliction of this child, and observed in sundry fits very strange effects, and operations, either proceeding from some naturall unknown causes, or of some Diabolicall practises: We thinke it convenient and fit for the ease and deliverance of the said child, from his said grievous affliction, that Prayer be made publikely for him, by the Minister of the Parish, &c. And that certein Preachers, namely these following: M. Gerrard, M. Harvy, M. Pierson, &c. these and none other to repaire to the said chi[l]d by turnes, as their leisure will serve, and to use their discretion for private Prayers and Fasting, for the ease and comfort of the afflicted, &c.[116]

Vaughan's licence insisted that the vicar of Northwich should be central to the dispossession, offering public prayers in the parish church. In this way the exorcism was integrated into, rather than placed outside, existing structures of ecclesiastical authority. However, although public prayers were to be offered for Harrison the fasting was to be private (unlike Parkhurst's 1574 fast), applying only to the Harrison household and the named preachers involved in the dispossession. This stipulation is perhaps an indication that Vaughan did not wish his licence to draw wider attention. However, although Vaughan's licence restricted the number of ministers involved in the dispossession (and identified them by name), it did not explicitly restrict the attendance of the laity, and Hinde reported that 'some 20 or 30' were present.[117] It seems unlikely that this was an unintentional omission; had Vaughan meant to discourage lay attendance he would have used a less ambiguous word than 'private'. The omission of any direct restriction on lay participation may have been a tacit acknowledgement that exorcism was a communal event.

Vaughan's exorcism licence – the sole Elizabethan example whose actual text survives – is highly significant, insofar as it shows that initial episcopal scepticism was not always followed by rejection of the reality of a possession, and that Vaughan's role as an investigator of possession did not preclude him from authorising an exorcism. The case of the 'Boy of Northwich' is evidence that Bishop Vaughan preferred to bring exorcism under his own control rather than outlaw it completely, although Harmes argued that Vaughan only licensed the exorcism 'grudgingly'.[118] However, Vaughan's warning that the ministers should 'forbear all forms of exorcism'[119] is scarcely remarkable, since 'exorcism' in this context meant the kind of imperative conjurations that were scorned by most Protestant ministers anyway. The form of dispossession by prayer and fasting authorised by Vaughan was identical to that practised by unlicensed exorcists, demonstrating that it was not the form of so-called 'puritan' exorcisms that offended the bishops, but rather their unauthorised character. The theology underpinning Vaughan's approach to exorcism was no different from that of Darrell, More and other advocates of exorcism; the only difference was that Vaughan was a bishop.[120]

THE EXORCISM OF MARY GLOVER

The last major case of 'puritan' dispossession in Elizabeth I's reign involved 14-year-old Mary Glover, who happened to be the granddaughter of a Gospeller burnt at the stake in Mary I's reign, Robert Glover.[121] The relationship was a significant one; it was no accident that John Foxe, the martyrologist and hagiographer of the

Marian Gospellers, had also set the pattern for godly exorcisms, which served as a form of substitute martyrdom.[122] Glover's possession was directly connected with a witchcraft trial, since she first showed signs of possession on the opening day of the trial of Elizabeth Jackson, who was accused of bewitching her, on 1 December 1602. The case prompted Bishop Bancroft to recruit the sceptical physician Edward Jorden, who attempted to convince the court that Glover was suffering from hysteria. The judge, however, 'convinced the land was about to be overwhelmed by witches', found Jackson guilty.[123]

The case of Mary Glover was a politically important one for Bancroft, because on 24 March 1603 Elizabeth I died and was succeeded by King James VI of Scotland, renowned throughout Europe for his interest in the subject of demonology. John Swan dedicated his 1603 account of Glover's exorcism to James, no doubt in the hope of recruiting him to the side of the exorcists.[124] However, James adopted a significantly more sceptical attitude to preternatural phenomena in his English reign. Although Freeman suggested that Bancroft managed to win James around to opposing the exorcists early in his reign,[125] James may already have been changing his mind on such issues by 1603, not because he disbelieved in witchcraft but because he was troubled by the evidential basis of many witchcraft trials.[126]

Supporters of exorcism received the conviction of Elizabeth Jackson as a significant victory. Swan confidently declared:

> Mary Glover was vexed by Satan, by means of a witch. Methinks I may safely say it, since the jury has found it, and the Honourable Judges determined so of it. And therefore I cannot think but that they did a charitable and warrantable deed that prayed for her.[127]

However, it did not follow that because the courts were zealous to punish witchcraft, and even accepted possession as evidence in witchcraft cases, that the exorcists had a right to conduct their ministry. Witchcraft was a criminal matter, while clerical exorcists were subject to canon law and the unsympathetic ecclesiastical authorities.

Swan covered himself by claiming he could not judge whether Glover was possessed or not, and when he claimed that the question in a recent disputation at Cambridge had been changed from

'There is no possession and dispossession of demons in these days' to 'There is no *ordinary* possession and dispossession of demons in these days' he was clutching at straws.[128] Swan was anxious to believe that some room for the practice of exorcism still existed within the ecclesiastical establishment.

Bancroft's reaction to the Glover exorcism was 'agitated and almost frenzied',[129] and when the minister Lewis Hughes went to see Bancroft he was called 'rascal and varlet', imprisoned by Bancroft in the Gatehouse for four months and deprived of his living.[130] Bancroft sponsored a campaign of anti-exorcism preaching early in 1603, with some preachers going so far as to deny the reality of all possessions since the death of the last apostle.[131] Nevertheless, the effort they made to persuade Bancroft testifies to the exorcists' loyalty to the Elizabethan religious settlement. The exorcism of Mary Glover concluded with 'a prayer general for the whole state' in which one of the ministers prayed for 'her Majesty, the Counsellors, Nobles, Magistrates, Ministers, [and] people' (although the omission of bishops from this list seems pointed).[132]

Although Harmes advances the case that the exorcists and their supporters 'challenged the reformed identity of bishops', texts refuting Harsnett and Bancroft's charges attacked the Bishop of London specifically rather than the episcopate in general.[133] Clearly, dissatisfaction with the institution of episcopacy was widespread among godly advocates of exorcism, but the exorcists were ultimately loyal to the Church of England. Arthur Hildersham, the exorcist of Thomas Darling, was so strongly opposed to separatism from the established church that he was known as the 'hammer of schismatics',[134] and (if the celebrated exorcist was indeed its author) a book by John Darrell denouncing the separatist Brownists was published in 1617.[135]

Swan wanted to claim that any dispossessions that took place were extraordinary providences of God, although he was hardly consistent in this regard since he also emphasised the frequency of possessions 'at Norwich, at Woolwich, at Nottingham, at Burton, at Colchester, in London, in Lancashire, and further off as I hear in Kent and Sussex'.[136] However, Swan's claim that possessions were simultaneously 'extraordinary' and common does make sense within the context of the apocalyptic tone of his account of the Glover exorcism: the last days were approaching, and Satan was showing his power by possessing the godly.[137]

EXORCISM FOR THE CHURCH OF ENGLAND?

In 1600 George More tried to reduce the performance of exorcisms to a straightforward contest of sacred power between the Roman Catholic church and the Church of England:

> [F]or if the Church of England have this power to cast out devils, then the Church of Rome is a false Church. For there can be but one true Church, the principal mark of which, as they say, is to work miracles, and of them this is the greatest, namely to cast out devils.[138]

More's use of the phrase 'Church of England' was pointed; godly Protestants in England often preferred to refer to themselves as the 'church of the Gospel' or simply 'Protestants' in order to emphasise their unity of faith with Continental Protestants. By using the term 'Church of England', More was inviting the bishops to take up the weapon of exorcism against Catholicism as an official ministry of the established church. Even as late as 1602 the exorcists of Mary Glover were anxious to inform Bishop Bancroft of events and solicit his support. Protestant exorcists in sixteenth-century England did not want to be rebels against the establishment: they wanted the Church of England to accommodate exorcism.

During the exorcism of Mary Glover one of the exorcists, Master Barber, 'complained that we might not, but in fear of men, meet together to perform such duties, and such means as God has sanctified, and the Church heretofore practised in such cases'.[139] While Barber's words were, on one level, an expression of discontent with the bishops (and Bancroft in particular), the exorcists' willingness to appeal to tradition ('the Church heretofore practised') as well as scripture was unusual for puritans, who were usually content to rely exclusively on the authority of the Bible. Another exorcist, Master Badger, alluded to 'the practice of his Church and children from time to time in such cases'.[140] It is unclear whether Barber and Badger were appealing to the practice of the preceding 30 years (beginning with Foxe) or to a practice of the early church, but the exorcists' claim that they acted within a legitimate tradition was an element of their efforts to defend themselves before the bishops.

There was no compelling theological reason for 'puritans' to be especially interested in possession and exorcism, since the tendency of Continental Calvinism was to downplay such phenomena. As Oldridge has argued, by engaging in dispossession, exorcists 'were inevitably influenced by traditional beliefs and conventions associated with the phenomena'.[141] The Bible makes no mention of the connection between witchcraft and possession so earnestly advocated by Darrell, whose practice was closer to the Roman Catholic exorcists than he would have cared to admit. Likewise, Samuel Harsnett's rigorous theological cessationism was just as much a part of the 'puritan' inheritance as Darrell's credulity.

The survival (or revival) of Protestant exorcism in post-Reformation England was an example of creative accommodation of popular belief, and a striking instance of the Church of England's *via media* in action. In his speech to Thomas Darling on the right approach to exorcism, Arthur Hildersham was exquisitely cautious and circumspect. A sectarian historiographical paradigm of 'puritan exorcism' is unhelpful in trying to understand a contested phenomenon that, at least until 1604, belonged to the established church. Furthermore, the very reasons why the bishops wanted to suppress exorcism were the reasons why it was more than just a 'puritan' phenomenon. As Freeman observed, exorcisms attracted crowds 'well outside of godly circles',[142] and exorcism allowed ministers 'to build devoted followings from beyond the ranks of the godly'.[143]

If Protestant dispossessions were, in and of themselves, an example of 'Anglican' compromise, why then were they sometimes so vehemently opposed by the bishops whose role it was to steer the Church of England's middle course? It is a truism that bishops disliked exorcism because it was a charismatic ministry they could never truly control. Exorcism, by definition, was a charismatic ministry belonging to an earlier stratum of Christian practice that predated any attempts by hierarchies to control and regulate it.[144] An episcopal desire to curb exorcists' tendency to rely on their own authority was by no means unique to the Church of England; similar concerns led to canonical restrictions being imposed on Roman Catholic exorcists in 1614 and, in the early eighteenth century, led to the banning of all rites other than the *Rituale Romanum*.[145] It is unfair to interpret the practice of exorcism as anti-episcopal simply because it was charismatic in nature, since the church has struggled to hold in tension the hierarchical and charismatic authorisation of ministries in every age.

Oldridge's observation that the effectiveness of Protestant exorcists 'depended more on their personal faith and knowledge of scripture than the institutional power of the church'[146] likewise holds true of Catholic exorcists as well. In medieval and post-medieval Catholic theology, exorcism was not a sacrament automatically effective because a priest performed it, but rather a *sacramental* whose effectiveness depended on the holiness of the exorcist.[147] William Weston and his fellow Catholic exorcists acted outside of any established ecclesiastical authority – to an even greater extent, in fact, than their Protestant counterparts, since there were no Catholic bishops in England until 1625. The difference between Catholic and Protestant exorcists in sixteenth-century England was the reluctance of the latter to use imperative forms of conjuration, although Protestant exorcists were inconsistent even in this. It is also not possible to mark out Protestant exorcists as 'puritan' because of their interest in witchcraft. Although anti-puritan bishops tended to discourage witchcraft accusations, preoccupation with witchcraft in the 1590s and 1600s was scarcely confined to the godly.

For Harmes, the defining feature of puritanism was the holding of 'views inimical to episcopacy',[148] but although the actions of specific bishops were frequently denounced in pamphlets supporting exorcism, advocates of exorcism did not use dispossessions to challenge the existence of bishops. The effectiveness of exorcism had never been dependent on bishops' licences, although Harmes may be correct that bishops suppressed dispossessions because they involved unlicensed behaviour – notably preaching, fasting and gatherings of the faithful. Furthermore, his overall thesis that exorcists were yet another challenge to the embattled authority of bishops caught between the monarch and the ministry is convincing.[149] Exorcism empowered ministers at a time when episcopal authority was weak, and a clash was inevitable.

Freeman has argued that the bishops' efforts to suppress exorcism, even though they resulted in a canon that virtually ended the practice, were not an unqualified success. By deploying the entire machinery of the early modern church and state against the exorcists Bancroft exposed its limitations, since 'By marginalising dissent, [the bishops] weakened it, but they also perpetuated it'.[150] In other words, Bancroft and Harnsett created sectarianism where it had not previously existed. In modern terms, they were profoundly 'un-Anglican' because, rather than allowing exorcism a space to exist within the Church of England, they tried to exclude it altogether and thereby empowered it as an instrument of sectarianism.

Furthermore, there was a structural weakness in Harsnett's strategy of argument against exorcism, because in a Church of England where the authority of scripture was unquestioningly accepted, scepticism about possession and exorcism would never be thoroughly convincing.[151] Faced with the apparent reality of possession and the apparent effectiveness of exorcism, English Protestants raised on a literal reading of the New Testament would naturally interpret these phenomena within a biblical worldview. However, Freeman also noted the limitations of Darrell's defence of exorcism in his 'failure to present any explanation of how or why possession or exorcism worked'.[152] This may have been down to the fact that the Bible offered few details about possession or exorcism, meaning that biblical literalism furnished a somewhat minimalist demonology. However, the absence of any thoroughly worked-out demonology amongst Protestant exorcists may also be an indication that their practice was largely a response to popular demand.

CONCLUSION

The Reformation neither increased nor diminished fear of the devil in early modern England, and the Protestant reformation of demonology involved 'a subtle realigning of emphasis, rather than an overt process of reform'.[153] The reformation of exorcism, however, was more thoroughgoing. After a hesitant beginning that left the baptismal exorcism intact in the 1549 Prayer Book, the 1552 and 1559 Prayer Books eliminated liturgical exorcism altogether.

The Reformation did away with pilgrimages to the shrines of exorcist saints and re-focussed popular demand for dispossession on the clergy. Hybrid exorcisms containing both Protestant and Catholic elements in the 1560s and 1570s gave way, in the 1590s, to godly exercises of prayer and fasting that, in spite of protestations to the contrary by the exorcists, were closer to the old practice of imperative conjuration than they seemed.

Protestant exorcisms were communal events, often instigated by puritan ministers (and sometimes authorised by bishops) but involving people of all persuasions. The collaboration of John Dee and John Darrell – a conjuring ritualist and a puritan dispossessor – in the case of the Lancashire Seven is a demonstration that the theological base of exorcism in sixteenth-century England extended beyond puritanism. However, the similarity of exorcistic 'exercises' to illegal conventicles and their use of unlicensed fasting meant that they were perceived as a threat by bishops, who did all they could to discredit the exorcists. Glyn Parry has argued that Archbishop Whitgift's hostility to exorcism in the 1580s ought to be seen as part of a conservative counter-reaction to puritanism, and while this may be true, opposition to exorcism existed among the bishops as early as the 1570s. Neither side, however, was completely victorious in the Elizabethan exorcism controversy. Protestant exorcism was driven underground and out of the established church, but Whitgift, Bancroft and their acolytes failed to convince the population at large that possession and exorcism were fraudulent. Roman Catholic missionary priests and cunning-folk stepped into the space vacated by the clergy of the established church in order to meet the demand for dispossession. Furthermore, as will be shown in Chapter 2, Bancroft failed to embed unambiguous rejection of exorcism as an unequivocal doctrinal commitment of the Church of England, thereby leaving room for both continuation and revival.

CHAPTER 2

Exorcism Marginalised,
1604–1852

From 1604, episcopally approved exorcisms of the demonically possessed were curtailed for more than three centuries, since no bishop was prepared to issue a licence for a dispossession. However, the intervening period was far from a hiatus in the history of the Church of England's engagement with exorcism. Some clergy ignored the restrictions on exorcism; others may have circumvented them by exorcising ghosts rather than demoniacs; and separatist and semi-separatist Anglican groups such as the Nonjurors and Methodists began experimenting with exorcism again in the eighteenth century. The climate of scepticism that prevailed in the Enlightenment Church of England was by no means universal, and while many clergy held out-and-out cessationist views, others adopted a variety of more nuanced theological positions.

Cases of demonic possession continued unabated in the seventeenth and eighteenth centuries, although there was often a gap between folk belief – which made no distinction between exorcism and bewitchment – and clerical interpretations steeped in biblical interpretation. As Owen Davies explains:

> [W]hile many of the clergy ... shared with folk culture the same belief in the power of possession, it did not necessarily share the same expressions, etiological concepts, and healing rituals pertaining to that basic belief. Clerical perceptions of witchcraft and possession were based on old elite, theological conceptions of diabolism. When

confronted by instances of witch-induced possession, the clergy saw the witch merely as an instrument of the Devil, and this directed their attentions more towards Satan than his earthly vassals. On the other hand, in the folk conception of witchcraft, the Devil was largely in the background, and was not generally cited directly as an agent in cases of popular witchcraft. When attributing blame for their possession by evil spirits, people looked no further than the witch.[1]

In the seventeenth century, clerical involvement in diagnoses of possession-bewitchment could lead to witchcraft prosecutions, as indeed it had done in the sixteenth. After the repeal of the 1604 Witchcraft Act in 1735 clerical interest shifted (if it had not already done so) from witches to the devil. The arrival of clerical spectators consequently often elicited a shift in the behaviour of demoniacs, who 'would begin to talk less of witches and more and more of devils, usually multiple devils, conversing in different voices, or supposedly communicating in different languages'.[2]

Possession and exorcism were decidedly minority interests among the clergy of eighteenth- and early nineteenth-century England, but this did not stop ordinary people attributing supernatural powers to the clergy in both folklore and reality. Owing to the unique position the church occupied in English rural society, perhaps combined with the half-remembered practices of the pre-Reformation church, in Davies's view 'the Church of England, unwillingly, and often unwittingly, ... contributed more to the survival of witchcraft and magical beliefs than Methodism ever did'.[3] The roles projected onto the clergy by popular belief sometimes drowned out the clergy's own interpretation of their role, and more than one unsuspecting curate ended up being persuaded to say 'prayers' that were ascribed magical significance by the laity. The Enlightenment Church of England tended to cessationism on both theological and philosophical grounds, trying to serve a population whose belief in the preternatural was undimmed, it seems, by the efforts of sixteenth-century reformers. Both tension and misinterpretation were inevitable.

CANON 72

Archbishop Whitgift died on 29 February 1604, and when the Convocation of Canterbury met on 20 March it was presided over, on

King James's instructions, by Bishop Richard Bancroft.[4] Convocation met in order to ratify a set of reformed canons, completing a process that had been begun, but never finished, in the reigns of Henry VIII, Edward VI and Elizabeth.[5] The Convocation of Canterbury ratified the canons in April, although the Convocation of York did not follow suit until 1606. One canon that Bancroft personally drafted was Canon 72, forbidding fasting and exorcism without episcopal permission. Bancroft's draft prohibited 'any privatt fastinge and prayer under pretence of Castinge out Devilles under payne of suspension and deprivation from the ministre'.[6] Bancroft's original draft contained no provision for an episcopal licence, and King James himself may have been responsible for adding 'the significant qualification that an exorcism could be performed with episcopal permission, which at least granted that a genuine and legitimate exorcism was possible'.[7]

The canon's Latin title contained the word *exorcismos*, although the text of the canon itself simply referred to attempts to eject (*eiicere*) or expel (*expellere*) a demon:

> No minister or ministers shall, without the licence and direction of the bishop of the diocese first obtained and had under his hand and seal, appoint or keep any solemn fasts, either publicly or in any private houses, other than such as by law are, or by public authority shall be appointed, nor shall be wittingly present at any of them, under pain of suspension for the first fault, of excommunication for the second, and of deposition from the ministry for the third. Neither shall any minister, not licensed, as aforesaid, presume to appoint or hold any meetings for sermons, commonly termed by some prophecies or exercises, in market towns, or other places, under the said pains: nor, without such licence, to attempt upon any pretence whatsoever, either of possession or obsession, by fasting and prayer, to cast out any devil or devils, under pain of the imputation of imposture or cozenage, and deposition from the ministry.[8]

Since the Latin rather than the English version of the canon was definitive, the appearance of the word *exorcismos* in the title is an indication that the canon suppressed imperative conjurations of the Roman Catholic type as well as Protestant dispossessions – although whether this usage also meant that a bishop could authorise an imperative conjuration is unclear. The absence of any authorised rite of exorcism from the 1559 Prayer Book did not, in and of itself, constitute a prohibition of the practice, since other 'unestablished ceremonies' of the Church of England (such as the consecration of churches and the coronation of monarchs) continued to exist outside the Prayer Book.[9] Furthermore, exorcisms were never directly prohibited by canon or statute because they were 'Catholic', as Harmes seems to suggest.[10] It was merely assumed that no minister of the established church would ever attempt such a thing. In the eighteenth century the Convocations of Canterbury and York became obsolete, since they were invariably prorogued as soon as they convened, and consequently the canons (including Canon 72) became largely unenforceable.[11] By 1700 the canon was an indication of the Church of England's official position on the issue of exorcism, but little more.

It is important to note, however, that exorcism and dispossession were not even the main targets of Canon 72. Patrick Collinson drew attention to the fact that Canon 73, following immediately after the restrictions on exorcism, prohibited 'conventicles and secret meetings of priests and ministers'. He suggested that Bancroft regarded all gatherings of believers outside of services in an authorised place of worship as schismatic.[12] Since a dispossession by prayer and fasting involved, by definition, a gathering outside of the context of a normal service (often including several ministers), it constituted a conventicle in Bancroft's eyes. The suppression of exorcism in Canon 72 reads almost as an afterthought appended to a canon aimed against a variety of schismatic activities, primarily unauthorised fasting. Although, as Freeman noted, 'to the ecclesiastical authorities the issues of fasting and exorcism were as intertwined as snakes on a caduceus',[13] it is not appropriate to read Canon 72 as a theological condemnation of exorcism.

THE IMPACT OF CANON 72

Although James may have prevented an outright ban on exorcism, the king's new sceptical stance was sealed in August 1605 when he examined the counterfeit demoniac Anne Gunter at Oxford. Having been committed to the custody of Bancroft, by October Gunter had confessed her fraud to the king.[14] The combination of royal scepticism with determined archiepiscopal opposition made it virtually impossible for a bishop to take advantage of the provisions of Canon 72, and indeed there is no evidence that an episcopal licence for dispossession by prayer and fasting was ever granted in England after 1604.[15]

Licences were, however, granted outside England under English episcopal authority. In 1629 the governor of Bermuda, Roger Wood, proclaimed a public fast for the dispossession of a young man named Roger Sterrop, and many of the island's inhabitants participated in the day-long 'exercise' of prayer that dispossessed him.[16] Wood, like all governors of English colonies, was exercising quasi-episcopal authority under the bishop of London – although it seems highly unlikely that the governor consulted William Laud on the matter. Furthermore, English Protestants continued to cite successful dispossessions in a controversial context. When visiting Brussels circa 1605 Joseph Hall (1574–1656), a future bishop of Exeter and Norwich, entered into a discussion of possession and exorcism with a Jesuit named Costerus. According to Hall,

> [Costerus] slipped into a choleric invective against our Church, which, as he said, could not yield one miracle; and when I answered, that, in our Church, we had manifest proofs of the ejection of devils by fasting and prayer, he answered, that, if it could be proved, that ever any devil was dispossessed in our Church, he would quit his religion.[17]

Cunning-folk and other lay practitioners of unbewitchment had been competing with Protestant exorcists before 1604, such as Edmond Hartley, the cunning-man executed for his attempted unbewitchment of the Starkie children in 1596. The popularity of cunning-folk may well have rested on their willingness to use traditional methods such as herbs and conjurations which were condemned by Protestant exorcists. As Owen Davies observed, 'The void left by the clergy's partial withdrawal from popular magic may ... have led to the proliferation of cunning-folk'.[18] The withdrawal of most clergy of the established church from the field of exorcism left it wide open to lay practitioners who 'borrowed from Catholic practices'.[19] In a world where belief in possession was so widespread, people were forced to improvise when the clergy refused to help, with one man even exorcising his own daughter.[20]

Although they were less numerous than lay practitioners on account of the difficulty of reaching England (and staying out of captivity when they got there), Roman Catholic missionary priests also did their best to supply the demand for exorcism. However, Catholic missionaries did not attempt another campaign of exorcism like that of William Weston in 1585–6. Not all priests supported exorcism as a method of proselytism, and even the Jesuits often opted for simple unbewitchments using holy water, relics of Jesuit saints or confession rather than the full rite of exorcism prescribed by Rome in 1614.[21] Exorcism was also practised by Protestant sectaries, who finally won the day in 1646 when Parliament abolished bishops and replaced the Prayer Book with the *Directory of Public Worship*.[22] The religious freedom of the Interregnum meant that sects such as the Quakers were free to practise exorcism as they chose.[23]

In 1650 Bishop Hall, living in rural Norfolk as the ejected bishop of Norwich, inveighed against Roman Catholic imperative exorcisms, 'a power more easily arrogated than really exercised',[24] denying that 'the Church hath any warrant from God to make any such suit, where [there is] any overture of promise to have it granted'.[25] Hall rejected the perceived automatic effectiveness of imperative exorcism, and while he accepted that the apostles had been able to command demons, he condemned imperative conjurations as prayers to demons:

> [F]or us, we that have no power to bid, must pray; pray, not to those ill guests that they would depart … but to the great God of heaven, who commands them to their chains. This is a sure and everlasting remedy: this is the only certain way to their foil and our deliverance and victory.[26]

However, although he rejected any form of imperative conjuration, Hall's anti-Catholic polemic contained no suggestion of cessationism with regard to demonic possession. Hall was prepared to accept that prayer for the possessed might be authorised. Hall, who had been suspected of puritanism by Archbishop Laud, was considerably more open to the possibility of dispossession than his predecessor Samuel Harsnett.

Furthermore, in spite of the effective suppression of exorcism itself, behaviours traditionally associated with exorcism continued as tools of 'diagnostic demonology' for dealing with the possessed and bewitched. In 1622 Bishop Thomas Morton of Lichfield and Coventry read different texts from a Greek New Testament in an effort to expose the counterfeit demoniac William Perry.[27] Morton may have been sceptical, but just by applying such a test he was stepping into the role of an exorcist, since the test implied the possibility that a demoniac might understand strange languages. Similar tests were used in witchcraft trials; Elizabeth Throckmorton's symptoms of possession stopped when Agnes Samuel was made to say the words, 'I charge you, you Devil, as I love you and have authority over you and am a witch, and guilty of this matter, that you allow this child to be well at this moment'.[28] Here, unbewitchment by an accused witch played much the same role as exorcism and served to incriminate the suspect.

In addition to the cunning-folk, Roman Catholic priests and dissenting ministers who continued to practise exorcism, at least some clergy of the Church of England chose to ignore or circumvent Canon 72 and exorcise anyway. In 1634 Anthony Lapthorne, rector of Tretire with Michaelchurch, Herefordshire, attempted the dispossession of an 'ungodly' parishioner.[29] Richard Napier (1559–1634), the rector of Great Linford, Buckinghamshire, obtained a licence to practise medicine from the archdeacon of Buckingham and established himself as a popular astrological physician.[30] Napier specialised in the treatment of the mentally ill, and although he did not often resort to exorcism, he occasionally 'either used Catholic formulas or composed his own texts to remove their Popish connotations'. Napier's diary recorded the formula he used for the exorcism of Edmund Francklin of Bedford in 1630:

> Behold, I God's most unworthy minister and servant, I do charge and command thee, thou cruel beast, with all thy associates and all other malignant spirits in case that any of you have your being in the body of this creature, Mr. E. Fr[ancklin], and have distempered his brain with melancholy and have also deprived his body and limbs of their natural use, I charge and command you speedily to depart from this creature and servant of God, Mr. E. F[rancklin], regenerated by the laver of the holy baptism and redeemed by the precious blood of our Lord Jesus Christ, I charge you to depart from him and every part of his body, really, personally.[31]

As Michael MacDonald observed, Napier 'was unusually ready to set aside scruples about the legitimacy of natural magic and ritual exorcism', suggesting that Napier's success as a physician may have emboldened him to do so.[32] At a time when medical licences could be issued by bishops and their commissaries, the line between medical and ecclesiastical sanction may have been blurred for both Napier and his clients. Napier was no puritan, and his practice of exorcism should be located in the private, therapeutic tradition of John Dee.[33] Although Napier made use of his status as an ordained minister to command the spirit in the exorcism of Edmund Francklin, he acted first and foremost as a physician and this may have led him to imagine that his actions lay outside the restrictions of Canon 72.

Owen Davies has argued that Napier's status as a clergyman may have helped him to attract custom. People knew the difference between a clergyman who unbewitched and a cunning-man or woman who unbewitched, and they sometimes went to Napier when they thought they had been bewitched by cunning-folk. Ironically, however, Napier was alarmed when he was called a conjurer, in spite of the fact that he was doing exactly this – conjuring (commanding) spirits.[34] Napier viewed his practice in the context of a learned tradition of astrological medicine and was unable to see that his prescriptions often resembled those of less learned popular magicians.

Clerical involvement in exorcism continued after the Restoration. In 1671 the astrological physician Joseph Blagrave reported that a clergyman had attempted to exorcise the daughter of a Basingstoke turner whom Blagrave subsequently delivered success-fully. On meeting the girl, Blagrave immediately diagnosed possession and advised her father 'to get one godly Minister or other to try what he could do by his means, and devotion'. The father reported that he had already done this, without success:

For the Minister of the Parish, whose name was Mr Webb one reputed to be a very honest, godly, and Learned man did undertake to do it: and came to his house two several times to that purpose, but could not prevail; notwithstanding he spent about three hours time in tryal thereof at his first coming, yet he was forced to desist: but withal, told her father, that at the next coming he would be better prepared, and accordingly he did come the second time, but could not prevail then neither, during all the time that he was in action about this business, the Maid was extreamly tormented, it being as before near three hours before he ended, who then said to her Father, *Lord have mercy upon me I cannot do it, wherefore I advise you to look out farther, per adventure you may meet with one another who may have strength of faith, and a gift to do it, and likewise to cure her distemper.*[35]

The minister in question is most likely to have been Thomas Webb (d. 1691), rector of Hannington, Hampshire between 1663 and 1691, who was at one point licensed to preach throughout the diocese of Winchester (Hannington is around seven miles northeast of Basingstoke).[36] If this identification is correct it is an indication that impeccably orthodox clergy could still be drawn into exorcism, since a licence to preach throughout a diocese was hard to come by and would only have been issued to a full-throated supporter of the Restoration religious settlement. Blagrave's account needs to be treated with considerable caution, primarily because his book was an extended advertisement for his business. Webb's supposed words, admitting his failure, are clearly preparing the reader to appreciate Blagrave's superior gifts as an exorcist. On the other hand, if Blagrave had fabricated the entire story it is unlikely that he would have named the clergyman in question.

EXORCISM AND ANTI-SADDUCISM

The movement in the Restoration Church of England that historians have called anti-Sadducism takes its name from Joseph Glanvill's *Saducismus triumphatus* ('Sadducism conquered', 1680), whose title alluded to the ancient Jewish sect which denied the resurrection and the existence of angels and demons. For Glanvill and other anti-Sadducists, Commonwealth sectaries such as the mortalist Muggle-tonians (who believed the soul died with the body) were modern day Sadducees, but the anti-Sadducists' principal target was Thomas Hobbes (1588–1679), who denied the existence of spirits altogether.[37] The anti-Sadducist case was essentially a 'slippery slope' argument: if people stopped believing in well attested manifestations of the spirit world, such as ghosts, demons and the effects of witchcraft, they were liable eventually to disbelieve in the supreme spirit, God himself.

The anti-Sadducists departed from earlier Protestant approaches to the preternatural by placing empirical evidence ahead of theological speculation,[38] and there is some truth in the claim that Glanvill was the first 'ghost-hunter',[39] and the ultimate ancestor of contemporary 'paranormal investigators'. Yet Glanvill's preoccupation with proof of the preternatural also harked back to earlier exorcists who practised 'diagnostic demonology', testing demoniacs and developing diagnostic criteria for possession. Glanvill defended a literal understanding of the exorcisms of Christ and St Paul and derided attempts to reinterpret biblical possessions,[40] even going so far as to assert that 'there were persons possessed with Devils some Ages after Christ', without specifying when.[41] In spite of his credulity Glanvill was ambiguous with regard to the possibility of demonic possession in the present, and made no reference to post-apostolic exorcisms.

Anti-Sadducists 'were seeking to walk a line between popery and nonconformist enthusiasm and using witchcraft and the spirit world to vindicate Anglicanism against both threats'.[42] They were determined to provide evidence of the reality of the spirit world, but at the time they were handicapped in collecting such evidence by the very fact that they were clergymen of the Church of England. In his *Pandaemonium, or the Devil's Cloyster* (1684) Richard Bovet reprinted a letter from the clergyman John Boyse describing the activities of the 'demon of Spraiton' in tormenting a young male servant of the Furze family. Boyse was forced to admit, however, that he had not personally visited the Furze household, since 'they have called to their assistance none but Nonconforming ministers, [and] I was not qualified to be welcome there, having given Mr Furze a great deal of trouble the last year about a conventicle in his house, where one of this parish was the preacher'.[43]

The Church of England's equivocal position on exorcism was a source of puzzlement to dissenters such as the congregationalist Thomas Jollie, who attempted to show that the clergy of the established church ought to be exorcising. Jollie appealed to Joseph Hall's non-cessationist views as well as the writings of Andrew Willet (1562–1621), whom Jollie claimed 'owns not only the extraordinary means, but this of Fasting, and Prayer; whereby saith he, we doubt not but even in these days, when it pleaseth God, Satan is chased from the Possession of Christ's Members'.[44] Jollie also appealed to Canon 72 as evidence that the Church of England accepted the possibility of possession:

> I am told there is a Canon of the Convocation, which prohibits the attempting this way of dispossessing Satan, without the License of the Ordinary; which necessarily implies that the Episcopal Clergy did believe there then was such a thing as Possession, and Dispossession. I am told Mr. T[aylor] was informed of the said Cannon, and thereupon reformed the first Leaf of his Preface.[45]

Jollie was alluding to Zachary Taylor (1653–1705), rector of Croston, whose *Surey Imposter* (1697) was the target of his own polemic. By showing that the Church of England countenanced dispossession, Jollie aimed to discredit Taylor as a minister unfaithful to his own church.

Jollie was hitting on a sore point. The outright cessationism of Bancroft, Harsnett and their followers was less common after 1604, although whether this had anything to do with Canon 72 is unclear. Jeremy Taylor, in his *Dissuasive from Popery* (1664–7), was extremely critical of the impiety of Roman Catholic imperative exorcisms, but stopped short of denying the possibility of possession and exorcism altogether. He simply observed that the burden of proof lay with the exorcists: 'We do not envy to any one any grace of God, but wish it were more modestly pretended, unless it could be more evidently proved'.[46] Anglican commentary on possession and exorcism was perpetually walking a tightrope between outright cessationism and belief, although virtually all Anglicans remained cessationist in practice.

Thomas Waters has argued that a kind of attenuated anti-Sadducism survived into the late eighteenth century (and even the early nineteenth) as the conviction of some conservative clergy that 'vivid supernaturalism, orthodox Christianity, and political loyalty went together'. Some clergy opposed discouraging belief in bewitchment among ordinary people, even if they did not share such belief, because the introduction of rationalism risked provoking the freethinking which might lead to revolution.[47] In 1838 a West

Country newspaper blamed 'those Tories who have so effectually resisted popular education' for allowing belief in witchcraft to continue, and attacked the clergy for failing in their duty. Witchcraft belief became associated with Anglicanism and Toryism, while dissenters and Whigs regularly renounced 'superstition'.[48] It is clear that the Church of England rarely if ever did anything to encourage belief in bewitchment and possession, but in the eyes of its critics the church did not do enough to proactively discourage traditional beliefs among the faithful.

CONJURING PARSONS: FOLKLORE AND REALITY

The figure of the 'conjuring parson', a clergyman who was able to command and lay spirits, is a common one in English folklore. Technically, Canon 72 did not prohibit the laying of ghosts, since it was focussed on casting devils out of people. This distinction may have been appreciated by ghost-laying clergy; or they may simply have been acting, as Theo Brown put it, 'at a prudent distance from the Bishop's Palace'.[49] However, the question of whether ghosts were really the spirits of dead people or devils in disguise was never resolved in Anglican theology, rendering the application of Canon 72 to ghost-laying ambiguous.[50]

The ghost-laying parsons of folklore usually acted in groups of nine or twelve,[51] were trained at Oxford University,[52] and were preferably learned in Latin, Greek, Hebrew and Arabic.[53] Parsons might banish a spirit to a magic circle, otherwise known as a 'gallitrap' or 'Lob's pound'.[54] These might be invisible or marked out with bands of iron taken from barrels (owing to the belief that spirits cannot pass iron). A clergyman could protect himself from harm by being in the presence of a pregnant woman or a baby, since it was believed that spirits could not harm the innocent.[55] A spirit could also be banished by throwing consecrated graveyard earth, which was believed to absorb the bodies of the dead and was therefore 'doubly potent'.[56] Indeed, Brown argued that 'in post-Reformation times it took the place of holy water' as a spiritual disinfectant.[57]

The parsons of folklore might also exorcise by 'reading down' a spirit into a small bottle or container, an idea that probably derived from medieval stories about John Schorne, a thirteenth-century rector of North Marston in Buckinghamshire who became a popular folk-saint in late medieval England and was often portrayed on the dados of rood screens confining the devil to a boot.[58]

> [A] company of parsons assembles in church, and they stand in a circle, each with a candle, and read the Psalms through over and over again throughout the night. The candles get dimmer and go out one by one, until there is only one left burning, that of the most powerful and most learned of the group. At this point the spook collapses and shrinks down and down, until he is so tiny he can trot into a little box or bottle.[59]

Sometimes, the folkloric exorcism would also involve an excommunication of the spirit with bell, book and candle; a bell would be tolled, the Bible slammed shut and a candle extinguished.[60] Once confined in a bottle or box, a spirit would usually be confined in a deep pond or well, and exorcism legends were often associated with such places.[61] The spirit might be set an impossible task, such as spinning ropes of sand, in order to keep it occupied.[62] The securest place of all to send a spirit was the Red Sea, a tradition that Davies traces back to 1650.[63] Sometimes it was necessary for the exorcists to make an offering to the spirit, such as the 12 parsons at Walford, Berkshire, who were said to have banished a spirit from a barn by tempting it with two cockerels (which it tore to pieces).[64] The offering of cockerels to spirits was a staple of early modern necromancy. Storms in the West Country were often attributed to a parson conjuring a spirit in the area, and lightning strikes on church steeples blamed on spirits being dispatched to the Red Sea.[65]

Folktales of ghost-laying are sometimes ambiguous about whether the spirit is a demon or a ghost. When the spirits are ghosts, they are 'the stubborn, malevolent spectres of local evildoers (often gentry) which disturb the whole community',[66] and not ordinary ghosts who appear to right an injustice and then go to their rest. In one Cheshire story a parson exorcises a 'boggart', which could mean 'either a troublesome goblin or a ghost' but in this case is the malevolent ghost of a local grocer. With the assistance of villagers the parson corners the boggart in a circle drawn with chalk, and 'they fair bet [beat] 'im an' smothter 'im wi' prayer, for th'devil was druv [driven] out o' 'im'.[67] The language suggests that the grocer was possessed by the devil before he died and this was why his spirit could not rest – in which case the parson was performing both a ghost-laying and an exorcism in the proper sense. Evil spirits and ghosts of wicked people may have been elided in the popular mind.

English folklore about ghost-laying parsons is interesting for what it reveals about popular attitudes to and perceptions of the clergy. As Davies observed, at a time of declining influence for the Church of England nationally, 'the legends … reflect the continued rural perception of the Anglican clergy as a protective, unifying parochial force'.[68] Furthermore, Davies noted 'the paucity of nineteenth-century legends regarding lay exorcists, compared with the profusion of clergymen', which suggested that 'Ghost-laying was evidently one area of supernatural interventionism where the Anglican clergy had a decided edge over cunning-folk in popular perception'.[69]

However, although legends about ghost-laying sometimes accumulated around real clergymen,[70] there is 'frustratingly little concrete evidence of the clergy laying ghosts'.[71] Theo Brown described John Ruddle (c.1637–99) as 'the most authentic conjuring parson of the seventeenth century',[72] since Ruddle left a sketchy account of his laying of the 'Botathen Ghost' in 1665 (Botathen was an alternative name for South Petherwin, located just southwest of Launceston, Cornwall). Ruddle was the son of Ralph Ruddle, a clerk of Stoke Dry, Rutland, although he was born at Bishops Cannings in Wiltshire. After receiving his education at Uppingham School he matriculated at Gonville and Caius College, Cambridge in October 1654 (thereby defying the stereotype of conjuring parsons being Oxford men). Ruddle was vicar of St Mary Magdalene, Launceston from 1663 until his death, as well as running the local school and serving as vicar of nearby Altarnun. In 1665 he was described as 'well affected to the government', which suggests he was without puritan tendencies. In 1680 he received preferment, becoming a prebendary of Exeter Cathedral.[73]

In January 1665 the ghost of Dorothy Dinglet was troubling the son of a Mr Bligh of Botathen as he walked across the fields to reach his tutor. Ruddle went to the field and

> after due thought … addressed the ghost quite simply and discovered that the cause of the haunting was some 'unfinished business' on earth.

He at once attended to it ... Then he returned to the scene of the haunting, reassured the ghost and dismissed her in words not recorded.[74]

Ruddle's behaviour was typical of many reported early modern ghost encounters, which usually involved the 'unfinished business' of the dead. It can hardly be classed as an exorcism, although by allaying their fears about the ghost, Ruddle was acting pastorally on behalf of his congregation. In subsequent re-tellings by Daniel Defoe and nineteenth-century folklorists 'Parson Rudall' became a skilled ritual magician who drew a magic circle and a pentacle, wielded a 'crutch of rowan', wore a brass ring engraved with the *scutum Davidis*, and chanted conjurations in Syriac from a parchment scroll. Later accounts also had Ruddle asking the bishop of Exeter for permission to exorcise the spirit (which of course he had no need to do).[75]

The case of John Ruddle demonstrates that clergy were genuinely pastorally concerned about their parishioners' beliefs about troublesome ghosts, but it has little or nothing to reveal about exorcism. Henry Bourne (1694–1733), a clergyman antiquary in Newcastle, recorded popular beliefs about banishing spirits in the northeast of England, and went so far as to translate and publish a week-long ritual for exorcising a haunted house by the Italian Franciscan friar Valerio Polidori.[76] Bourne's justification for publishing the rite was ambiguous: 'not that [Catholic priests] are envied for their Art of conjuring, but that it may be seen, how well they deserve the Character they go under'.[77] The 'character' Bourne was referring to was the widespread reputation of Catholic priests as exorcists. Bourne described Polidori's approach as 'whimsical forms of exorcising':

'Tis ridiculous to suppose that the Prince of Darkness, will yield to such feeble Instruments as Water and Herbs and Crucifixes. These Weapons are not spiritual but carnal: Whereas, in resisting this potent Enemy, we must put on the whole Armour of GOD, that we may be able to resist him: which is such a Composition, as is entirely free from the least Allay or Mixture of any such Superstitions.[78]

It is striking that, rather than condemning exorcism outright, Bourne merely criticised Polidori's *form* of exorcism as 'whimsical' (a word that scarcely implies the strongest religious censure). Recounting another story, Bourne suggested that prayer alone was sufficient to drive the devil away, and that the accoutrements of Catholic exorcism were simply unnecessary. Bourne was in no doubt that the devil and demons could take up residence in places and needed to be driven away, and in this respect he was more sympathetic to exorcism than many of his fellow clergy. Furthermore, by translating and publishing Polidori's rite of exorcism of a haunted house, Bourne must have realised that he was making it accessible to some people who would be more than happy to use it, and Paul Monod suggests that Bourne's belief in the devil's physical presence in places led him to include the translated rite.[79]

Ultimately, there is no real evidence (if folklore can be discounted) that 'reading down' of spirits by the clergy ever took place; nor is there any evidence that clergy drew magic circles to confine spirits. Yet some clergy in rural areas did compete with cunning-folk and provided similar magical services. In 1826 the Cornish clergyman Richard Polwhele claimed he 'could mention the names of several persons, whose influence over their flock was solely attributable to this circumstance'.[80] In 1914 J. F. Chanter reported that a famous 'black book' belonging to a real clergyman of North Devon active in the 1820s (identified by Chanter only as 'Parson Joe') had been discovered. The 'black book' turned out to be a manual of astrology containing a few questionary horoscopes cast by Parson Joe. Chanter concluded that 'we can well understand that anyone possessing a knowledge of that art would be credited by the peasantry with the possession of supernatural powers'.[81]

The case of Parson Joe suggests that rumours of 'black books' may not have sprung up entirely without cause, since Parson Joe was genuinely interested in occult knowledge. However, Theo Brown's suggestion that ordinary people regarded *any* learning as occult knowledge is not altogether plausible, and credits rural people with too little intelligence.[82] The fact that some clergy were content to allow a reputation as a ghost-laying conjurer to build up around them does not mean that they actually attempted to lay ghosts. On the other hand, it is hard to see why folklore of ghost-laying was so persistent if no clergy ever agreed to attempt it. It is not hard to imagine some incumbents assuaging the fears of their parishioners from time to time by attempting – or pretending – to deal with the unquiet dead. Owen Davies has pointed to the poverty of the rural clergy, which may have created 'the temptation ... to exploit their spiritual position, not only out of cynical cupidity, but also out of a charitable Christian sense that they were helping their parishioners'.[83]

But clergy found it increasingly difficult, in spite of the decline of the church courts, to engage in 'moonlighting enterprises' as the eighteenth century wore on. The church was acutely aware of the threat posed by Methodism and 'the social distance the expanding middling classes were putting between themselves and what was deemed the "vulgar" beliefs and practices of the lower orders'.[84] By the early decades of the nineteenth century conjuring parsons were a vanishing breed, 'partly due to a new intellectual climate, and partly because of commercial and professional developments'.[85] Yet, on remote Exmoor, local people were still ascribing magical powers to one clergyman as late as the 1930s.[86]

NONJURORS, METHODISTS AND HUTCHINSONIANS

With the exception of possible instances of ghost-laying in rural areas, exorcism disappeared as a ministry of the parish clergy of eighteenth-century England. However, it continued to exist at the margins of Anglicanism. The Nonjurors were those clergy who refused to swear allegiance to William and Mary as Supreme Governors of the Church of England in 1689 because the exiled James II was still alive. The Nonjurors, who were mostly of a strongly high church persuasion, soon acquired their own bishops, chapels and congregations and began to experiment liturgically. Most Nonjurors abandoned the *Book of Common Prayer* as unacceptable because it now contained a service of thanksgiving for the arrival of William of Orange in England in November 1688, and some reverted to the 1549 Prayer Book and its associated ceremonies. This produced an internal split within the Nonjuring church between 'usagers', who were prepared to adopt ritual usages found in the 1549 Prayer Book, and 'non-usagers' who rejected them. The dispute spawned more than 40 tracts written by opposing Nonjurors between 1717 and 1725.[87]

One of the issues on which usagers and non-usagers disagreed was exorcism.[88] The most determined advocate of the usages was Thomas Deacon (1697–1753), who made his living as a physician in Manchester but was also a Nonjuring minister. Deacon, who was consecrated to the episcopate by Bishop Archibald Campbell of Aberdeen in 1732, was an avid liturgical scholar. In 1734 he produced an expanded version of the Prayer Book liturgy augmented with additional rites. Deacon's liturgy of baptism restored the *effeta* (in which the priest blew in the candidate's face), pre-baptismal signing with the cross and an exorcism closely based on the 1549 Prayer Book:

> I command thee, thou unclean spirit, in the name of the Father, and of the Son, and of the Holy Ghost, that thou come out of and depart from these infants, whom our Lord Jesus Christ hath vouchsafed to call to his holy Baptism, to be made members of his body, and of his holy congregation. Therefore, thou cursed spirit, remember thy sentence, remember thy judgment, remember the day to be at hand, wherein thou shalt burn in fire everlasting, prepared for thee and thine angels: and presume not to exercise any tyranny towards these infants, whom Christ hath bought with his precious blood, and by this his holy Baptism calleth to be of his flock.[89]

In his catechetical work *A Full, True and Comprehensive View of Christianity* (1748), Deacon provided a commentary on his reintroduction of exorcism to baptism. Deacon stopped short of claiming that candidates for baptism were literally possessed, however, writing instead that 'the devil … is in possession [of them] by sin':

> After which follows the Exorcism, that is, the Priest blows in the Catechumen's face, signs him with the sign of the Cross, and pronounces authoritative words, commanding the devil to depart from this creature, of whom he is in possession by sin: Thus is that impure spirit constrained to give place to the Holy Ghost, the Spirit of purity, who is going to make this creature his temple. This is called by the Ancients the fire of Exorcism, because, as mixed metals are purged by fire, so does Exorcism purge the soul, and as it were fires the evil spirit from it, casting a terror upon him, making him fly from his possession, and leave it in a salutary state and hope of eternal life.[90]

Deacon classed exorcism as one of five 'Lesser Sacraments' associated with baptism,[91] and even included a lesson on exorcism in his catechism:

Exorcism is the ceremony of blowing in the face, signing the person with the sign of the cross, and using authoritative words: the design of this is to drive away the devil, that impure spirit who possesses all that are not possessed by the Spirit of God; and to constrain him to give place to the Holy Ghost, that Spirit of purity, who is going to make this creature his temple.[92]

The child was then to be interrogated on the subject:

Q. What is to be done before Baptism?

A. The person is to be exorcised.

Q. What is that ceremony?

A. It consists of blowing in the person's face, signing him with the sign of the cross, and using authoritative words.

Q. What is the design of Exorcism?

A. To drive away the devil, and make him give way to the Holy Ghost.[93]

In addition to the exorcism that was part of the baptismal liturgy, Deacon included prayers for 'energumens' (the ancient Christian term for baptised persons troubled by the devil):

[L]et us all earnestly pray for them, that God, the lover of mankind, would by Christ rebuke the unclean and wicked spirits, and deliver his supplicants from the dominion of the adversary. Let us pray, that he who rebuked the legion of demons, and the prince of wickedness the devil, would now also rebuke these apostates from goodness; would deliver his own workmanship from the power of Satan; and cleanse his creatures, whom he hath made with great wisdom.[94]

Deacon's description of energumens as 'vexed with unclean spirits' and 'apostates from goodness' made it ambiguous whether the energumens were literally bodily possessed, and partially conflated them with penitents. The 'blessing' of energumens followed:

O Thou, who hast bound the strong one, and spoiled his goods; who didst give thine Apostles authority to tread on serpents and scorpions, and over all the power of the enemy, and didst deliver the serpent, that murderer of men, bound unto them; at whose sight all things shake with fear, and tremble at the presence of thy power; who hast cast down Satan as lightning from heaven to earth, from honour to dishonour, by reason of his voluntary malice: thou whose looks dry up the deep, whose threatening melteth the mountains, and whose truth endureth for ever; whom infants praise, and sucklings bless, and angels celebrate and adore; who lookest upon the earth, and makest it tremble; who touchest the mountains, and they smoke; who rebukest the sea, and makest it dry, and driest up all the rivers; the dust of whose feet is the clouds, and who walkest upon the sea as on firm ground: thou only-begotten God, Son of the great Father, do thou rebuke these wicked spirits, and deliver the works of thine hands from the power of the adverse spirit. For to thee is due glory, honour, and adoration, and through thee to thy Father in the Holy Ghost, for ever and ever. Amen.[95]

It is striking that, while Deacon was prepared to revive the imperative conjuration of catechumens, the prayer for the energumens is not an exorcism proper. Instead, following the Protestant tradition established in the sixteenth century, it takes a deprecative form: 'do thou rebuke these wicked spirits'. The language used by Deacon to describe both catechumens and energumens suggests that he may not have believed in the literal bodily possession of either group. While Deacon presumably made use of his liturgy of baptism, it seems unlikely that the public prayers for energumens prescribed in his *Devotions* were ever read. Their inclusion was, rather, an antiquarian exercise for an individual preoccupied with reproducing the rites of the early church (as he interpreted them) as exactly as possible.

It may be significant that Deacon, like Richard Napier, was a physician, and his attitude to exorcism could be seen as akin to that of 'therapeutic' exorcists in the tradition of John Dee and Napier. Deacon included a consecration of oil of the sick in his *Devotions*, which appears to suggest that the oil might be used in therapeutic exorcisms: 'Grant that those who shall be anointed therewith, may be delivered … from all the snares, temptations, and assaults of the powers of darkness'.[96] However, Deacon does not seem to have considered it necessary to exorcise inanimate objects, and none of the consecrations of oil, milk and honey in his *Devotions* includes an exorcistic formula.

The reality of the ministry of Nonjurors, to small congregations in unlicensed backstreet chapels, was very different from the apostolic ideal they envisaged, and there is no evidence that any exorcism (apart from baptismal exorcisms) was performed by a Nonjuror. What mattered to the Nonjurors was that they maintained their right to exorcise because this was a practice of the early church. However, the Nonjurors were not alone in being troubled by the absence of any form of exorcism from the 1662 Prayer Book. In 1711 the liturgical scholar William Nicholls (1664–1712) published a supplement to his extensive commentary on *The Book of Common Prayer*, which included 'Offices out of the several Protestant Liturgies, and rituals, that are not in the Liturgy of the Church of England'.[97] Among these was a collection of material 'out of the Danish Ritual' for the deliverance 'Of Possessed Persons, and those who are vexed by the Devil, or any of his wicked Spirits'.[98]

Nicholls did not explain why he felt it necessary to include rites from foreign liturgies. However, like many clergymen in the church of Queen Anne, Nicholls was fighting a rearguard action against dissenters emboldened by the Toleration Act of 1689. Anglicans found themselves in a competitive religious market alongside dissenters, and as Thomas Jollie had proved in his dispute with Zachary Taylor, dissenters were prepared to use Anglicans' unwillingness to exorcise against them. It is possible that Nicholls wanted to supply the Church of England with a suitably 'reformed' procedure for exorcism which might serve as an 'unestablished ceremony' for occasional use. However, the Danish material Nicholls translated was a set of guidelines for ministers on diagnosing possession rather than a liturgical rite. It suggested scriptural passages and words of comfort to be said over a possessed person, recommended the administration of communion and instructed that 'the Minister shall conclude all with the Lord's Prayer, and the solemn Form of Blessing pronounced over the tempted Person, which he must always make use of when he departs from him'.[99]

Nicholls's Danish guidelines did not, in fact, prescribe anything that could be described as exorcism – or even dispossession, for that matter. In this sense their publication would have been less controversial than might first appear. However, the guidelines *do* presume the possibility of the reality of demonic possession in the present age. While most eighteenth-century Anglicans accepted that demonic possession had existed in the time of Christ, its continued existence was controversial. Ultimately, however, what mattered to high churchmen like Nicholls and Deacon was not that demoniacs were actually exorcised but that the church should vindicate itself by continuing to claim this power; Deacon's description of exorcism as 'authoritative words' is significant, coming from a man who held an elevated view of the priesthood.

Although Deacon's language of exorcism was steeped in scholarship of the early church (hence his use of the term 'energumens'), popular belief in the eighteenth century was focussed on possession as bewitchment. In 1735 the 1604 Witchcraft Act was repealed and replaced with a new law that made it illegal to 'pretend to exercise or use any kind of Witchcraft, Sorcery, Inchantment, or Conjuration'. The new act would remain in force until 1951. Famously, the Scottish MP James Erskine was the sole voice of opposition to the bill in Parliament;[100] yet this did not mean the act was universally welcomed. No one had been executed for witchcraft for 20 years, but some high churchmen opposed the repeal of the 1604 act on what were essentially anti-Sadducist grounds, arguing that if the law gave people permission to disbelieve in witchcraft, all faith in the unseen spiritual world was thereby imperilled.[101]

Jonathan Barry has questioned Keith Thomas's thesis of 'the decline of magic' from around 1700 onwards, and drawn attention to a prevalent double standard of 'public infidelity and private belief' in the supernatural amongst educated people in the eighteenth century.[102] The rise of Methodism, in particular, challenged the prevailing elite culture of public scepticism. Methodism began as a movement of devout 'societies' and chapels led by clergy of the Church of England, such as John Wesley's 'Foundery Society', established in 1739. Wesleyan Methodism's Arminian theology of salvation set it apart from previous evangelical movements, and both John and Charles Wesley were strongly influenced by the spirituality, theology and liturgy of the Nonjurors. John Wesley visited Thomas Deacon in Manchester in June 1733 and Deacon included an essay by Wesley in his *Compleat Collection of Devotions*.[103]

It is unclear whether the Methodists' willingness to adopt imperative exorcism was an inheritance of the Nonjurors. There is no evidence that John Wesley ever adopted baptismal exorcism from

Thomas Deacon.[104] However, Charles Wesley attempted an imperative conjuration as early as 1739, as described by his biographer John Telford:

> In December, 1739, when in Wycombe, Charles stayed with a Mr. Hollis, who spoke of the French prophets as equal, if not superior, to the Old Testament ones. While he and Charles Wesley were undressing, this man fell into violent agitations, and gobbled like a turkey-cock. Charles, in his terror, began to exorcise him with the words, 'Thou deaf and dumb devil,' etc. The man soon recovered, and they lay down; but Charles says, 'I did not sleep so very sound with Satan so near me.'[105]

On 1 October 1763 John Wesley recorded 'a very strange account' of possession and exorcism which he received 'from a man of sense as well as integrity'. The story concerned a woman known as M. S. who became possessed after witnessing an apparition of the devil, who took the form of her uncle and forced her to promise she would kill her father.[106] The woman attempted suicide on several occasions until her brother obtained a straitjacket from Bedlam. One of John Wesley's associates, John Sparke, the assistant curate at St Sepulchre-without-Newgate,[107] offered 'to fasten her so that she shall not get loose';[108] the clergyman's presence suggests that the woman's family already suspected a spiritual cause for her affliction. However, it was a physician who confirmed this when he said that the woman's 'disorder' was 'Partly natural, partly diabolical'.[109]

The woman's family and friends began to pray for her, which exacerbated her symptoms, until a 'Mr. W.' visited in September 1762. It is possible that this was Henry Washington of Queen's College, Oxford, one of the original members of the Wesleys' 'Holy Club'. Washington (if that was who it was) interrogated and then prayed with M. S. for several days. M. S. claimed that the devil was coming to fetch her away the next day; she asked John Wesley's informant (who seems to have been a clergyman) to stay with her:

> We began laying her case before the Lord, and claiming His promise on her behalf. Immediately Satan raged vehemently. He caused her to roar in an uncommon manner; then to shriek, so that it went through our heads; then to bark like a dog. Then her face was distorted to an amazing degree, her mouth being from drawn ear to ear, and her eyes turned opposite ways and starting as if they would start out of her head.

Presently her throat was so convulsed that she appeared to be quite strangled; then the convulsions were in her bowels, and her body swelled as if ready to burst. At other times she was stiff from head to foot, as an iron bar, being at the same time wholly deprived of her senses and motion, not breathing at all. Soon after her body was so writhed, one would have thought all her bones must be dislocated.[110]

The Methodists continued to take it in turns to pray for M. S., but some started to say that they needed to leave. Wesley's informant saw this as a form of weakness in the face of Satan:

We all saw the snare, and resolved to wrestle with God till we had the petition we asked of Him. We began singing a hymn, and quickly found His Spirit was in the midst of us; but the more earnestly we prayed, the more violently the enemy raged. It was with great difficulty that four of us could hold her down. Frequently we thought she would have been torn out of our arms.

After a while M. S. fell quiet, and the lead exorcist persuaded her to sing one of John Wesley's own hymns, 'O Sun of Righteousness, arise', which finally effected the exorcism:

I now looked at my watch and told her, 'It is half-hour past two; this is the time when the devil said he would come for you.' But, blessed be God, instead of a tormentor He sent a comforter. Jesus appeared to her soul, and rebuked the enemy, though still some fear remained; but at three it was all gone, and she mightily rejoiced in the God of her salvation. It was a glorious sight. Her fierce countenance was changed, and she looked innocent as a child. And we all partook of the blessing; for Jesus filled our souls with a love which no tongue can express. We then offered up our joint praises to God for His unspeakable mercies, and left her full of faith, and love, and joy in God her Saviour.[111]

At first glance, the exorcism of M. S. resembles the 'puritan' exorcisms of the sixteenth century. It was a communal event involving ministers and laity, avoiding imperative conjuration and consisting essentially of determined group prayer for the possessed person. However, on closer examination it is clear that the Methodists had a more confident belief in dispossession than earlier puritans. Arthur Hildersham, the exorcist of Thomas Darling, would certainly not have thought it acceptable to 'wrestle with God till we had the petition we asked of Him'. The Methodist exorcists' charismatic approach, summoning the presence of the Holy Spirit, differed markedly from the resigned approach of the puritans. Furthermore, the use of hymns in exorcism was distinctive of Methodists and no doubt reflected the importance of hymnody to Methodist spirituality.

Other than endorsing the integrity of his source, John Wesley did not comment on the propriety of the exorcism of M. S. However, John Wesley did not always regard exorcism in a positive light. One of the criticisms levelled against Thomas Maxfield and George Bell, who were expelled from the Methodist connection for their heterodox views, was that they had performed an exorcism.[112] Indeed, although John Wesley declared his belief in the reality of the possession of George Lukins in Bristol in 1788,[113] there is no evidence that John Wesley ever got directly involved in exorcism himself. Just as the Nonjurors regarded the power of exorcism as a demonstration of priests' sacramental authority, so Wesley may have seen it as a demonstration of charismatic power and the blessing of the Holy Spirit.

In addition to the backlash against latitudinarian modernisation represented by the Nonjurors and Methodists, Jonathan Barry has noted the popularity among many eighteenth-century English Christians of

> [P]ietist and anti-materialist philosophies, which attracted them to spiritual accounts of nature and its powers, as embodied in such movements as Hutchinsonianism, Behmenism and, later, Swedenborgianism and mesmerism ... they sought an ecumenical alliance of groups emphasizing biblical and Trinitarian ideas against deist and Unitarian tendencies within both dissent and Anglicanism.[114]

Mesmerism (or 'magnetism'), in particular, produced symptoms in those treated very similar to those displayed by demoniacs in an earlier era, and at least one of the students of the mesmerist Jean Bonniot de Mainauduc on his visit to London in 1788 was a clergyman of the Church of England.[115] Another of these 'anti-materialist philosophies', Hutchinsonianism, was Anglican in origin and was based on the writings of the anti-Newtonian natural philosopher John Hutchinson (1674–1737). Hutchinson made the Bible central to natural philosophy by arguing for an eccentric reading of the Hebrew language and a figurative interpretation of scripture.[116] Hutchinson's influential follower, the high churchman William Jones (1726–1800), perpetual curate of Nayland, Suffolk, defended the reality of demonic influence in a 1786 sermon on miracles:

> Another miracle of Christ, and one of the most considerable, is that of relieving the possessed by casting out evil spirits: the design of which is to teach us, that there is a spirit working in the children of disobedience ... which nothing but the power of the Gospel can cast out. When we observe how strangely men err in their judgments; how they hasten towards their own destruction ... we must conclude they are under the working of some malignant power, beyond the mere depravity of nature.[117]

Hutchinsonianism was just one among several reactionary anti-Enlightenment strands within eighteenth-century Anglican thought. Increasingly outspoken sceptics and liberal theologians who were prepared to adopt non-literal interpretations of scripture pushed some Anglicans towards a resurgent belief in witchcraft, as a reaction against the prevailing theological winds.[118] In 1761–2, the children of Richard Giles, landlord of the Lamb Inn, Bristol, were troubled by phenomena that the family interpreted as the result of witchcraft. On 7 January 1762 the local curate, James Rouquet, said prayers 'for the relief' of the children; on 9 January Henry Durbin, a local chemist, noted that 'a clergyman went to prayers, and [the affliction] ceased directly, and was quiet all night'.[119]

As Barry notes, the account 'fudges' the question of whether Rouquet was attempting to cast out devils as envisaged in Canon 72. Without the text of Rouquet's prayers it is impossible to judge whether he acted in breach of the Canon, which he would only have done if he had prayed explicitly for an evil spirit to be cast out. As has already been noted, Canon 72 did not prohibit 'diagnostic demonology', and when the headmaster of Bristol grammar school, Samuel Seyer (also an ordained minister), visited the Giles children on 10 February 1762 he 'asked many questions in Greek and Latin'.[120]

The bishop of Bristol at the time of the Giles possessions, Thomas Newton (1704–82) adopted an equivocal position on possession in his *Dissertation on the Demoniacs in the Gospels* (1775). Newton argued that possession was certainly possible and had taken place in apostolic times; it might also take place in the present day, but because the church no longer had the faculty of 'discerning spirits' it was impossible to tell true from counterfeit demoniacs.[121] Newton's view was a nuanced one, and raised epistemological challenges for exorcists rather than denying the existence of exorcism on *a priori* theological grounds; the difficulty was proving the reality of a given alleged possession.

THE EXORCISM OF GEORGE LUKINS

George Lukins, a 25-year-old tailor, began showing the symptoms of possession at Christmas 1769 while he was mumming in his home village of Yatton, Somerset.[122] Lukins spent time in several hospitals, but in 1787 he declared he was possessed by seven devils which needed to be cast out by seven ministers. In May 1788 Lukins's neighbour Sarah Baber approached Joseph Easterbrook, vicar of the Temple Church in Bristol, about the possibility of saying prayers over Lukins.[123] Easterbrook invited Lukins to Bristol. Easterbrook approached other Anglican clergy, but without success:

> I applied to such of the clergy of the established church (among those comprehended within the circle of my acquaintance,) as I conceived to be most cordial in the belief of supernatural influences, namely to the Rev. Mr. Symes, Rector of St Werburgh's; the Rev. Dr. Robins, Precentor of the Cathedral; and the Rev. Mr. Brown, Rector of Portishead; requesting that these Gentlemen would with me attend a meeting for prayer in behalf of this object of commiseration; but though they acknowledged it as their opinion, that his was a supernatural affliction, I could not prevail upon them to join with me, in this attempt to relieve him.[124]

On 13 June 1788 Easterbrook was joined by six Methodist lay preachers and eight others in the vestry room of the Temple Church, while a large crowd gathered outside. The exorcists began by singing a hymn,[125] which exacerbated Lukins's symptoms. The exorcists proceeded to interrogate the demoniac, demanding the name of the devil possessing him.[126] Easterbrook asked Lukins to try to say the name 'Jesus':

> During this attempt a small faint voice was heard saying, 'Why don't you adjure?' On which [Easterbrook] commanded, in the name of Jesus,

and in the name of the Father, the Son and the Holy Ghost, the evil spirit to depart from the man; which he repeated several times: – when a voice was heard to say, 'Must I give up my power?' and this was followed by dreadful howlings. Soon after another voice, as with astonishment, said, 'Our master has deceived us.' – [Easterbrook] still continuing to repeat the adjuration, a voice was heard to say, 'Where shall we go?' and the reply was, 'To hell, thine own infernal den, and return no more to torment this man.' – On this the man's agitations and distortions were stronger than ever ... But as soon as this conflict was over, he said, in his own natural voice, 'Blessed Jesus!' – became quite serene, immediately praised God for his deliverance, and kneeling down said the Lord's prayer and returned his most devout thanks to all who were present.[127]

The prominence of hymn-singing in the exorcism of George Lukins meant that it somewhat resembled the exorcism of M. S. in 1762, recorded by John Wesley. However, by far the most remarkable feature of the Lukins exorcism was Easterbrook's use of imperative conjurations, at the insistence of the demoniac himself. It was later alleged that the curate of Yatton, Samuel Teast Wylde, pronounced public prayers of thanksgiving for the deliverance of George Lukins in Yatton church on 15 June, although Wylde later denied this.[128]

The exorcism of George Lukins provoked a national pamphlet controversy, with one fellow clergyman citing Canon 72 as evidence that the Church of England had rejected the 'superstitious' practice of exorcism.[129] Barry argues that Easterbrook, who was ecumenical in outlook and regularly collaborated with both Methodists and Baptists, 'represented the public face of a powerful evangelical alliance in Bristol'.[130] Nevertheless, Easterbrook's opponents portrayed the exorcism 'as a victory for the Methodists and a questioning of the authority of the church'.[131] The involvement of Methodist lay preachers in the exorcism would prove significant. In 1794 the Methodist connection in Bristol was split between those who regarded episcopal ordination as necessary and therefore wished to remain in the Church of England, and those lay preachers who believed that they were directly ordained by God. As Barry notes, 'surely their sense of their own ministry and ordination by God can only have been heightened by their belief that they had delivered Lukins from the devil?'[132]

CONCLUSION

Clergy continued to be in demand for exorcisms (or more properly unbewitchments) well into the nineteenth century. In his 1869 edition of the Canons of 1604, Charles Henry Davis cited the case of 'a curate in Gloucester [who] was tempted to go through the form of exorcising an insane woman, at her earnest desire, as she believed that she should thus find relief' in 1840 or 1841. Similarly, in around 1867, a curate in Wales was summoned by a woman who believed herself to be bewitched. He eventually agreed to 'read a chapter of the Bible, and offered up a prayer', and was later informed by the woman that 'he had broken the spell'. A Victorian rector of Enville, near Birmingham, prayed for a bewitched woman while also treating her with port wine and soup.[133]

Davis cited with disapproval the opinion of 'Presbyter Dunensis', published in *The Church Intelligencer* in 1843, that it was 'the implied belief of the Church [that] with the licence and direction of the bishop a minister can cast out devils', claiming that 'the practice [of exorcism] was effectually put down' by Canon 72. Davis excused the canon's ambiguity on the grounds that Convocation 'would have raised up a host of enemies' by an outright ban on exorcism.[134] In reality, Canon 72 created two competing narratives about the place of exorcism in the Church of England that continue to this day. The canon effectively outlawed exorcism, and no exorcisms were subsequently licensed; and yet, because it permitted a bishop to sanction exorcism, the language of the canon also implied that possession and dispossession were real and possible in the present age.

Until the advent of modern biblical criticism in the late nineteenth century, it was difficult for clergy of the established church to deny the possibility of demonic possession altogether. The threat from sceptical deists and Unitarians, combined with competition from dissenters who had no qualms about dispossession and a population committed to the reality of bewitchment, put the Church of England in an awkward position. The church could not be seen as credulous, yet at the same time it needed to head off the dissenters and defend orthodox Christianity against 'heretical' movements. As a consequence, many Anglicans adopted nuanced views on possession and exorcism. As Barry observed, the controversy following the exorcism of George Lukins in 1788 saw 'many attempts to find middle grounds which could incorporate some belief in the reality of devils and spirits without requiring acceptance of any particular instance'.[135] This is, in fact, a good summary of the Church of England's approach to the issue throughout the eighteenth century.

Owen Davies argues that while people believed that a clergyman of the established church could unbewitch by saying 'a few words' over someone, 'the popular reasoning behind this belief differed radically from the conception of exorcism', since 'People invested the clergyman himself with the magical power to cure'. Methodists, by contrast, held that it was 'only the power and the word of God that could heal supernaturally inspired illnesses'.[136] In other words, neither the Church of England nor the Methodist church was exorcising in the true, imperative sense in the eighteenth and nineteenth centuries – both because the proceedings of clergy were not truly exorcistic, and because the perceived problem they were dealing with was bewitchment, not demonic possession.

CHAPTER 3

Spiritualism and the Return of Exorcism, 1852–1939

The appearance of Spiritualism in Britain in 1852 marked the beginning of an important shift in discussion of preternatural phenomena in the Church of England. Both advocates and opponents of claimed mediumistic phenomena were prepared to use traditional demonological language, although Enlightenment language of 'superstition' continued to dominate Anglican discourse on the preternatural. The rise of the spiritual healing movement in the late nineteenth century, feeding into early Pentecostalism, similarly placed a renewed focus on demonology, while the growth of Anglo-Catholicism predisposed many Anglicans to take seriously the rites of the Roman Catholic church, including rites of anointing and exorcism. Finally, colonial missionary activity brought Anglicans into contact with phenomena they chose to interpret as demonic possession. All of these factors contributed to the re-emergence of exorcism as a ministry (albeit a fringe practice) in the 1920s. Nevertheless, a diverse range of views on exorcism remained among bishops and lower clergy alike. Scepticism still predominated, and early experiments in exorcism were tentative and (in Britain at least) did not involve attempts to deliver the demonically possessed.

Spiritualism presented apparent evidence for the survival of the soul beyond death and posed a dilemma for the established church. Should the church condemn Spiritualism as sinful dabbling with the occult, or seize upon any evidence of an unseen world in order to convince a doubting generation? The Church of England largely held back from unambiguous condemnation of Spiritualism, and Janet Oppenheim argued that this negotiation provides 'a fascinating glimpse of the Establishment's ongoing pursuit of a *via media*'.[1] The revival of charismatic healing of the sick during the interwar years convinced some clergy that, in a small number of cases, people were in need of exorcism. However, the return of exorcism within the Church of England should also be set against the background of rising popular demand for it as one of the pastoral services expected by the laity from clergy who increasingly saw themselves as parish priests rather than parsons. Furthermore, the reluctance of the Roman Catholic church in England and Wales to engage with exorcism during the period allowed Anglican clergy to move into the vacated pastoral space.[2]

There is no evidence that any exorcisms were conducted in England by Anglican clergy until after World War I, when interest in exorcism stimulated by Spiritualism and occultism coincided with the rise of spiritual healing, of which the ministry of deliverance was one aspect. However, exorcisms of places continued greatly to outnumber exorcisms of possessed persons, and some clergy used the word 'exorcism' somewhat freely to refer to a range of prayers and blessings for several different purposes. Furthermore, the immersion of many English missionary clergy in indigenous cultures that accepted spirit possession and exorcism as a matter of course seems to have eroded the Church of England's traditional practical cessationism. In this respect, the return of exorcism to England was, at least in part, a legacy of the British Empire. Focussing primarily on the attitudes of a series of archbishops of Canterbury and on the testimony of practising exorcists, this chapter examines the range of views on exorcism that existed within the nineteenth- and twentieth-century Church of England, and charts the gradual return of exorcism as a component of the church's ministry.

A POSSESSION IN BARBADOS

For much of the nineteenth century the archbishop of Canterbury was metropolitan not only of the Province of Canterbury but also of the British colonies, so matters that colonial bishops could not easily resolve were referred to him. Amongst these is a rare example of a request for authorisation of an exorcism, which is revealing both of the archbishop's approach to the matter and prevailing views in the mid-nineteenth century. In 1877 the bishop of Barbados, John Mitchinson (1833–1918), wrote to Archbishop Archibald Campbell Tait, asking for advice in the case of a member of his clergy who appeared to be demonically possessed, N. H. Greenidge:

> Early this year an estimable \but eccentric/ Clergyman in my diocese, the Rev. N. H. Greenidge, partly thrown off his balance by the riots of 1876[3] partly by the sudden death of an excellent wife, became disordered in mind, & was obliged to give up his Curacy. After some aberrations, the malady suddenly took the terrible form of the conviction that he was possessed by a Devil. At first he was terribly violent and destructive in his paroxysms & was removed to the Lunatic Asylum where he now is. Some time ago he sent through the Physician of the Asylum to beg me to visit him. I did so. It was a very terrible sight. He certainly exhibited all the phenomena of demoniacal possession which we read of in the Gospels: – the same tendency to tear off clothes, the constant grinding of the teeth and distressing working of the maxillary muscles; above all the strange duality of consciousness, with a constant struggle between the two wills, – even a duality of vocalization, Mr. Greenidge from time to time talking in his natural voice, & then suddenly (and often with blasphemous expressions utterly alien to his natural disposition) in a totally different voice & a totally changed expression of countenance. Since then I have frequently visited him, and I notice that he is quieter than heretofore and less liable to demoniacal outbreaks. Oddly enough except for this 'possession' he is as rational as you or I. His memory is entire, his powers of reasoning clear & vigorous, and his hold upon the doctrines & duties of religion strong and persistent, in spite of [*illeg.*] interruptions during prayer & at the mention of Holy persons & things from his devil-half. He is painfully conscious of this, and, complaining that the Devil would not let him think consecutively in unpremeditated prayer, I composed for him some forms of private prayer, suitable to his case.[4]

Mitchinson's reason for writing to Tait was to ask if an exorcism would be appropriate:

> But from my first visit he has constantly implored me to exorcise him, declaring that he is satisfied that he must be thus authoritatively

exorcised to be relieved, and trying to prove to me that I have the power to set him free. I have reasoned much with him (for he is quite capable of argument) to shew him that I see no evidence that this extraordinary gift was continued to Christs Ministry along with the Ordinary gifts of the Spirit, & we have thoroughly discussed the question together. I have tried to make him believe that in answer to united & persistent prayer the relief will be granted in Christs time in Christs way: but he still has set his heart on exorcism, and I have promised to refer the question to you & to abide by your dictum in the matter.[5]

Greenidge's demand for exorcism is suggestive of Anglo-Catholic tendencies on his part that do not seem to have been shared by Bishop Mitchinson, who adhered to the practical cessationism conventional in the Church of England since 1604. However, it is also possible that Greenidge's long exposure to Afro-Caribbean culture, in which possession and exorcism were commonplace, had convinced him of the efficacy of exorcism. Demands to be exorcised that came from the demoniacs themselves were a frequent feature of nineteenth-century exorcisms even in the Roman Catholic church, at a time when the church still retained much of the sceptical caution of the eighteenth century.[6]

In his reply to Mitchinson, Tait showed great sympathy towards Greenidge and even went so far as to recommend that Mitchinson use a form of deprecative exorcism, although the archbishop implicitly distanced himself from imperative exorcisms in the traditional form:

Under all the circumstances I cannot think you w[oul]d do wrong in yielding to his desire for a formal service of the nature of Exorcism. Of course such words as you w[oul]d use w[oul]d all be in the form of prayer – and if he desires that you sh[oul]d in a set form of words call upon God, in prayer, to deliver him, in His mercy from this terrible seizure or disease – there can, I think, be no reason ag[ain]st you doing so – from what you say of the poor man's present state he is evidently quite capable of understanding the nature of such a service, wh[ich] he w[oul]d not suppose to be an exercise of Miraculous power on your part, but an invocation of the aid of Almighty God to bring his suffering to an end. So long as he understands that the operative power is God's and not man's he may call it exorcism if he will. And it w[oul]d seem hardly right to deny him – in his present distressing condition – the special form of relief wh[ich] he craves.[7]

What mattered to Tait was not so much whether the service was described as an 'exorcism' but whether it was thought to be an exercise of miraculous power that might compromise the Church of England's traditional practical cessationism. Furthermore, Tait was recommending that the form of words used be sufficiently ambiguous to allow for a naturalistic interpretation of Greenidge's affliction, while at the same time giving sufficient comfort to Greenidge to be of pastoral benefit to the sufferer. However, Tait seems to have been committed to the idea that a priest (or bishop in this case) had a role to play in ministering to those who believed themselves possessed by evil spirits, even if it was not the role of the traditional commanding exorcist.

Beginning in 1865, the Church of England began to grapple with the issue of revising the largely obsolete canons of 1604. Attempts to appeal to the authority of the canons in the nineteenth century were unsuccessful,[8] and by the same token, the canons (including Canon 72) were largely unenforceable. It is unlikely that this fact emboldened priests to attempt exorcisms, however. The old canons retained some moral authority, but the main stumbling block to most clergy when it came to exorcism was the perception that such practices were either superstitious, Roman Catholic, or both. Archbishop Tait's approach, as outlined in his letter to Mitchinson, struck a moderate note – although we cannot know whether Tait would have been equally sympathetic to such a rite being performed on English soil.

THE CHURCH OF ENGLAND AND SPIRITUALISM BEFORE 1920

For almost a century, between the arrival of Spiritualism in England in 1852 and World War II, the Church of England was riven with disagreement over the issue of Spiritualism, perhaps the most significant popular religious movement of the period in Britain. The appeal of Spiritualism was by no means confined to devout lay Anglicans; clergy were involved in séances from the very start,[9] a phenomenon that should probably be set in the context of the 'declericalised' character of the Anglican clergy.[10] For many clergy of the period, the clerical state represented a profession rather than a sacred character; and few at this early stage seem to have perceived Spiritualism as a competing theology with that of the Church of England. Furthermore, like its antecedent 'animal magnetism', Spiritualism was largely received (and presented itself) within mid-Victorian society as a would-be-science rather than as a revival of occultism.

Georgina Byrne has divided Anglican criticism of Spiritualism into three categories: concern for the 'mental, moral and physical welfare' of people who attended séances; scepticism about 'physical séance phenomena'; and 'scornful criticism of the theology and ideas of Spiritualism'.[11] Early Anglican responses to Spiritualism were dismissive, with Bishop Samuel Wilberforce of Oxford describing claimed supernatural phenomena in 1853 as 'the work of the Evil Spirit only so far forth as all frauds are'.[12] In 1866 another clergyman, John Henry Elliott, criticised Spiritualist claims as 'debasing and puerile' and described Spiritualism as pernicious, but the import of his attack was that Spiritualism was empty, worthless and made false promises.[13] However, the Church of England's concern about the 'danger' to mental health presented by involvement in séances eventually spilled over into concern about the spiritual dangers of mediumship. Criticism of this kind was muted at first; to attack Spiritualism as demonic deprived the church of the opportunity to denounce it as fraudulent, and clergy who took this path were always at risk of being accused of 'superstition' themselves. However, from the late 1890s critics such as Alfred H. Burton and John Godfrey Raupert became bolder in using traditional demonological language to denounce Spiritualism and mediums.[14] In 1893 Archbishop Whately of Dublin, confirming his belief in the real powers of some mediums, described Spiritualism as 'necromantic practices'.[15]

The anti-Spiritualist movement within the Church of England, much like the anti-Sadducism of the seventeenth century, created an intellectual space in which it was possible to discuss demonology once again, on the grounds that Spiritualism supposedly presented a real danger to the faithful. Such discussion riled theological liberals. Ernest William Barnes (1874–1953), then Master of the Temple, preached in 1917 that 'Our Lord's language with regard to possession by evil spirits ... must be regarded as symbolism, patient of a crudely literal interpretation, but not demanding it'. Barnes accused the leading Anglo-Catholic anti-Spiritualist Lord Halifax of 'meeting superstition with superstition' and went on to argue that 'We cannot again fetter Christianity to demonology ... Evil is real enough on this earth. We need not personify evil forces, attach them to definite persons, and assume them to give to those persons supernatural evil powers'. The *Church Times* observed acidly, 'It is evident that Dr Barnes has no firsthand knowledge of spiritualism, nor of certain other ways in which evil is working today, which he would not have to go far from Cambridge to find'.[16]

Defenders as well as opponents of Spiritualism appealed to traditional demonology as evidence that the church had not always been contemptuous of the preternatural. Charles Maurice Davies (1828–1910), who continued to style himself 'a clergyman of the Church of England' in spite of his association with various free churches,[17] wrote to Archbishop Tait in 1881 to appeal for recognition of Spiritualists as orthodox Anglicans, quoting the words of a fellow priest who had converted to Roman Catholicism:

> Where is the bishop who now reminds the missionaries whom he sends forth of their title to ... miraculous powers? Who are the Christians who believe in them except as things of the past? Why have they ceased to be a part of the inheritance of the saints? Why is the Church so mundane in its aspect, so eager to disown its essential prerogatives, so cankered by a profound scepticism, so zealous for rigid dogma, yet so careless withal of signs and wonders which are the evidence and the cause of faith? Jesus Christ is the same yesterday and today and for ever; and if His ministers relied on Him now as they did of old they would speak with tongues, and cast out evil spirits, & disease and pain would fly before them.[18]

Alluding to Canon 72, Davies added, 'It is surely not without pertinence that the canons of our Church of England contain a proviso that no clergyman shall exercise [*sic.*] without special licence from ~~the~~ his Bishop', with the implication that this was a sign of the church's unwillingness to fulfil its original mission. Davies's lengthy letter to Archbishop Tait is an intriguing example of how a supporter of Spiritualism could draw on both the testimony of Roman Catholic converts dissatisfied with the Church of England's practical cessationism whilst also claiming that Spiritualists were 'those persons ... who may, I think, be rightly described as believing that the Pentecostal powers still remain with the Church, and that Christ's promises, made during the great Forty Days, are yet being literally fulfilled in our midst'.[19] Davies also compared Spiritualist séances with 'the "prophesyings" of the old Reformers',[20] alluding to the puritan discussions prohibited by the Elizabethan church in the 1570s.

The established church's equivocal response to Spiritualism was epitomised by Edward White Benson (1829–96), archbishop of Canterbury between 1883 and 1896. Benson had been a founding member of the Cambridge 'Ghost Club' in 1851 and two of his sons, Edward Frederic Benson and Robert Hugh Benson, became celebrated writers of ghost stories.[21] On 15 June 1893 the leading journalist W. T. Stead, editor of *The Review of Reviews*, wrote to Benson announcing his intention to start publishing the quarterly *Borderland*, 'which is to be exclusively devoted to the study of the phenomena which lie on the borderland which Science has hitherto, for the most part, contemptuously relegated to Superstition'. *Borderland* was, in fact, a popular magazine about Spiritualism – a word Stead studiously avoided using in his communication with the archbishop. Stead asked Benson for 'any conclusions at which you may have arrived as to the utility and expediency of such studies, and with any word of counsel as to what you believe may be the most helpful, or the least harmful, method of dealing with the phenomena of the BORDERLAND?'[22]

Instead of replying directly to Stead, Benson sent the journalist a copy of an earlier private letter to a third party in which he had given his thoughts on Spiritualism. He may have done so because he did not have time to write a separate reply to Stead, but his decision to share a personal letter says much about the archbishop's ongoing interest in parapsychology. Benson subsequently received a request from D. M. Image, a friend or employee of Stead's, asking for permission to quote from it. In an attempt to convince Benson, Image warned that unless Stead received the help of eminent authorities, 'he is driven to seek sympathy from some ignorant people – who will not ridicule him'.[23] However, the pencil annotation '?controvert' by one of Benson's chaplains on the letter probably meant 'controverted', a warning for the archbishop to stay away from a sensitive subject. The issue was not whether Benson was prepared to comment on Spiritualism, but whether he should do so publicly.

The archbishop replied to Image immediately, asking why Stead wanted to publish the letter. Image continued her efforts to persuade Benson to give his permission, arguing that 'it is calm & unbiased & exactly expresses the attitude that a large number of people feel the right one to take in regard to the subject'. Image even asked for a personal meeting with the archbishop.[24] Benson sought the advice of Randall Davidson, then bishop of Rochester (later archbishop of Canterbury), who replied,

> My view is that your letter, which so admirably puts the case, might with advantage become public. But I think you c[oul]d only consent to this if it is made quite clear in giving it publicity that it was written with no view to publication but as part of a private correspondence many months ago.

Davidson further advised that it should be left to the recipient of Benson's letter to allow Stead to publish it, '& that if it appears in such journal it is the recipient's doing & not yours'.[25] Davidson's response suggests that it was the potential reputation of *Borderland* as a sensational journal which made it inappropriate for the archbishop to contribute directly, but there was no issue with the archbishop expressing a view on the matter. Benson followed Davidson's advice and his letter appeared in the first number of *Borderland* in July 1893.

Benson described the manifestations of séances as 'phenomena of a class which appears mostly in uncivilised states of society, and ... in persons of little elevation and intellect', and argued that they could be explained in terms of 'thought transference'. He also cautioned against involvement in Spiritualism just in case demons might be implicated:

> If it were really believed that the impression was produced by spiritual beings of a bad or mean or foolish order, it would be at least as unworthy a course to seek their intimacy as to seek that of degraded human creatures, and ... more likely to be 'dangerous', so to speak, to a struggling moral nature.[26]

Benson's letter made clear his acceptance of parapsychological phenomena such as telepathy, as well as hinting at belief in demonic involvement – although the archbishop's use of the subjunctive, 'If it were really believed ...', served to conceal his personal views. Byrne is critical of Oppenheim for taking Benson's letter as representative of Anglican opinion on Spiritualism at the time – or indeed as representative of Benson's own views – and Byrne cautions against 'the easy assumption that condemnation of spiritualist séances was the same as condemnation of *any* communication between the living and the departed'.[27]

The mass bereavement of World War I heightened the importance of a response to Spiritualism from the church, as so many people sought solace in communications with fallen relatives. Spiritualism was on the agenda of the Lambeth Conference of 1920. The bishops resolved that:

> [T]he practice of spiritualism as a cult involves the subordination of the intelligence and the will to unknown forces and personalities and, to that extent, the abdication of the self-control to which God calls us.[28]

The Lambeth declaration on Spiritualism was ambiguous, allowing for the interpretation of mediumship as psychic activity ('unknown forces') but it also strongly implied a potential demonic element ('unknown ... personalities'). What is most remarkable about the declaration is that it made no allusion to Spiritualism as fraud and appeared to accept that Spiritualists were either psychic or in contact with departed spirits (or demons). It is easy to see, therefore, why the Lambeth Conference's conclusion emboldened rather than shut down Anglican advocates of Spiritualism.

SPIRITUALISM AS A CAUSE OF POSSESSION: A SICILIAN EXORCISM

An early instance in which a clergyman of the Church of England directly linked a case of possession with involvement in Spiritualism occurred in the English expatriate community of Messina, Sicily, in 1902. The Anglican chaplain at Messina, Charles Hulleatt, wrote to Archbishop Frederick Temple asking for advice on how to proceed in the case of a man he called 'W. M.' who had apparently become demonically possessed as a result of acting as a medium in séances.

Hulleatt's decision to write directly to Temple immediately raises the question of why he did not ask the advice of his ordinary, the bishop of Gibraltar (then Charles Waldegrave Sandford). Since Hulleatt made no reference to the bishop of Gibraltar in the letter, however, it seems likely that the bishop either did not reply to Hulleatt or did not give him the answer he wanted, causing Hulleatt to go over his head and write directly to Temple. Hulleatt reported:

> Shortly after taking up my work here as British Chaplain, in October last [1901], I was enabled by God's grace to reclaim a victim of sin, whom I will call 'W M'. Mr M (now about 30 years old) is the youngest son of a former chaplain, who seems to have been a man of singular ability & piety. This son however managed to entangle himself in various ways social & financial & had sunk to the lowest verge of respectability. He managed to retain his sobriety & general truthfulness (I think) but otherwise his conduct was disgraceful & he was generally ostracised. He was however still sought after & valued by one set of people on account of his affording unusual results at spiritualistic séances – & at the time of my arrival was not far off paying the usual penalty, madness.[29]

Hulleatt reported that W. M. had changed his ways after being dissuaded from his involvement in Spiritualism, although the Spiritualists continued to pressure him into acting as a medium:

> On his steadily refusing to act as medium the spiritualistic circles demanded from him proof of his assertion that (as I had shown him) the spirits so far as any were present were evil & lying spirits. I furnished him with notes giving proofs from Scripture, which proved so effectual that several persons present refused to have any longer connection with the proceedings – & one, a Roman Catholic priest, copied the notes, & though reluctant to use a 'heretic's' arguments, preached a sermon from them which converted at least one person.[30]

As a consequence of Hulleatt's opposition, another medium in the group declared that he was an obstacle to their work. A few days later, having acted as a medium for the Spiritualists once again (although Hulleatt was unaware of this), W. M. displayed what Hulleatt considered symptoms of demonic 'obsession' (he wrote and then crossed out 'possession') while playing chess at the local sailors' rest with Hulleatt and three other men (two analysing chemists and a businessman):[31]

Then quite suddenly Mr M & his chair fell tipped over backwards ... in what we thought was a fit. We loosened his collar, laid him on a long cushioned seat, & put cold water on his forehead – but so far from being a fit, it was an 'possession' obsession by evil spirits in all respects similar to those described in the New Testament. The evil spirits sometimes spoke as Mr M, & some as claiming him, but there was no difficulty in discerning their utterances, from his own personal ones ... They wished to force him to <u>write</u>. His hand moved convulsively in the effort, but we <u>held</u> his hands so that he couldn't & I prayed for his deliverance. They asked before I had said anything 'Why do you call us evil?' He was in a cataleptic trance at the time but his ordinary knowledge of what I had previously taught him <u>might</u> account for that. They said 'We have come to claim this our servant' I replied 'He is no servant of yours but of the Lord Jesus Christ' ... The first ten minutes or so of the seizure was occupied in this matter of dispute, & ... the rest – nearly an hour – in his efforts to write & our unvarying restraint of him.[32]

A doctor arrived halfway through the exorcism (he had been sent for when the men thought W. M. was simply having a fit) who wrote a prescription for a 'bromide draught', but 'The spirits observed when in Italian when he wrote the prescription, "This is no doctor for he does not know what is the matter"'.[33] Hulleatt further described W. M.'s symptoms of possession:

Mr M's legs were absolutely rigid the whole time, but his arms moved & from time to time he turned his head violently, & in the extreme paroxysms his body was like a rigid arch. He bit his tongue or cheek bringing blood, & two or three times endeavoured to strangle throttle himself, when thinking him quiet we loosed him to let him come to more easily. He did not however offer any violence to any one else – not do I think that he was in any way responsible, but that simply the evil spirits having been baffled were endeavouring to wreak their rage where alone they could, on his body – Their utterances were in his natural voice & language ... except that the tone was level & quiet, & the language simple, whereas he is inclined ordinarily to scream ... & to use fantastic words.[34]

In an appendix to the letter, Hulleatt wrote that he thought the spirits had been sent to possess W. M. by 'Mr. A.', the leader of the Spiritualist circle:

They sent 'three more powerful spirits' who were baffled by our proceeding, in (i) refusing to turn down the lights (ii) withholding paper

& pen (iii) holding M's hands (iv) praying. These spirits resent the insult put on them, & the 'cabinet' has been destroyed in its power of 'manifestations' by our resistance.[35]

Hulleatt concluded by asking Temple,

Does your Grace consider that I should treat him now as a transgressor or a victim? If he desires the Holy Communion, should I encourage him as one needing so greatly spiritual food & refreshment or should I have regard to the recent sin, & scandal of his backsliding? Also is it desirable that either in person or by in writing he should make public renunciation of such doings & seek forgiveness (as in the Commination)?[36]

Hulleatt approached demonic possession and exorcism from an evangelical theological standpoint; he had trained for ministry at Wycliffe Hall, Oxford,[37] and used the phrase 'prayed for his deliverance', which suggests he avoided anything resembling an imperative exorcism. Hulleatt characterised his own theological views when he declared that 'what I yesterday saw and heard simply confirmed in the strongest way and in every detail my previous belief based on the minute investigation of the Word of God only as authoritative'.[38] Nevertheless, Hulleatt was clearly very concerned that his account would not be believed, since he took pains to present himself as an unbiased observer at the start of the letter and provided a copious list of clergy (including bishops) who could testify to his character and respectability.[39]

Hulleatt wrote that he had formerly 'concurred in Archb[ishop] Trench's statement ... and believed such cases no longer existent unless perhaps where idolatry still survived',[40] but this conviction had been shaken by his experience of an actual possession. Hulleatt was referring to *Notes on the Miracles of Our Lord* (1846) by Richard Chenevix Trench (1807–86), dean of Westminster from 1856 and archbishop of Dublin from 1864. Trench's views on possession developed over time. In the first edition of his *Notes*, he described the Gadarene demoniac as a 'maniac' whose sins admitted 'Satanic influences' into his soul.[41] By the fifth edition of 1856, however, Trench had come to accept 'the real presence of another will upon the will of the sufferer' in cases of possession.[42] He unambiguously affirmed the reality of possession, clearly distinguished it from mental illness and rejected the cessationist position that exorcism and possession had ended with the death of the last apostle. The principal influence that changed Trench's view seems to have been the testimony of missionaries, and he alluded to the experiences of a Lutheran missionary in India. However, Trench continued to believe that possessions did not take place in the Christian world. Hulleatt was probably thinking of this passage when he alluded to Trench's views:

> [T]he might of hell has been greatly broken by the coming of the Son of God in the flesh; and with this a restraint set on the grosser manifestations of its power ... His rage and violence are continually hemmed in and hindered by the preaching of the Word and ministration of the Sacraments. It were another thing even now in a heathen land, especially in one where Satan was not left in undisturbed possession, but wherein the great crisis of the conflict between light and darkness was finding place through the first proclaiming there of the Gospel of Christ. There we should expect very much to find, whether or not in the same intensity, yet manifestations analogous to these.[43]

Trench did not even rule out the possibility that some inmates of a British 'madhouse' might be diagnosed as demonically possessed by 'one with apostolic discernment of spirits',[44] and his attitude marked a decided shift from the inherited practical cessationism of the eighteenth century. The problem for Trench was not how to discredit 'superstition' without denying the truth of scripture, but how to account for the fact that possessions like those recorded in the New Testament did not appear to take place in Victorian England. Trench moved from practical cessationism to a sort of 'localised cessationism' in which possession and exorcism happened in foreign places. Ironically, belief in witchcraft, bewitchment and unbewitchment was alive and well in rural areas of Victorian England;[45] Trench may have been unaware of this, or else he ignored it as insignificant 'superstition' because it did not fit his interpretation of the scriptural model of possession and exorcism. Hulleatt was evidently surprised to come across such a manifestation in Sicily, which he must have considered part of the 'civilised' world.

Hulleatt did not write to Temple without an agenda. His decision to use the technical word 'obsession' rather than 'possession' in his letter suggests a pre-existing interest in demonology. His closing sentence, 'I think that a knowledge of the consequences [of mediumship] might deter any who were inclined to toy with this evil',[46] suggests he hoped the archbishop would publicise the case in the anti-Spiritualist cause. Yet Temple, unlike his predecessor Benson, clearly had no interest in preternatural phenomena; nor, unlike his predecessor Tait, did he have any sympathy for those who believed themselves demonically possessed. In his reply to Hulleatt, Temple reverted decisively to the Church of England's traditional attitude of contempt for 'superstition', although some knowledge of the burgeoning science of psychology lent a little more subtlety to his approach:

> I do not find in the very painful account that you have given me anything supernatural or anything to justify the supposition that the lunatic you describe is suffering from the attacks of evil spirits. The forms of madness are very many and very various [and] as far as they have been studied, they appear to be entirely physical and such as no treatment other than medical can touch. The delusions are generally semiconscious and the patient finds a strong attraction in the attention which is paid to him and in the astonishment and alarm he creates.

Temple suggested Hulleatt seek advice from an experienced physician, as the archbishop was unable to counsel him in such a case. However, Temple also took a cessationist theological swipe at demonic possession:

> In the times of the New Testament there was much that was supernatural, much that was miraculous; but miracles are not wrought now, and we have good reason to believe that one result of the preaching of the Gospel has been that many of the things abnormal and outside the range of nature have altogether disappeared. We cannot heal diseases by a word or a touch, and there are no devils except the great Devil called Sin that we are able in any manner or degree to cast out.[47]

While not quite an outright denial of the existence of evil spirits, Temple's view was that demonic possession no longer occurred and that the clergy had, in any case, no power of exorcism. However, Temple's letter is more remarkable for what it does *not* say than for what it does. Temple does not tell Hulleatt that he ought to have asked the bishop of Gibraltar's permission before attempting the 'deliverance' of W. M. Indeed, at no point does Temple suggest that Hulleatt did not have complete discretion to act as he did – a surprising omission since, as a chaplain under the jurisdiction of the bishop of Gibraltar, Hulleatt had (in theory) less canonical freedom than a beneficed clergyman in England. For all his disapproval of exorcism, Temple made no attempt to invoke Canon 72.

Temple's highly unsympathetic response to the Sicilian case was in stark contrast to Tait's approach to the Barbados possession in 1877. As well as revealing differences in the character of the two archbishops, the responses of the two men show that senior clergy could not be relied upon even to believe in the possibility of possession, let alone authorise an exorcism at the turn of the twentieth century. Hulleatt's enthusiasm for 'prayer of deliverance', on the other hand, shows that a great potential for interest in deliverance existed amongst devout Anglican evangelicals. It may be that this interest could only develop into the full-blown practice of exorcism when removed from the social constraints placed on such a ministry in Victorian and Edwardian England.

THE CHURCH OF ENGLAND AND SPIRITUALISM AFTER 1920

In the years after World War I critics from both the evangelical and Anglo-Catholic spectra of Anglicanism began to marshal the traditional biblical condemnations of sorcery and mediumship against the Spiritualist movement. On the Anglo-Catholic side, Charles Rouse concluded that Spiritualism was of the devil, while Viscount Halifax asked of mediumistic utterances, 'may they not be the utterances of agencies intending to deceive?'[48] Believing that Spiritualism was a satanic deception of humanity was not necessarily the same, of course, as believing that mediums were directly in contact with, or possessed by, demonic agencies. However, leading evangelical opponents of Spiritualism in the 1920s such as Charles Frederick Hogg, William Sheppard and Cyril Dobson were unashamed to denounce mediumship as 'witchcraft', 'necromancy' and 'divination', comparing it with Saul's sin of consorting with the Witch of Endor.[49]

In contrast to Spiritualism's Roman Catholic critics, Anglican opponents did not make the accusation that mediums might be demonically possessed, primarily because the Church of England had no remedy for such possession in the form of an accepted ministry of exorcism. However, a growing belief in parapsychology also held critics back from launching into a full-blown demonological discourse of condemnation. Many clergy attended séances for 'research' as members of the Society for Psychical Research and believed that the alleged phenomena of Spiritualism called for scientific investigation.[50] Furthermore, interest in parapsychology and demonology were not mutually exclusive. Indeed, two of the twentieth century's leading Anglican exorcists, Max Petitpierre (usually known by his monastic name of Robert) and Donald Omand, believed themselves to be 'psychic' and embraced parapsychology (although later in life Petitpierre attempted to suppress his psychic abilities, believing they conflicted with the promptings of the Holy Spirit[51]). Parapsychology allowed the exorcists to explain away the majority of alleged preternatural phenomena as paranormal and to distinguish them from 'genuine' (and rare) cases of demonic involvement.

Max Petitpierre's approach to Spiritualism was to criticise it as 'dangerous', but not because it was always demonic. Rather, most mediumship was based on 'telepathic links', although he acknowledged that 'an evil spirit might break through into a séance ... where the people present are lacking in moral fibre or are perhaps sinful, self-centred, self-concerned and self-interested'. Even Petitpierre did not suggest that a medium might become demonically possessed.[52] Like Rouse and Viscount Halifax in the 1920s,[53] Petitpierre believed that the rise of Spiritualism stemmed from the Church of England's neglect for prayer for the dead within its inherited reformed liturgy.[54]

The argument about Spiritualism raged throughout the 1920s and 1930s, with most in the church unwilling to condemn practices favoured by otherwise faithful Anglicans that gave comfort to the bereaved and sustained belief in a future life. In the 1930s the bishop of London banned Spiritualist meetings in churches and church halls,[55] but there was no obvious way to discipline clergy who involved themselves in Spiritualism; such activity was not obviously covered by any of the existing canons, nor were the canons readily enforceable. Finally, in 1936, the archbishop of Canterbury, Cosmo Gordon Lang, convened a small committee chaired by the dean of Rochester, Francis Underhill, 'To investigate the subject of communications with discarnate spirits and the claims of Spiritualism in relation to the Christian faith'. The members of the committee visited séances and questioned psychic researchers.[56]

Seven of the ten committee members concluded that it was more probable than not that at least some Spiritualist 'communication' came from 'discarnate spirits'; the other three disagreed and continued to maintain that mediums were either fraudulent or deluded. A report based on the majority view was presented to Lang in January 1939. The archbishop wrote to Underhill expressing his regret that the report had not laid greater stress on the dangers of Spiritualism, and in July the bishops agreed that the report should remain unpublished.[57] In 1939 Lang received a letter from 'The Confraternity of Clergy, Ministers, Laymen and Spiritualists' enquiring about the outcome of the committee's investigation.[58] Byrne has shown that the 25 Anglican clergy who signed this letter not only continued their ministry in the Church of England but, in some cases, received preferment in spite of their (in some cases very public) commitment to Spiritualism.[59]

By early 1940 the conclusions of the Church of England's report on Spiritualism had been leaked, and Lang was forced to issue a statement explaining that 'in respect of practical guidance to Christian people on a subject fraught with grave dangers, it did not seem to be so clear or conclusive as to make its publication desirable'.[60] This response marked the end of the Church of England's engagement with Spiritualism, and after World War II Spiritualists largely parted company with the established church, setting up their own churches and congregations. However, both the pro- and anti-Spiritualist movements within the Church of England prepared the way for a more accepting attitude towards possession and exorcism. Spiritualism changed the terms of internal debate about the preternatural within the Church of England, replacing the eighteenth-century dichotomy of 'superstition' versus reason with a debate about whether mediumistic phenomena were parapsychological or demonic in nature, or even whether the spirits contacted by mediums were good or evil. In the debate on Spiritualism, traditional Anglican scepticism was largely sidelined.

Oppenheim argued that, irrespective of the 1939 report's suppression, Spiritualism was 'accommodated' within the Church of England: 'The fact that the accommodation was unenthusiastic is less significant than the accommodation itself'.[61] The difficulties faced by the Church of England in accommodating Spiritualism in the early twentieth century were not dissimilar to the challenge of accommodating puritan 'exercises' in the sixteenth century (with the difference that the twentieth-century church was without means of coercion). As in the sixteenth century, the established church risked creating separate Spiritualist 'conventicles' if Spiritualism were not accommodated. There was a strong instinct among many Anglicans against turning Spiritualism into a rival religious movement, but the feelings of anti-Spiritualists were equally intense. Yet as Byrne has shown in her analysis of the Church of England's gradual drift towards authorising prayer for the dead during and after World War I,[62] the established church was, to some extent at least, obliged to accommodate popular spiritual movements in order to remain relevant to modern society.

EXORCISM AND THE SPIRITUAL HEALING MOVEMENT

A source for the revival of exorcism in Anglicanism that was completely separate from the Spiritualist and anti-Spiritualist movements was the holiness movement, a spiritual awakening that began in Britain at Keswick, Cumbria in the 1850s and influenced both evangelical and high church Anglicans. In 1907 Alexander Boddy (1854–1930), the vicar of All Saints', Monkwearmouth (who had been involved in the Keswick holiness movement) travelled to Oslo with his wife Mary to hear the preaching of the English missionary Thomas Barratt, one of the early founders of Pentecostalism. Alexander and Mary Boddy experienced 'baptism in the Holy Spirit', and Barratt subsequently visited Monkwearmouth where an 'outpouring of the Spirit' led to 'many exorcisms of a dramatic nature'.[63]

Boddy became editor of the Pentecostal periodical *Confidence* between 1908 and 1926 and Monkwearmouth quickly developed into the centre of British Pentecostalism, hosting the 'Sunderland Conventions'. The Dutch Pentecostalist Wilhelmine Polman, who received 'baptism in the Spirit' at a Sunderland Convention in 1908, reported to Mary Boddy that there had been several successful exorcisms at her meetings in Amsterdam. Spiritualists were attracted to Polman's meetings and some were exorcised[64] – an indication that, in spite of their differences, both Spiritualists and Pentecostalists shared a craving for material evidence of the supernatural, whether in the form of mediumistic phenomena or healing miracles.

Exorcism does not seem to have played a very significant role in the Boddys' own ministry, although it should be noted that Pentecostalist theology does not tend to make a very clear distinction between exorcism and other forms of healing ministry. Mary Boddy emphasised the power of the blood of Christ to give 'Perfect Victory over sin, disease, and all the powers of darkness', while Alexander Boddy declared that 'sickness is *generally* from Satan and his emissaries'.[65] For Pentecostal Anglicans, therefore, *all* healing ministry was by definition a ministry of exorcism. Alexander Boddy described his somewhat minimalistic rite of anointing in *Confidence* in 1922:

> [The Elder] rebukes the sickness, and all the evil powers behind the disease (Luke 4:39), next placing the sufferer under the Precious Blood for cleansing ... [and for] protection from all evil powers and for victory (Rev. 12:11) ... [Then], pouring a few drops of olive oil into his left palm, the Elder prays that God will graciously sanctify the oil, and that He will use it as a channel of spiritual blessing to the sufferer for Christ's sake ... Then with a finger of his right hand dipped into the oil, he touches the forehead in the 'Name of the Lord,' and then in the full name of the Trinity, placing his left hand with the oil in it on the head of the sufferer, with such oil as remains. As in Mk. 16:18, he lays on both his hands, and asks that the hands of Christ – the Pierced Hands – may also rest on the sick one to impart His Life.[66]

Whether Boddy's 'rebuke' of disease and evil powers should be considered an exorcism is debatable, since Boddy does not explicitly state whether he commanded a demon of sickness to come out of the sufferer. It is curious that, in spite of his evangelical theology,

Boddy felt it necessary to pray for the sanctification of the oil before using it – effectively a blessing (or exorcism) of the oil that was dropped even from the 1549 Prayer Book that retained the rite of anointing itself. This is just one example of how the desire for tangible contact with the divine led Pentecostalists into a kind of sacramentalism, even if they were using very different language from high church sacramentalists.

Some medical professionals were attracted to the spiritual healing movement. In 1908 a medical doctor and supporter of faith healing, Charles Williams, reported that successful exorcisms were taking place at Bethshan, a non-denominational spiritual healing centre in Highbury, London which had been active since the 1880s, and in which some Anglicans were involved.[67] Williams recommended the establishment of dedicated sites for exorcism of the mentally ill, as well as urging medical professionals to have the courage to recommend exorcism:

> [A]s there are many in the medical profession to-day who are not ashamed to, in an emergency, baptise a new-born infant, or suggest sending for a minister of religion when patients under their care become critically ill, so too, I hope, there will not be wanting those who, now that this method has been brought to their notice, and the reasonableness of it pointed out, so I hope, and indeed am confident, that there will not be wanting at least *some* who, in a suitable case of this dire and intractable malady, Insanity, will not be ashamed to show the same courage.[68]

Williams's views were at (or perhaps beyond) the fringe of Edwardian psychiatric opinion, but rather than adopting a sectarian approach to exorcism as proof of the truth of a particular variety of Christianity, he advanced a pragmatic argument that exorcism seemed to relieve the symptoms of the mentally ill. Unlike the public, evangelistic exorcisms of the sixteenth century, these proposed twentieth-century exorcisms were to be private and therapeutic in nature.

At the same time as some on the evangelical wing of the Church of England were being drawn towards spiritual healing and exorcism by the holiness movement and Pentecostalist influences from across the Atlantic, Anglo-Catholics were becoming increasingly dissatisfied with the absence of a rite of anointing of the sick from

The Book of Common Prayer. In 1910 one of the Cowley Fathers, F. W. Puller, argued that the sacramental ministry of anointing had not originally been confined to the dying (as in Roman Catholic practice) and that prayers for the consecration of oil and anointing should be added to the Prayer Book.[69] Puller had been a missionary in South Africa, and it is possible that his experiences of African Christianity heightened his awareness of the need for a more tangible rite of healing. In 1915 the Guild of St Raphael was formed under the patronage of the archbishops of Canterbury and York, dedicated to the sacrament of anointing by priests and the laying on of hands and prayer for healing by laypeople.[70]

Liberal Anglicans were appalled by what the dean of St Paul's, W. R. Inge, described as a 'craze for miracle mongering' and 'a widespread recrudescence of superstition among the half educated'[71] – a comment that was probably intended as a swipe at Spiritualism as well. In 1925 Herbert Hensley Henson, bishop of Durham, coupled spiritual healing with exorcism in his denunciation of the practice: '[The] crude demonology, the childish literalism, the abject fear, the preposterous science, the debased sacramentalism, scarcely superior to the fetish-worship of Africa; these lie behind the exorcisms, unctions, and the benedictions of the Church in the early centuries and in the Middle Ages'.[72] However, one colonial bishop supplied the shortfall himself; *Divine Healing* (1921) by Herbert Walsh, bishop of Assam, India, included a rite for anointing on which Alexander Boddy based his practice.[73]

The twentieth-century debate about anointing of the sick and exorcism in the Church of England was partly an antiquarian one. In his *Exorcism and the Healing of the Sick* (1932) Reginald Maxwell Woolley collected the evidence for ancient Christian rites of exorcism and anointing. Woolley noted in his preface the contemporary relevance of his book, owing to 'the request made by the Lower House of the Convocation of Canterbury for the provision of a Form for the anointing of, or laying hands on, the sick'. Woolley claimed to treat his subject 'from the purely historical point of view' but nevertheless made a theological judgement by claiming that exorcism and the healing of the sick 'are so closely connected as to form two aspects of one and the same thing, a fact that has, I think, hitherto been largely overlooked'.[74]

Woolley's conclusions about the purposes of exorcism in the New Testament were, similarly, applicable to present-day situations:

> Our Lord regarded all ill of soul and body as due to one common cause, the presence of evil. Disease and sin are two different forms or manifestations of one and the same thing. So the expulsion of the evil from the person vexed delivered him entirely from the possession of evil generally, both in soul and body, both from sin and disease. Our Lord exorcised the sufferer generally by the laying on of hands or by some form of touch; sometimes, in exceptional cases, by a word.[75]

By interpreting the New Testament as teaching that 'ill of soul and body' were one and the same thing Woolley approached perilously close to Christian Science. However, he denied that all Christians possessed healing power and described it as 'charismatic': 'This charisma, the gift of healing, covered sickness of body and soul, and so the healing of bodily sickness, and the exorcism of evil from either body or soul, represent different aspects of the same thing'.[76] However, Woolley seems to have been advocating the exorcism of the oil of the sick when he gave a form of blessing from the Gregorian Sacramentary, noting that 'To this may be added the ancient prayer which is still to be found in the *Roman Rituale*, under the heading of *Benedictio olei simplicis*'.[77] This formula, which had also been recommended by Puller as the basis for a future rite of blessing of holy oil, began with an exorcism (*Exorcizo te creatura olei* ...[78]). It is hard to see why Woolley should have inserted the instruction 'to this may be added' in an antiquarian study unless he expected clergy to make practical use of the formulae in his book.

It is unclear whether Anglo-Catholic supporters of anointing of the sick followed John Dee in believing that the exorcism of oil made it effective for exorcism in a wider sense, but some members of the spiritual healing movement were also interested in ghosts. In 1929 the Anglo-Catholic spiritual healer Dorothy Kerin opened St Raphael Home, known as Chapel House, opposite the family home of Max Petitpierre in Ealing.[79] Just after Easter 1931 Petitpierre celebrated mass at Chapel House, and Kerin saw the chapel crowded with the spirits of Franciscan friars – although no attempt was made by Petitpierre to exorcise the place. Nevertheless, the incident was a formative one for Petitpierre as a budding exorcist.[80]

LAYING GHOSTS

The practice of ghost-laying, which may never have died out entirely among clergy of the Church of England, continued in the first half of the twentieth century. Some 'exorcisms' of haunted houses in the 1930s are well known, such as those attempted at Borley Rectory, but interest in exorcism of haunted houses in the interwar years extended even to the most senior clergy in the Church of England. In 1937 Alan Campbell Don (1885–1966), then chaplain to Archbishop Lang but later dean of Westminster, received a letter from his friend Philip Worsley enquiring,

> Do you believe in laying 'ghosts'? I know your great chief[81] does, or at any rate did so believe. I am interested in a haunting of an old monastic house in Suffolk, which has some connection with a <u>nun,</u> & which is therefore probably founded on the obvious kind of misdemeanour. The people who live in the house are of the kind who would be spiritually helpful if their help was needed. The haunting is not one of the very dreadful kind, but wakes nearly everybody up at 2.30 am. pretty regularly, so is not a very popular affair![82]

Worsley wanted Don to get involved because 'very intense concentration of prayer is part of the "treatment" and you will forgive me for saying that you are one of the few people I know who could help in this way if you believe that "ghosts" care to be exorcised'. Don replied by recounting a ghost-laying he had performed in Dundee:

> [O]n one occasion when I was in Dundee I tried the experiment of laying a ghost, or whatever you like to call it, with apparently excellent results. The house in question was not an old house, but there was something queer about it in that three people quite independently told me that in a certain portion of the house they were conscious of experiencing a feeling of eeriness amounting almost to terror, a sensation which was, strangely enough, shared by a dog which belonged to one of the parties in question. I made up my mind that something must be done, and accordingly on the occasion of one of my weekly visits to the house, for the purpose of celebrating the Holy Communion (it was a Rescue Home more or less under my charge) I walked through the part of the house where the trouble lay, together with one of my staff and the Matron of the Home, and recited a prayer in each of the rooms.[83]

Don recommended that Worsley seek the help of 'one or two clergy who are specially interested in psychical matters' and offered to put him in touch with them, but Worsley declared himself suspicious of 'definite psychical experts, however divine'.[84] There is no surviving evidence that a ghost-laying ever took place or that Don was involved in it, but the case demonstrates that, by the late 1930s, what Inge called the 'recrudescence of superstition' had penetrated as far as Lambeth Palace.

GILBERT SHAW: FATHER OF EXORCISM

The Irish-born Anglo-Catholic priest Gilbert Shaw (1886–1967) can with some justification be considered the father of modern exorcism in the Church of England. During his lifetime Shaw was renowned as an authority on mystical prayer, on which he wrote prolifically, but unlike other exorcists such as Petitpierre, Donald Omand and Christopher Neil-Smith, he did not publicise his practice of exorcism. Shaw's interest in the supernatural seems to have begun with an encounter with the notorious occultist Aleister Crowley when Shaw was still an undergraduate at Cambridge in 1908.[85] Later, in 1916, Shaw was introduced to mystical spirituality by Hugh Trotter, curate of St John's church, Newbury. Trotter had been a Roman Catholic monk before his ordination as an Anglican priest in 1911, and he became Shaw's spiritual director.[86] Shaw subsequently became associated with a religious community at Glasshampton and conducted preaching missions in the English countryside, often recruiting students from Oxford to help.[87]

One of the students recruited for a mission at Eynsham, Oxfordshire in the summer of 1922 was Max Petitpierre, who had matriculated as an undergraduate at Merton College, Oxford the previous year. Trotter was also part of the mission. Petitpierre claimed that:

> Eynsham lies under an ancient Stone Age site and it appears a gang of black magicians began activities there. Allying themselves with evil spirits, they attacked Eynsham with psychic force. Shaw and his helpers carried out several exorcisms, the majority of which, I think, were of a minor and antiseptic nature ... and their ministrations appeared to be effective.[88]

On 1 August (Lammastide) Petitpierre and the priests were surprised to discover that the entire population of the village made its way to Eyn Hill, which they danced round anticlockwise chanting 'Jack Tar! Jack Tar!'. Petitpierre, who linked the name of the village to the Norse god Odin, believed that the words were a corrupted invocation of the Anglo-Saxon god Tyr, albeit 'the majority of people involved in these rites had no idea of their origin, nor were they attempting to revive (or perhaps a better word would be continue) pagan practices'.[89] Shaw was an anthropologist by training, and he may well have been aware of Margaret Murray's recently published *The Witch Cult in Western Europe* (1921) which developed the argument that medieval and early modern witchcraft trials were evidence of the survival of an ancient pagan fertility cult. Shaw would have been trained within the methodological assumptions (long since academically discredited) that underpinned Murray's work and derived from Sir James Frazer's *The Golden Bough*. Both Frazer and Murray were convinced that pagan ritual survivals were to be found everywhere, often concealed under innocuous or modern guises.

Shaw himself was unwilling to speak about what happened at Eynsham, saying only 'I once had my nose bitten by the devil'. This was an allusion to something that happened when he and Petitpierre admitted to one another that they shared a 'sharp psychic awareness' of 'some kind of psychic disturbance associated with an ancient Roman settlement on the outskirts of the town'. Whatever happened at Eynsham, it resulted in a mental breakdown for Shaw that confined him to bed for weeks.[90] The following year Shaw began training for ordination at Westcott House, Cambridge and in 1924, while still a layman, he was asked to become vice-principal of St Paul's Missionary College at Burgh-le-Marsh, Lincolnshire.[91]

Meanwhile Petitpierre, having been introduced to exorcism at Eynsham, became involved in another exorcism at Merton College itself in 1923. The ghost of a man in Tudor costume was reportedly appearing in Mob Quad, so an undergraduate who was an ordained priest conducted an exorcism from the window of the room of Petitpierre's friend Dix, which looked out into the quad:

> Dix himself stood on the priest's right hand side with holy water and I on his left holding the book from which the priest read the Roman Catholic rite of exorcism. All went quite normally until the priest issued the words of command to the evil spirit to depart in the name of Christ. What happened then defies rational explanation. Everything on Dix's washstand began to shudder and rattle in the most alarming and inexplicable way.[92]

Petitpierre reported that the exorcism was successful, although his account of it does not make a great deal of sense. 'The Roman Catholic rite of exorcism' (assuming that Petitpierre is referring to the *Rituale Romanum* of 1614) was intended for the exorcism of persons, not places. Indeed, until one was published in the 1950s,[93] no rite for the exorcism of places was accessible, except to the most determined scholar of demonology. It is possible that Petitpierre's priest friend made use of Pope Leo XIII's general 'Exorcism against Satan and the Apostate Angels', although this is a general exorcism of evil influences in the world rather than a directed ritual of any sort.[94] On another occasion, Petitpierre reported that Hugh Trotter exorcised a college room after one student seriously assaulted another, and there were rumours that a ghost from an adjoining churchyard had entered the college. Petitpierre, although then still a layman, was sent by Trotter to carry out further exorcisms 'two or three times a week until the end of term'.[95]

In 1926 Shaw invited Petitpierre to join St Paul's Missionary College to train for the priesthood, giving the two men an opportunity to continue their experiments with exorcism.[96] On one occasion they exorcised a local church where they believed the nave was troubled by the souls of the dead desiring a requiem mass.[97] According to Petitpierre, Shaw believed that ley lines (an idea only recently coined by Alfred Watkins in his book *The Old Straight Track* (1925)) were 'lines of magic' used by megalithic people, who 'Gathered together in a ritual meeting ... would generate a force of energy or excitement which their priests or druids would help direct along these ley lines in a psychic attack against their enemies'.[98] However, Watkins never made supernatural claims regarding ley lines (an idea that only emerged in the late 1960s), and it seems likely that Shaw's beliefs about projected psychic energy derived from nineteenth-century occultism.

During the General Strike of 1926 Shaw and Petitpierre became convinced that the Soviet Union was making use of psychic techniques to stir up industrial unrest similar to those they believed were employed by ancient peoples, since they felt 'quite intense psychic pressures passing through the college chapel and, so far as we could ascertain, coming from the east'. Shaw believed that Burgh-le-Marsh was on a ley line running between Russia and Snowdonia and decided to exorcise the ancient tumulus in the middle of the village.[99] This seems to have been the first occurrence in the modern Church of England of the exorcism of ancient pagan sites – later frequently practised by Donald Omand – which echoed the practices of Anglo-Saxon saints such as St Guthlac and St Botolph, who settled in remote locations troubled by devils and drove them out.[100] Many years later, Shaw alluded to 'peasant magic that might have been found in the rural districts before the spread of education and may indeed survive in Lincolnshire fens',[101] which may be an allusion to experiences he had at Burgh-le-Marsh.

Traditional belief in bewitchment persisted in England well into the twentieth century, to the extent that doctors in some parts of the country felt they were still competing with professional unwitchers in the early 1900s,[102] and medical opposition to cunning folk may have been one reason for their eventual demise. Thomas Waters has argued that the disappearance of cunning-folk, who had originally replaced the exorcists in the sixteenth and seventeenth centuries, was one factor that enabled the reappearance of exorcists: 'The increasing regulation of healthcare combined with the liberalization of religion were … responsible for a shift in the practice of counter witchcraft: it went from being largely medicinal in character to being largely religious'.[103] Waters identified the revival of exorcism in the second half of the twentieth century as part of a 'supernatural turn' in the Church of England, 'made possible by the passing of the "respectable", austere, self-improving Protestantism which had dominated … the Church of England … since the early nineteenth century'.[104]

Indeed, although Gilbert Shaw may have been almost alone in using the vocabulary of 'exorcism' to describe his ministry, he was not alone among the clergy in attempting to combat spiritual evil. In January 1926 Charles Kent, the vicar of Merton, Norfolk 'prayed for the removal of a curse supposedly levied on the nearby village of Sturston, and for a parishioner who feared that she was "bewitched"'. Kent opined to a local newspaper that 'there may be something in witchcraft'.[105] Similar suspicions even reached as far as the bishops, with Bishop Bernard Heywood of Ely publicly blaming 'discarnate rebellious spirits' for a blight on fruit trees in his diocese in June 1938.[106] Waters has argued that ideas about psychic attack like those held by Shaw and others influenced by nineteenth-century occultism subsumed and reinterpreted older and more primal beliefs about witchcraft, simply attaching pseudo-scientific terminology to old ideas.[107] On this interpretation, Shaw may not have been as radical a figure in the interwar Church of England as he first appears.

In 1929 Shaw was introduced to a woman known as 'Pauline', living in the East End of London, who believed she was suffering magical attacks from a mysterious Italian defrocked priest. Shaw became convinced that the Italian was an adept in black magic who belonged to a global 'Satanist Society' which had perfected means of psychic control using animal sacrifice and ancient centres of magical power in the landscape. Shaw apparently made many of his 'discoveries' about the Satanists when he experienced spiritual opposition in prayer, and came to believe that he could use prayer to disrupt the psychic energies projected by the black magicians.[108] Shaw's belief in organised Satanism resembled developments in the Roman Catholic church in the late nineteenth century, when Pope Leo XIII's belief that Freemasonry was a global Satanic conspiracy became the church's official stance.[109] Although the idea of organised devil worship had a precedent in the European myth of the witches' Sabbath, nineteenth-century Satanic conspiracy theories had a global scope never seen in the early modern era. The old rites of exorcism were no longer fit for purpose in dealing with this supposedly ubiquitous spiritual threat, leading Pope Leo to compose a new general exorcism,[110] and the same sense of pervasive spiritual evil (as opposed to traditional demonic possession) lay behind Shaw's practice of psychically 'disrupting' black magic. In this sense, Shaw was a very modern exorcist.

CONCLUSION

Owing to a variety of influences, including the anti-Spiritualist movement, the holiness and Pentecostal movements and contact with global Christianity, by the 1920s there existed a small number of clergy in the Church of England who were prepared to experiment with, and accept the efficacy of, exorcism. Yet there is no compelling evidence that any clergyman of the Church of England performed an exorcism in Britain before World War II of a person believed to be demonically possessed. Instead, early experiments with exorcism included exorcism of oil (by Anglo-Catholics), a generalised practice of exorcism of all sickness by the Anglican Pentecostalist Alexander Boddy, and several instances of exorcism of places by Anglican clergy.

A striking feature of the history of exorcism in the Church of England in the late nineteenth and early twentieth centuries is the extent of convergence between different wings of the church that, in other areas, were becoming increasingly estranged by ritual and theology. Furthermore, exorcism was a practice with considerable 'ecumenical' potential, since Anglicans who supported it were generally very open to inspiration from other traditions and even other churches. Most importantly for the subsequent history of exorcism in the Church of England, Gilbert Shaw and his protégé Max Petitpierre set themselves up as the first 'professional exorcists' in the established church since the days of John Darrell, thereby preparing the ground for the revival of exorcism as a specialist ministry from the 1960s onwards.

CHAPTER 4

The Rise of the Anglican Exorcists, 1939–1974

In the years after World War II, the pioneering Anglican exorcist Gilbert Shaw waged a determined one-man campaign to achieve recognition for this ministry. In 1958 he succeeded when proposed guidelines for the authorisation of exorcisms (without guidance on what an exorcism should actually involve) were included in a report of the archbishops on healing. Shaw's disciple Max Petitpierre repeatedly brought exorcism to the media's attention in the 1960s and 1970s, culminating in an influential report on exorcism commissioned by the bishop of Exeter and edited by Petitpierre in 1972. Furthermore, the Anglican charismatic movement of the mid-1960s revived the use of Pentecostal-style exorcisms in some Anglican churches. The new General Synod finally replaced the canons of 1604 in 1969, abolishing Canon 72 but putting nothing in its place.[1] Fuelled by anxiety about rising interest in the occult as well as a sense that the church needed to do more to engage with people's concerns, exorcism took off spectacularly between 1969 and 1974. No longer an outlandish preoccupation of one or two priests, exorcism was on the way to becoming an accepted ministry of the Church of England, with many bishops appointing a diocesan exorcist after 1972.

While the Church of England may have agonised and dithered for decades over other changes to its liturgy and practice, the normalisation of exorcism was extraordinarily rapid and overturned centuries of Anglican caution and reticence in demonological matters. This Anglican embrace of exorcism coincided with the Roman Catholic church's near complete withdrawal from the ministry, meaning that the Church of England became the first port of call for those desiring exorcism. However, as might be expected from a movement that sprouted almost from nowhere, there was little consistency in the approach of Anglican exorcists. The Exeter Report embodied an 'orthodox' approach to exorcism derived from Gilbert Shaw and was grounded in the Anglo-Catholic tradition, although John Richards made some effort to make the approach palatable to Protestant Anglicans. However, Anglican charismatics adopted a contrasting approach, derived from the Pentecostal tradition, that was far more open to spontaneous action. Other clerical exorcists were prepared to draw on other spiritual traditions, relying on everything from 'vibrations' to psychic mediums and sacred lots to guide their ministry.

THE LATER CAREER OF GILBERT SHAW

In 1940 Gilbert Shaw, the pioneer of exorcism at St Paul's Missionary College in Lincolnshire, moved to St Anne's, Soho, which was destroyed by two high explosive bombs on 24 September of that year. The congregation relocated to nearby St Anne House, and had a particular mission towards the London intelligentsia, including T. S. Eliot and Dorothy L. Sayers among its members.[2] Throughout this time Shaw continued his attempts to deliver 'Pauline', whom he believed was being controlled by a 'Satanist Society' even after the death, in 1935, of the mysterious Italian black magician whom Shaw blamed for the trouble.[3] Max Petitpierre described Shaw's exorcism of a woman who may have been 'Pauline' in the basement of St Anne House in 1943, which Petitipierre considered the sole case of 'genuine demonic control' of a person he encountered during his entire career as an exorcist.

> The case concerned a lady who was no more than 5 feet 5 inches tall. She had been involved with certain drug gangs operating at that time in London's East End. I do not believe that she actually *took* drugs herself. But she was unquestionably mixed up in an evil business and it seems

clear that at times she came under demonic control. The symptoms are varied, generally involving continual blasphemy, often a display of telepathic knowledge beyond the ken of either the victim or those trying to cure him or her and frequently accompanied by a display of abnormally violent strength ... Gilbert Shaw, I, and the others concerned with the lady's case had satisfied ourselves that her case lay beyond medical help.[4]

Petitpierre claimed that the woman was under 'psychic attack' from the 'drug group', and as a result she would go into trances.

One day we managed to get her down into the basement room of the parish house – a large room about forty by twenty feet. For almost an hour Shaw, myself and a deaconess prayed for her, calling her back to normality. At last she recovered and then suddenly she stood up and stuck one foot out in front of her. We grabbed her but with her foot still stuck out straight and hopping on one leg she *dragged all three of us round* that big room three times ... Eventually we managed to sit her down again and Gilbert Shaw performed a major exorcism, exhorting the demon to depart and harm no one ... As the prayers ended, an amazing transformation took place. This wild, violent little figure suddenly became tranquil, serene, and normal. It was [as] though she had sloughed off an enormous weight or come out of a deep sleep. She herself acknowledged the demon's control.

'Cor – that was a demon, wasn't it?'[5]

According to his biographer R. D. Hacking, Shaw was anxious to appear circumspect in his ministry of exorcism and established personal rules of conduct for himself:

Almost invariably Gilbert was satisfied after examination that some alternative explanation could adequately account for the manifestations. He believed scepticism to be the only proper way to approach such work, an attitude he strongly commended to all who were drawn to this form of ministry ... As the workload grew he adopted a policy of accepting requests for help only from bishops, and when he was engaged in an investigation or an exorcism, he always ensured that the diocesan was kept fully in the picture.[6]

Shaw also ensured that 'a Christian doctor' participated in his exorcisms, but he encountered a complete lack of practical experience of exorcism in the Church of England 'and an equal absence of theory'. Accordingly, Shaw turned to Roman Catholic formulae, translating and adapting them for Anglican use, 'and it is his work which underlies all the liturgical forms relating to the ministries of deliverance used within the Church today'.[7] After Petitpierre joined Nashdom Abbey in 1947 Shaw had difficulty recruiting new apprentice exorcists who did not 'become unhealthily interested in what they imagined to be the sensational nature of the work'.[8] Shaw toured the country in a one-man attempt to equip the clergy in knowledge of demonology, although his views were often rejected out of hand.[9] In 1947 he warned a group of clergy in the diocese of St Davids against undue curiosity about the occult:

> Curiosity and credulity because a subject appeals to the natural instincts as being exciting or uncanny, is entirely out of place ... It will help us to approach the subject to possess not only the detachment of religion but also the detachment of the scientific temper which will ruthlessly tear down the barriers of illusions and suggestions behind which the father of lies would work his evil and preserve his kingdom of discordance.[10]

One consequence of Shaw's concern about the unhealthy interest of exorcists was that he increasingly believed the ministry should be brought under the control of bishops.[11] However, although Shaw cautioned scepticism when it came to the work of the devil and evil spirits, he did not adopt this attitude towards claimed psychic powers. Shaw believed himself to be psychic and portrayed this as a natural ability, arguing that 'The psychic is only the observation of immaterial reality that belongs to the created world of time-space ... the psychic can be dealt with reasonably and rationally and can be discriminated and educated just as any other part of our make up'.[12] Shaw's approach would become the accepted orthodoxy among Anglican exorcists, for whom paranormal and parapsychological theories became the norm even if great caution was exercised in attributing phenomena to the devil or demons.

Shaw did not always heed his own warnings about personal involvement; according to Hacking, 'in an effort to communicate something to others, at a time when he was feeling isolated, he undoubtedly tended to talk too much about the more sensational aspects of the work'.[13] In the early 1950s Shaw fell out with Petitpierre, criticising the younger exorcist for sensationalising the ministry, talking too much about ghosts and not placing sufficient emphasis on the reality of evil behind magic. Shaw even warned the exorcists he trained against having any contact with Petitpierre.[14] Nevertheless, Petitpierre's practice remained firmly grounded in the approach he had learnt from Shaw and he can be considered the continuator of Shaw's tradition.

In 1947 Shaw left Soho and moved to Southwark, where he formed a friendship with the Russian Orthodox priest Anthony Bloom (1914–2003), then chaplain to the Fellowship of St Alban and St Sergius, an organisation founded in 1928 to foster understanding between the Anglican and Orthodox churches.[15] Bloom would go on to lead the Russian Orthodox church in Britain for many years as Metropolitan of Sourozh. Shaw was drawn to Orthodoxy's unreserved acceptance of the reality of angels and demons, in contrast to the scepticism he so often encountered among Anglicans. Shaw contributed a paper on practical demonology, 'Angels and Demons in Human Life', to a conference of the Fellowship, which was published in 1952.[16] In 1954 Shaw and Petitpierre were invited to give evidence to a subcommittee of the Church of England's commission on healing, specifically concerned with demonology. Shaw built a relationship during the 1950s with the bishop of Jarrow (and later Wakefield), John Ramsbotham (1906–89), who headed the Guild of St Raphael. It seems likely that Ramsbotham, for whom Shaw prepared detailed guidelines on exorcism to be used in his own diocese,[17] was the means by which Shaw was introduced to the episcopate as a whole as the Church of England's principal authority on demonology, possession and exorcism.

Shaw was accepted as an authority on demonology by Lambeth Palace as early as 1953, and the correspondence regarding his involvement in cases passed to him by the archbishop's office well illustrates his approach. On 23 October 1953 Shaw was contacted by E. G. Jay, one of the chaplains of Archbishop Geoffrey Fisher, about a Hungarian woman who claimed to be under magical attack from other members of the Hungarian émigré community. Jay was informed of Shaw's unique expertise by Noel Davey, an editor at SPCK.[18] Shaw told Jay that he would need to meet with the Hungarian in order to establish the reality of her accusations:

I am afraid it is true that there are groups of perverts and evil-minded people who give themselves up to this kind of thing. It is probable that they are more common on the Continent than in this country and if there is reality in what your visitor complains of it may be a recent importation. The practical question which we may have to discuss is how far she is herself involved with the group and, if she is, how to get her clear. The seriousness or not of this business depends a good deal on the character of the group, whether it is merely a collection of perverted exhibitionists or whether they have a more sinister purpose of gaining power over others definitely to spread moral breakdown and subversive activity. If we have any suspicion of the latter I think I can get it looked into in ways other than by the ordinary police.[19]

Shaw noted that, unless practitioners of black magic were serving or selling drugs or alcohol without a licence, the police could not arrest them.[20] Shaw paid a visit to Jay on 29 October, who noted, in a briefing paper prepared for Archbishop Fisher, that 'Nashdom Abbey holds a whole file on this subject, including more or less all that is known of the activities of these groups'.[21] This was presumably a file compiled by Max Petitpierre. Jay also expanded on Shaw's dark allusion to 'ways other than by the ordinary police', claiming that 'One or two persons in M.I.5 keep a look out for any news of activity as in some cases the exponents of black magic aim at getting people within their power with subversive intentions'.[22] Whether Shaw really had such contacts with MI5 is unclear; according to his biographer, Shaw had been called in during the War to assess the Nazis' capabilities in psychic warfare.[23]

Jay gave the names and addresses of four other Hungarians who had been accused by the woman concerned, and noted that 'Gilbert Shaw said that the name of Mr. Gardner might be kept in mind as being connected with some of these groups in the past'.[24] Shaw was probably referring to Gerald Gardner (1884–1964), the founder of the Wiccan religion, who was widely publicising his activities in the early 1950s; another possibility is Edward Gardner (1869–1969), a leading Theosophist. On 17 November Shaw reported to Jay on his meeting with the Hungarian woman, describing the entire affair as 'a mare's nest' and attributing it to 'persecution mania' on the part of the woman concerned, who had imagined that a group of people interested in Spiritualism and crystal-gazing were also directing black magic against her.[25]

Jay drew on Shaw's expertise a second time in March 1954 when another woman in north London wrote to the archbishop claiming to be under the influence of black magic. Shaw described the woman's claims as 'suggestion', which was the result of 'primitive magic' being practised against her. He recommended a meeting between the woman and her parish priest: 'In the old days belief in GOD and the efficacy of the priestly blessing was probably sufficient, and it is something on that line that should be carried out'. Shaw argued that the only certain way of combatting a powerful suggestion of magic was an equally powerful counter-suggestion.[26] Jay referred a third case to Shaw in the same month regarding a woman from Brighton who claimed to be under magical attack.[27]

Archbishop Fisher seems to have taken such matters seriously, writing personally to each of the women concerned, and Jay reassured the woman from Brighton that 'Church authorities, and indeed the Police, are not unaware of the activities such as you mention, and a very close watch is kept on those who dabble in Black Magic'.[28] For Jay and Shaw, the church's role was not only a pastoral one; in dealing with supposed 'black magic groups' it acted almost as an extension of law enforcement. Shaw's role reinforces Thomas Waters's argument that belief in 'black magic' (sometimes called witchcraft) persisted as an undercurrent in twentieth-century British society.[29] In a 1971 television interview, Theo Brown claimed she had heard of a recent case (presumably in the West Country) when 'a bishop went to remonstrate' with a woman who boasted of having bewitched her neighbour's cows.[30]

In his last years Shaw contributed several articles to the Guild of St Raphael's magazine *St Raphael Quarterly*, expounding his approach to exorcism. In a 1961 article he declared that 'The essential condition for exorcism is the cognition of that which is to be cast out', warning that 'a vague good will and intention to benefit sufferers' was unlikely to work.[31] In another article Shaw warned that exorcism had to be approached with complete faith, since 'thoughts of doubt, anger, disgust, or impatience as expressions of selfhood, may provide contact for the demonic spirit to act upon the exorcist, to weaken his prayer and even nullify his action'.[32]

Gilbert Shaw's influence on the future direction of exorcism in the Church of England was immense; it would be no exaggeration to say that he single-handedly re-invented the ministry. No doubt he would have remained an eccentric figure on the fringes of the church unless he had won the trust of the bishops via his work with the Guild of St Raphael, as well as his insistence that exorcisms should be firmly under episcopal control. Shaw established the idea that using rituals and prayers to rid a place of a perceived evil influence was indeed exorcism, and that this form of 'exorcism' would be the one primarily practised in a pastoral context within the Church of England. By translating the formulae of the *Rituale Romanum* into English, Shaw also established that Anglican exorcism would be a liturgically rooted practice in the sacramental tradition, imitative of Roman Catholicism. By doing so he imported Roman Catholic demonological language into Anglican practice, and later exorcists would refer to 'major' and 'minor' exorcisms. Anglican exorcism need not have gone in the direction Shaw took it; the fact that Shaw belonged firmly to the Anglo-Catholic tradition strongly affected his approach to exorcism, and the exorcisms of Shaw, Petitpierre and their disciples bore little or no relation to the Protestant exorcisms which had briefly flourished in the Church of England in the sixteenth century. But neither Shaw nor Petitpierre showed any awareness of, or interest in, pre-existing Anglican traditions of exorcism, and they proceeded on the assumption that it would be necessary to borrow and adapt Roman Catholic material.

'THE CHURCH'S MINISTRY OF HEALING'

The report produced by the demonology subcommittee which Shaw joined in 1954 was finally published in a much condensed form in 1958 as part of *The Church's Ministry of Healing*. Before publication, the demonology report was submitted to Ian Ramsey (1915–72), Nolloth Professor of the Philosophy of Religion at Oxford (later bishop of Durham). Ramsey objected to the report on the grounds that it relied too much on unverifiable claims derived from experience alone.[33] However, publication of a stripped-down version of the report went ahead as an appendix to a much larger report that represented the culmination of a process of theological reflection on healing dating back to before World War II. The report acknowledged the difficulty of attempting 'any really exhaustive investigation' of exorcism, noting that a thorough study of theology, psychology and medicine 'together with a review of evidence available from the records of the work of the Church overseas particularly in Africa and India, and some study of the work of the Society for Psychical Research' would have been necessary for a complete report. The subcommittee therefore decided to restrict its scope to 'evidence available in Great Britain'.[34]

The report complained of 'the general ignorance of the subject [of exorcism] which apparently prevails throughout the country' and the difficulty of finding 'competent witnesses'. Language was also a challenge; some witnesses used theological terms while others used medical terms to describe the phenomena of possession, making it difficult to be sure people were talking about the same phenomena. The report concluded that 'From the evidence available it is clear that some form of exorcism is at present used in this country; very infrequently in the case of persons, but rather less infrequently in the case of places'.[35] The report noted the difficulty of 'the discernment of demons'; its claim that 'reliance had, in the last resort, to be placed on the exorcist's spiritual discernment of the presence of a demon' was what provoked Ian Ramsey's concern. The report warned against the misuse of exorcism and advocated 'the doctor and the priest working in close collaboration', as well as recommending extensive spiritual preparation for the exorcist and 'pastoral care for the patient afterwards'.[36]

Like the Church of England's committee on Spiritualism in 1939, the subcommittee on demonology was divided, with some members 'not persuaded that demons may cause or complicate any malady'. However, all members agreed 'that medical knowledge is not, and cannot be, comprehensive, and they would not like to assert *a priori* that no case will ever be found of such an unusual character as suggests the need for exorcism'.[37] The subcommittee made the following recommendations regarding exorcism in the Church of England:

(1) That the Archbishops of Canterbury and York be respectfully asked to consult with the appropriate medical authorities with a view to setting up an advisory panel consisting of priests and doctors.

(2) That the following procedure should be adhered to before exorcism of persons is authorised, and should apply to the exorcism of places insofar as the health of any person has been affected by them:

  (a) That any priest or doctor who has reason to suspect that a certain case demands exorcism should refer it to the diocesan bishop before taking action.

  (b) That if the bishop is satisfied, after such investigation and consultation as he thinks fit (involving reference to the medical authorities in charge of the case and the parish priest or chaplain concerned) that a *prima facie* case has been made for exorcism, he may refer the case to the panel for diagnosis.

  (c) That the considered report of the panel should be submitted to the diocesan bishop who, in the light of it, would authorise action appropriate to the case.

  (d) That exorcism should be practised only with the authority of the diocesan bishop, given in each case separately, and after the foregoing procedure has been complied with.

These proposals were essentially Shaw's, and although the guidelines were never actually implemented (since the proposed archbishops' panel was never set up), they set the tone for future approaches to exorcism in the Church of England. Indeed, the 1958 guidelines were considerably stricter than subsequent guidelines – stricter, indeed, than Canon 72 – since they obliged diocesan bishops to refer suspected cases to the proposed archbishops' panel of clergy and medical professionals. The guidelines did not oblige the bishop to follow the panel's advice, merely stating that he 'would authorise action appropriate to the case' in the light of it. The report gave no indication of what an exorcism was expected to involve, nor did it seek to define what exorcism was. However, the procedure it recommended, if implemented, would have been immensely longwinded – a deliberate proviso, perhaps, to ensure that any fraudulent or spurious demoniacs would be deterred from seeking attention.

The Church's Ministry of Healing attracted the notice of the press because it contained a short section on exorcism, and Shaw was interviewed on the BBC's *Panorama* programme as well as receiving full-spread treatment in several newspapers.[38] The attention was understandable, given that the report was the Church of England's first official statement on exorcism since 1604. However, as Hacking noted, the work of the demonology subcommittee had been confined primarily to considering the metaphysical question of whether demons intervened in the physical world,[39] and gave little practical consideration to the *practice* of exorcism. This preoccupation reflected the theological debates of the day, which tended to focus on the reality (or otherwise) of the devil and demons.[40]

The renewed interest in exorcism provoked by the report also prompted the Convocations of Canterbury and York, in July 1960, to request greater episcopal oversight of exorcism to prevent 'misuse and wrong diagnosis'.[41] Agendas of bishops' meetings at Lambeth Palace show that exorcism was discussed five times in the 1960s and 1970s: on 26–27 January 1961 (along with Canon 72),[42] 13–16 June 1966,[43] 15–18 June 1970,[44] 14–17 June 1971[45] and, together with 'Satanism and Black Magic', on 18–19 June 1975.[46]

DONALD OMAND

One of the few Anglican exorcists not trained by Gilbert Shaw was Donald Omand. Omand was born in Perth, Scotland in 1903, the son of a minister of the Church of Scotland. Omand obtained a doctorate in the Philosophy of Religion and lectured in Berlin in the 1930s, acting as a correspondent for the British press (which led him to interview Adolf Hitler three times). He was ordained as a Free Church minister in 1937 and became an adviser on ecclesiastical history to a film studio. One day Omand encountered a circus troop on the studio lot looking for a minister to perform weddings and baptisms. Omand agreed to do this and became the country's first circus chaplain.[47]

Omand's involvement in exorcism began when a circus strong-man started displaying personality changes that led some of the other performers to believe he was possessed. The strongman's behaviour disturbed the lions, who killed their trainer during a performance; the lions then started displaying uncharacteristic behaviour and the performers believed the spirit previously possessing the strongman had entered the animals. They asked Omand to perform an exorcism on the lions, which he did.[48] In 1954 Omand was ordained as an Anglican priest by the bishop of Oxford, who dispensed him from further study. In spite of his unusual background, Omand followed a more conventional path in the Church of England than Gilbert Shaw, serving as rector of Winterbourne Abbas 1956–9 and then vicar of Chideock 1959–71, both parishes in Dorset, during which time he served as exorcist of the diocese of Portsmouth.[49]

Like Shaw and Petitpierre, Omand believed himself to be personally 'psychic', claiming that it was his 'feyness' (a claim to 'second sight' inherited from his Hebridean ancestors) that gave him the power to exorcise.[50] Unlike some other Anglican exorcists, Omand was convinced that exorcism was a personal talent; indeed, he compared it to musical ability.[51] When his biographer Marc Alexander asked him, 'What is it that gives you as an exorcist authority over evil?', Omand made no mention of the authority of the church in his answer, although he acknowledged that the permission of a bishop 'put[s] some sort of brake on it'.[52] Omand's techniques were similar to Shaw's and Petitpierre's, concentrating primarily on house blessings, including celebrations of the eucharist in people's homes.[53]

Omand shared Shaw's preoccupation with the exorcism of ancient sacred sites, and his experiments with exorcism became more extreme over time. Only a third of Omand's exorcisms involved exorcising a person; the rest involved places or objects, and Omand pioneered exorcism of 'accident blackspots' as well as attempting to exorcise both the Loch Ness monster and the Bermuda Triangle.[54] His preferred formula of exorcism was a translation from the *Rituale Romanum*: 'Go forth thou deceiver, full of all evil and falsehood, the persecutor of the innocent. Give place thou wicked one; give place thou evil one; give place to Christ'.[55]

In spite of his more bizarre activities, Omand enjoyed episcopal support. Anselm Genders, bishop of Bermuda, both authorised and wrote in support of Omand's exorcism of the Bermuda Triangle,[56] and John Phillips, bishop of Portsmouth (1910–85) wrote a foreword for Omand's book *Experiences of a Present Day Exorcist* (1970), reporting that all of Omand's exorcisms within his diocese had been accomplished 'with complete effect'.[57] The bishop of Hereford, Peter Mumford, supplied a 'personal commendation' to Alexander's 1978 biography of Omand, writing that:

> Christians need to keep their nerves steady. On the one hand in the face of those who are cynical about the Church's traditional ministry of deliverance from evil, and on the other hand before those who feel called to minister without any reference to authority and experience in the field of medicine or in the Church.[58]

Omand was an eccentric character, like most of the pioneering Anglican exorcists, although several exorcists adopted even odder practices and beliefs than he did. His emphasis on exorcism as a personal talent put him at odds with Shaw, Petitpierre and John Richards, who all warned against this belief, but he was essentially an exorcist priest practising what Collins describes as 'the gentle Anglican version of sacramental exorcism'.[59]

THE LATER CAREER OF MAX PETITPIERRE

Max Petitpierre, who entered the Benedictine Nashdom Abbey in 1947 and took the name Robert, had been Gilbert Shaw's protégé from his very first experiments with exorcism in the 1920s. By the time of Shaw's death in 1967 Petitpierre was generally regarded as the Church of England's leading expert on exorcism, and was invited to join the committee on exorcism convened by the bishop of Exeter in 1964. After the Exeter commission published its report (edited by Petitpierre) in 1972, the commission continued its work under the name of the Christian Exorcism Study Group (CESG), with Petitpierre as chairman.[60] John Richards served as secretary and Petitpierre stepped down as chairman, to be succeeded by Alan Harrison, in

1974.[61] In 1976 Petitpierre published an account of his 50 years' experience as an exorcist, *Exorcising Devils*, in which he explained his views and the techniques he employed.

Generally speaking, Petitpierre's approach as a demonologist was to play down the power of the devil and demons, referring to demons pejoratively as 'little devils'. Petitpierre criticised the use of the term 'possessed' to describe demonised people, suggesting that the idea of exorcism as a dramatic casting out of the devil dated from the sixteenth century:

> [N]obody can be possessed by anybody but God ... this way of looking at exorcism is a mistaken one. Previously [to the sixteenth century], exorcism had been a far from dramatic action – simply a prayer to the Lord to cleanse persons of evil influences. And it is in this sense that the words 'Christian exorcism' should normally be used. There are, of course, cases of demonic attack, although they are rare. Even in these cases, there is no need for dramatic behaviour – no need to shout or to command in a loud voice. It is only necessary to say quietly, 'In the name of the Lord Jesus I command you to go, harming no one' – and go the demon must.[62]

Petitpierre claimed that cases in which a person was 'controlled' by a demon constituted no more than one per cent of what an exorcist had to deal with.[63] In the vast majority of cases, Petitpierre was called upon to perform 'antiseptic' or 'minor' exorcisms in which he believed any prayer would do to banish spiritual 'bugs' from people or places. Petitpierre used blessed oil or holy water for such exorcisms. He adopted a classification of hauntings that would become standard among Anglican exorcists, distinguishing between 'place memories' and 'earthbound spirits', and recommended the celebration of a requiem mass as the most effective means of removing the annoyance of ghosts.

Petitpierre was somewhat influenced by Spiritualism in his approach to the cleansing of 'earthbound spirits' from places, arguing that some people 'do not quite realize that they have died' and have to be helped to move on to the afterlife.[64] Petitpierre condemned the Church of England for failing to teach the doctrine of the Communion of Saints in its Catholic form and blamed the rise of Spiritualism on the church's refusal to pray for the dead.[65] Petitpierre also considered it acceptable for two priests to administer absolution to a ghost, a significant deviation from conventional sacramental theology.[66] He uncritically accepted as factual the parapsychological claims of Joseph Rhine and Uri Geller, an attitude which was not unusual in the 1970s.[67]

In May 1975 the bishop of St Albans, Robert Runcie, reported that 'I have virtually put exorcism into the hands of Dom Robert Petitpierre who only operates according to my specific instructions and then he deals with areas which think in this sort of language'. Although Runcie was personally sceptical about exorcism, he justified his use of Petitpierre on the grounds that 'he manages to satisfy one or two people who have places with strange atmospheres,' reporting that 'He doesn't do more than celebrate Communion and say some strange prayers'.[68] Runcie's approach suggests that Petitpierre was tolerated rather than welcomed by the bishops. On the whole, however, Petitpierre's approach was 'orthodox' within the context of the Anglo-Catholic tradition established by Shaw, even if he was more willing than his teacher to publicise his activities.

EXORCISM IN THE EARLY ANGLICAN CHARISMATIC RENEWAL

The charismatic renewal (sometimes called neo-pentecostalism) was a global movement within existing mainstream Christian denominations to recognise and welcome the gifts of the Holy Spirit, including 'baptism in the Spirit', glossolalia (the gift of tongues) and miraculous healing (including exorcism). Among Anglicans, the charismatic renewal began in Episcopalian churches on the western seaboard of the United States in the early 1960s. In the Church of England, charismatic renewal began at All Souls, Langham Place in London, where a curate, Michael Harper (1931–2010), received 'baptism in the Spirit' in 1962. In 1963 another former curate at All Souls, John Collins, was appointed incumbent at St Mark's, Gillingham, which thereby became the Church of England's first charismatic parish.[69]

From the very beginning, Harper was convinced that welcoming the active work of the Holy Spirit would result in 'spiritual warfare'. Early in his ministry a man and a woman expressed their desire to be filled with the Holy Spirit but the woman confessed to being involved in witchcraft, 'begging for deliverance', while the man started making animal noises. Harper 'bound the powers of darkness which were tormenting the man, and cast out evil spirits until he was completely freed'.[70] Harper regarded 'discerning and expelling of evil spirits in particular' as just 'one part of the total conflict',[71] which was much broader than exorcism alone. Harper and other early Anglican charismatics adopted the Pentecostal approach to exorcism as a form of healing for both physical and spiritual sickness, and were much preoccupied with a perceived threat from the occult, which Harper dubbed 'the Devil's Pentecost'.[72] Nevertheless, Harper displayed some caution, suggesting that the local bishop's permission should be sought to exorcise, if not for every individual exorcism.[73]

Harper was not alone in his caution among the early charismatics. As Graham Smith observes,

> All the pioneers saw dangers in the field of spiritual warfare to a greater or lesser extent, whether from a paranoid dualism ..., supernatural deception, or inexperience ... [M]ore than one practitioner cautioned that those claiming to have an evil spirit most often did not ... [C]asting out non-existent demons can leave damaging feelings of guilt; some can wrongly minister with never-ending lists of demons; there can be a lack of clear spiritual authority in this ministry (though the Anglican system helps here considerably); and there can be a lack of common sense, or the use of strange practices lacking proportion and decency.[74]

The extent to which 'the Anglican system' helped mitigate potential excesses of charismatic exorcisms is unclear. Even the most enthusiastic Anglican exorcists in the sacramental tradition, such as Petitpierre, Omand and Neil-Smith, acknowledged the 'extraordinary' nature of exorcism and treated it as a specialist ministry. Charismatic evangelicals, by contrast, often regarded discernment and casting out of spirits as a gift of the Spirit available not only to any member of the clergy but to the laity as well; and since spiritual warfare was constant and unrelenting, it was appropriate to minister 'deliverance' in regular prayer meetings and services. It is difficult to see how Harper's suggestion that episcopal permission for exorcism should be sought was practical in a charismatic context. Indeed, as Smith notes, all of the charismatic Anglican pioneers agreed that the greatest danger in the field of spiritual warfare was a minister's reluctance or refusal to minister 'deliverance'.[75]

Andrew Walker has described the tendency of charismatics to attribute a huge range of social, familial, psychological and medical problems to demons as their 'paranoid universe'. A dualistic world-view in which God and Satan are permanently at war within human beings produces deep-seated insecurity which leads in turn to the demonisation (and ultimately persecution) of others, as well as contributing to over-reliance on the leadership and discernment of spiritual 'strong men'.[76] Graham Smith has disputed Walker's analysis, arguing that if demons are real then spiritual warfare is justified, and that if deliverance is seen in terms of an encounter with truth rather than a confrontation between opposing powers it carries less potential for harm. However, even Smith acknowledged that 'going back and looking for "demonic strongholds" which do not exist ... could increase anxiety'.[77] J. M. Collins observed that a key difference between the approaches of Anglican charismatics and 'sacramentalists' like Petitpierre is the charismatics' tendency to demonise all 'paranormal' activity, while Petitpierre opted for 'pseudo-scientific' explanations of many phenomena, such as poltergeists.[78]

Anglican charismatics were not unique in being preoccupied by the threat from the occult, although they placed a particular emphasis on ideas of Satanic conspiracy. Without understanding or enquiring into its tenets, Christian demonologists in the 1960s and 1970s usually uncritically accepted that the Wiccan religion, first publicised by Gerald Gardner in 1954, involved Satanic worship, and they believed that Satanism existed as an organised movement. In reality, apart from their adoption of the terminology of 'witchcraft' and their belief in magic, most twentieth-century pagan witches bore no relation to their early modern predecessors, and were bound by an ethical principle (the Wiccan rede) that specifically forbade cursing.

Nevertheless, the publicity given to self-proclaimed 'Satanists' such as Anton LaVey, who founded his 'Church of Satan' in California in 1966, fed the demonologists' fears of organised Satanism. Yet Ronald Hutton has argued that British Satanism was never anything more than a rumour stirred up by journalists.[79] Indeed, a spate of acts of sacrilege in churches in the late 1960s seems to have been inspired by sensational media reports of alleged 'Satanism' rather than vice versa.[80] No convincing evidence for organised Satanic worship in Britain has ever been brought forward, although Bill Ellis has noted that some acts of sacrilege during an early outbreak in 1963–4 showed some knowledge of folk magical practices.[81] In the twentieth century, as in the sixteenth, it seems that the myth of Satanic worship as an inversion of Christianity served to create the enemy the demonologists required to legitimise their work.[82] By the 1980s, the exorcism of desecrated churches was a recognised part of the Church of England's 'deliverance ministry'.[83]

In spite of the very different approach to exorcism adopted by charismatic Anglican churches compared with the 'mainstream' techniques of exorcism developed by Gilbert Shaw, specialist exorcists within the Church of England would go on to be influenced by charismatic ideas. These included belief in 'territorial spirits' (demons having an influence over a particular geographical area), ancestral demonisation (demonic activity passed down from a person's ancestors) and the belief that demons might cause physical illness. Unlike their Protestant predecessors, twentieth-century charismatics were comfortable with direct imperative conjurations; for example, the theologian Michael Green advocated dispossession by prayer and fasting before he 'experienced renewal in the Holy Spirit' in the early 1970s, after which he began to adjure.[84] Many of the characteristic features of the charismatic approach were direct borrowings from Pentecostal practice, although charismatics might argue that Alexander Boddy was already borrowing in this way in the early 1900s. Nevertheless, no genetic link existed between Boddy's Anglican Pentecostalism and the charismatic movement of the 1960s.

THE EXETER REPORT

Perhaps the most influential of the Church of England's reports on exorcism in the last 75 years was *Exorcism: The Report of a Committee Convened by the Bishop of Exeter* (usually referred to as the Exeter

Report), published in 1972. Although the report had no official status (except in the diocese of Exeter), it aspired to provide a framework for exorcism for the whole Church of England. In his foreword to the report Bishop Robert Mortimer claimed to have been 'much disturbed by the unhealthy and near-hysterical publicity given by the national press to the question of exorcisms in the Church of England' in the early 1960s.[85] Mortimer may have been thinking, at least in part, of a 1965 article in *Life* magazine which reported that he had exorcised a haunted house at Abbotskerswell, Devon in November 1963.[86] Graham Smith traces the origins of the Exeter Report back to John Richards's lectures on deliverance ministry at Queen's College, Birmingham in 1971–2 and the 'doubts and anxieties' raised by the rise of the charismatic movement and the 'stupendous deliverances' that accompanied this.[87]

Mortimer noted that he was receiving a large number of requests for exorcism, but 'It had become apparent that there were very few people indeed in the Church of England who had any knowledge or experience of the subject'. He regretted that most clergy regarded exorcism as 'an exercise in white magic or a survival of medieval superstition' and as a 'purely negative action'. He believed that exorcism's 'positive aspect as an extension of the frontiers of Christ's Kingdom' justified its reconsideration,[88] although the bishop offered no historical examples from the Church of England or elsewhere to show that exorcism could have the 'positive aspect' he advocated. The committee convened in 1964 does not seem to have questioned the assumption that exorcism was a potential good. In addition to Petitpierre and Omand the committee consisted of three other clergymen: M. H. B. Joyce, who was also a medical doctor and a consultant psychiatrist; the leading Anglo-Catholic philosopher and theologian Eric Mascall, and Patrick Ferguson-Davie, who served as the committee's secretary. The committee also included two Roman Catholic priests, the Jesuits Thomas Corbishley and Joseph Crehan. Corbishley was a well-known spiritual writer and supporter of ecumenism based at the Church of the Immaculate Conception, Farm Street, while H. J. A. Sire described Crehan as the English Jesuit Province's 'best-known theologian'.[89]

The neo-Scholastic philosopher Eric Mascall had previously acted as a consultant for Gilbert Shaw; according to Hacking, Shaw used Mascall 'to confirm that what Gilbert was discovering [about demonology] made sense within the boundaries of theological and philosophical discourse'.[90] Mascall had also been one of the editors of the 1952 volume of proceedings of the Fellowship of St Alban and St Sergius that featured Shaw's article on demonology.[91] Crehan provided a theological overview of exorcism in the New Testament,[92] but it is obvious from a comparison of the recommendations of the report with Petitpierre's *Exorcising Devils* (1976) that the monk of Nashdom was the principal author of the report itself.

The report defined exorcism as 'the binding of evil powers by the triumph of Christ Jesus, through the application of the power demonstrated by that triumph, in and by his Church', leaving open the possibility that such 'binding' could happen in more than one way. Petitpierre noted that, strictly speaking, only a demon could be exorcised from a person; it was not the person who was being exorcised, and exorcisms should be said 'over' a place 'in order to release it from the domination of any evil powers that may be there'.[93] However, while the report repeatedly appealed to the New Testament as justification for the exorcism of demoniacs, it offered no real justification for the particularly Anglican practice of 'exorcising' places.

Petitpierre elided baptismal exorcism, exorcism of objects and exorcism of demoniacs, noting that 'all that comes into the Church needs to be freed from the domination of evil'.[94] Petitpierre rejected the concept of 'possession',[95] and portrayed all exorcisms as being on a continuum of seriousness, from the merely symbolic exorcism of catechumens at one end of the spectrum to the solemn exorcism of demoniacs at the other. One of the Exeter Report's more eccentric claims (which has found its way into subsequent literature) was that prayers for liberation from evil (including the Lord's Prayer) could be considered 'exorcisms',[96] and the report even included 'A Note on the Occurrence of Exorcism Prayers in the Book of Common Prayer'.[97] Since no liturgical scholar would recognise the prayers cited as exorcisms in any sense, the inclusion of this material created the highly misleading impression that *The Book of Common*

Prayer contained exorcisms and thereby falsely implied that a liturgical tradition of exorcism existed within the Church of England.

The Exeter Report recommended that 'All forms of [exorcism] in ordinary use should contain, in the context of either prayer or command, an order to the demon (i) to depart (ii) to harm no one and, most importantly (iii) to depart to its own place, there to remain forever'.[98] It is not clear how someone was supposed to order a demon without using a 'command', and Petitpierre does not seem to have considered that some Anglicans in the Protestant tradition might have been unwilling to address a demon directly. Petitpierre suggested the following formula:

> I command you, every unclean spirit, in the Name of God the Father Almighty, in the Name of Jesus Christ his only Son, and in the Name of the Holy Spirit, that harming no one you depart from this creature of God, N., and return to the place appointed you, there to remain forever.[99]

Petitpierre provided alternative imperative formulas taken from the *Rituale Romanum*, the baptismal liturgy of the 1549 Prayer Book and the East Syrian rite, but no deprecative alternatives.[100] In fact, these forms of exorcism had originally been translated and compiled by Shaw, something that Petitpierre failed to acknowledge in the report.[101] With no obvious authority, the report urged that 'Although the liturgical forms for exorcism vary from place to place and from age to age, those appended here should be considered normal for the province [of Canterbury], and so be used'.[102] For anyone unaware that the Exeter Report had no force outside Mortimer's own diocese this was a highly misleading statement.

Petitpierre cautioned that 'In the first place it should be assumed that the patient's illness has a physical or mental cause', and exhorted cooperation between the exorcist and medical professionals.[103] The report advised that exorcisms of persons should always be authorised, in each individual case, by the diocesan bishop – even citing the obsolete Canon 72. In addition, the report envisaged that only trained exorcists holding a more general licence from the bishop would perform this ministry. Witnesses should also be present.

Exorcism of places, on the other hand, might be a matter for an ordinary parish priest to deal with.[104]

The involvement of two Jesuit priests in a report that so wholeheartedly endorsed the ministry of exorcism is somewhat surprising, in the light of the contemporaneous theological direction of the Roman Catholic church (and the Society of Jesus) *vis à vis* exorcism. In the late 1960s and 1970s, in the wake of the Second Vatican Council, the Roman Catholic church began to downplay imperative exorcism, portraying it as a kind of prayer. The minor order of exorcist was abolished in 1972, and in 1975 the Sacred Congregation for Divine Worship described exorcism as 'a remotely possible service', while Jesuit theologians such as Herbert Haag, Henry Ansgar Kelly and Juan Cortés rejected traditional demonology altogether.[105] The practice of exorcism virtually ceased in many Roman Catholic countries, a decline hastened in Western Europe by the tragic death of a young German student, Anneliese Michel, following a lengthy series of exorcisms in 1976.[106] The Exeter Report advocated the establishment of joint training centres for Anglican and Roman Catholic exorcists;[107] it is scarcely surprising that this never happened, given the Roman Catholic church's lack of interest in (and even antipathy towards) exorcism at the time.

The Exeter Report's section on exorcism of places suggested that magic was real and effective, claiming that it could be 'in some measure substantiated' that magicians were able 'to instigate and operate "haunts"' and speculating that 'the influence of magicians' might be behind poltergeist phenomena. Further, it was claimed that the activity of magicians 'frequently revivifies ancient celtic sites such as tumuli, circles, and snake-path shrines'.[108] Exactly how any of this could be 'substantiated' was left unclear in the report. These claims reflected Shaw and Petitpierre's particular (and inaccurate) interpretation of prehistoric sites,[109] yet (presumably owing to Petitpierre's strong influence) they made their way into a report destined to have a significant influence on the Church of England's direction of policy. The Exeter Report was an eccentric document that reflected the particular demonological preoccupations of Petitpierre (and perhaps Omand as well).

The recommendations of the Exeter Report corresponded, to a large extent, to what many dioceses were already doing. John Richards reported that a former bishop of Durham had insisted, long before 1972, on a full case history of any subject of a proposed exorcism (including medical history) before he would authorise this ministry.[110] However, awareness and recognition of the ministry seems to have been patchy across the Church of England as a whole. One local report to emerge in the wake of the Exeter Report was prepared by Morris Maddocks, bishop of Selby in the diocese of York and published in March 1974. The York Report noted that 'All clergymen by virtue of their ordination have the right to act as exorcists', but added that in the diocese of York 'a full-scale exorcism may be carried out only by an authorised exorcist or under the personal supervision of such an authorised exorcist, and that a report of the case be sent to the bishop of the area in which the exorcism was administered'.

The York Report made provision for the authorisation of lay exorcists[111] and suggested that 'any Christian' might act as an exorcist in 'emergency cases'. The report emphasised the potential need for spontaneous ministry and urged ministers to 'extemporise' on the forms of exorcism provided.[112] The report recommended the use of phrases of the litany or the short exorcism 'In the Name of Jesus of Nazareth, Son of the Most High God, I bind you, evil spirit(s), and command you to leave this person N / this place, to harm no one, and to go to your own place, never to return'.[113] The York Report recommended that, after deliverance, the demoniac should make 'an act of renunciation' of involvement in occult practices,[114] and even suggested that 'Any object or book with occult or pornographic or evil connotation should be removed and if possible destroyed or defaced'.[115] The bishop of Selby became the first port of call for priests confronted with cases apparently demanding exorcism.[116] The York Report acknowledged that the cinematic release of *The Exorcist* was to blame for the apparent epidemic of possession,[117] and envisaged a church in which frequent exorcism was the norm, to the extent that it was even delegated to licensed lay ministers rather than the clergy. There does not appear to be any evidence, however, that such a licensing of lay exorcists ever took place.

JOHN RICHARDS

One of the most influential Anglican demonologists of the 1970s was John Richards, secretary to the CESG, whom J. M. Collins describes as 'a thoughtful but cautious charismatic'.[118] Richards was appointed to a one-year fellowship at Queen's College, Birmingham in order to complete his book *But Deliver Us From Evil* (1974), which provided the most thorough treatment of demonology and exorcism then available. Richards began by setting demonology within the wider context of the church's ministry of healing,[119] before devoting a chapter to what he called 'The Occult Explosion'[120] and two chapters to 'The Occult Journey',[121] exploring the ways in which he claimed people might be drawn into engagement with the occult. Richards then dealt with possession,[122] deliverance ministry in general,[123] and finally exorcism of people[124] and places.[125]

The 1970s were the decade that saw interest in the supernatural return to British society with a vengeance, yet ironically it was the church that was often the bastion of scepticism. As John Richards wrote in 1973,

> Had I, even in the nineteen sixties, ventured to suggest that exorcism should be a small but real part of the Church's ministry of healing, most opinion ... would have dismissed the suggestion as medieval superstition ... Today the task is much easier. While the spiritual and supernatural still remain unfashionable in many quarters of the Church, no informed opinion would hold that they are unfashionable in the contemporary society which the Church exists to serve.[126]

Richards saw exorcism as an aspect of healing ministry and described it as 'spiritual surgery', claiming that 'only those familiar with the healing ministry of the Church ... will be able to understand Christian exorcism'.[127] Richards defined exorcism as 'the Church's compassionate response to people (and places) needing spiritual surgery when, acting with Christ's authority, the Church – through individuals – makes his victory real in a particular situation'.[128] He saw exorcism as just one part of deliverance ministry, drawing an analogy between repairing the fabric of a house and ejecting unwanted occupants. Exorcism was the latter, whereas deliverance ministry as a whole was restorative of the whole person.[129] Indeed,

Richards maintained that exorcism would be ineffective if someone was unwilling to change a lifestyle that invited demonic engagement.[130]

This distinction between deliverance ministry and exorcism was not Richards's invention but derived from Henry Cooper (d. 1982), a prominent member of the Guild of St Raphael.[131] The distinction has not endured, judging from the contemporary Church of England's tendency to conflate exorcism and deliverance ministry in order to avoid using the controversial word 'exorcism'. Richards insisted that exorcism, although performed by an individual, was an act of the church; the question was not 'Where can I find an exorcist?', but 'What must *we* do for this suffering person now and in the future to ensure his full deliverance to God?'[132] Richards's use of the phrase 'deliverance to God' was significant, indicating a reversal of the usual notion of deliverance 'from evil'.

Richards maintained the importance of constructing a detailed case history for the subject of a proposed exorcism, on the grounds that this was necessary for a person's 'full healing'. The case history might be expected to involve exposing someone's entanglement with occult practices, including inherited influences.[133] Richards noted Shaw's view that it was possible to diagnose possession without the charismatic gift of 'discernment of spirits', but maintained that the gift of discernment was advantageous to the exorcist; what was needed was a complementary approach that valued reason and revelation equally.[134] Richards displayed a strong Pentecostal influence by rejecting a dichotomy between demonisation and illness; it was not a question of whether a person was mentally ill or demonised, for example, but whether the person's mental illness might be the result of demonisation.[135] Clearly, such an approach makes it possible to diagnose virtually any sick person as demonised.

Whilst Richards acknowledged that it was possible for a Christian to be possessed (a much disputed question among charismatic demonologists), he believed that 'those whose doors are "shut" to psychic, occult, magical or demonic forces and pressures' were 'immune' from demonisation.[136] This view was a development of the warnings of anti-Spiritualists of the early twentieth century, although Richards's view that some sort of occult involvement was a necessary precondition of demonisation was in stark contrast to the earlier Protestant belief that demoniacs might be innocent victims of bewitchment.

Richards cautioned of a potential 'danger of others being adversely affected' by exorcism and warned against 'the isolation of the act of exorcism, away from the care and prayer of the local Christian community'.[137] He argued that the dangers of exorcising someone who was simply mentally ill 'are much exaggerated by general ignorance and mistrust of what Christian exorcism involves'.[138] Richards advised that 'The avoidance of any sort of pact or agreement between minister and spirits is sound and essential' and sympathised with those who preferred to describe exorcism as dispossession, but noted that people always seemed to come back to using the word 'exorcism'. Richards rejected any claims that exorcism was a gift of 'psychically gifted' clergy; it was, rather, 'a demonstration in power and love of the Lordship of Christ over his world'.[139]

Richards recognised the distinction between imperative and deprecative exorcism: 'Christian exorcism may be either a *petition* to God, as in the Lord's Prayer and the tradition of the Eastern Churches, or a command addressed *not* to the demoniac but to the demon(s)'.[140] He argued in favour of distinguishing 'acute' and 'mild' cases of demonisation and noted the Roman Catholic church's use of the terms 'major' and 'minor' exorcism to be used against possession and obsession respectively. He was sceptical of exorcism at a distance or over the telephone, arguing that it might 'divorce the action from the Christian community and the patient from adequate after-care'.[141]

Richards was likewise wary of reliance on specific verbal formulas of exorcism: 'Whatever words [the exorcist] might use, they will convey the same message – *get out, and don't come back*'.[142] However, he specified three elements that any imperative formula of exorcism ought to contain: commands to the demon to harm no one, to come out of the person and to go somewhere else. It might be necessary, Richards considered, 'to add to this a prohibition to enter anybody else', but he rejected the notion that a spirit could be told where it was to go.[143] Although Richards recognised that exorcism could be both deprecative and imperative, he seemed to err on the side of imperative exorcism, averring that 'The demons will do what is said in the name of their Lord, but they are malign not benevolent intelligences, and an unquestioning response to suggestions and gentlemanly hints are not of much avail'.[144] Imperative exorcism is not in danger of becoming magic, according to Richards, unless the exorcist gives in to the spiritual temptation of pride, believing the devil is cast out by his own power rather than God's.[145]

Richards acknowledged that the question of whether to ask a demon its name, much debated by charismatic exorcists, was a 'puzzle'. He did not think that knowing a demon's name made the act of exorcism any more authoritative, but acknowledged that 'To find out the name of the demon (the name given might be Lust, or Hatred, or Anger, Witchcraft, etc.) enables the Church to see that such things are replaced by their opposites in the aftercare of the person'.[146] Richards also accepted the possibility of verbally 'binding' a demon to behave (or not behave) in a certain way,[147] but advised against the laying on of hands (preferring sprinkling with holy water) in case of 'some temporary evil transference'.[148] He denied that a recurrence of symptoms in a demoniac was an indication of a 'failed' exorcism; some people might require more than one 'spiritual spring-clean'.[149] However, some exorcisms did fail, and in this case it was most likely to be because 'the exorcism has been taken out of the context of deliverance and salvation'.[150]

Richards was reluctant to regard exorcism as a specialist ministry and thought it should be in the hands of individual parish priests.[151] He quoted with approval Henry Cooper's criticism of 'the episcopal assumption that the ministry of exorcism is a matter for specialists, for that presupposes that it requires a *gnosis*, a knowledge of a human kind'.[152] In the aftermath of the abolition of Canon 72 in 1969, Cooper appealed to the bishops to provide some guidance on exorcism in the *Church Times* of 8 May 1970, and Richards observed that 'Until there is some guidance, the situation will continue in which priests use their discretion according to the nature of the case drawing on the experience of the "Diocesan exorcists" if they feel the need to do so'.[153] Richards supported the principle of bishops granting a priest *general* permission to exorcise, on the grounds that 'exorcism has come to be regarded as the ministry of the Church and not a priestly ritual'. However, he warned that in many of the cases he had encountered 'obtaining episcopal permission was either impractical or unnecessary'.[154]

Richards cited Christian tradition, including John Wesley's practice, to defend the practice of fasting in association with exorcism.[155] Likewise, he advocated apotropaic use of the sign of the cross.[156] However, Richards rejected the notion of possession by departed spirits[157] and adopted a traditional Protestant attitude towards ghosts when he claimed that 'most apparently earth-bound spirits are undoubtedly lying spirits'.[158] Indeed, Richards was largely sceptical of the exorcism of places, remarking that it was 'usually a ministry to distressed people and the causes of their distress'.[159] Richards's achievement as a demonologist was not to offer anything new but to create an eclectic synthesis that brought together the insights of Roman Catholics, Anglo-Catholics, Anglican charismatics and even Pentecostals. Richards frequently quoted Michael Harper and Gilbert Shaw, but also referred often to the rubrics of the *Rituale Romanum* (which he even included as an appendix).[160] Richards's even-handed borrowing from different spiritual traditions may have created the impression for some readers of his book that a place existed for exorcism in the *via media* of the Church of England.

JOHN PEARCE-HIGGINS AND CHRISTOPHER NEIL-SMITH

In addition to those Anglican exorcists and demonologists who largely remained within the 'orthodoxy' on exorcism established by Gilbert Shaw (who included Petitpierre, Richards and Omand), other exorcists pursued still more eccentric paths yet continued to enjoy episcopal support. John D. Pearce-Higgins (1905–85), vice-provost of Southwark Cathedral, was appointed the diocese of Southwark's exorcist by bishop Mervyn Stockwood in the late 1960s or early 1970s. Pearce-Higgins studied at Gonville and Caius College, Cambridge before ordination in 1937. After service in World War II he served as a vicar in Worcestershire and London.[161] Pearce-Higgins did not subscribe to the 'orthodox' approach to exorcism articulated in the Exeter Report, and in an interview he gave in around 1974 he repudiated the title of exorcist. Pearce-Higgins believed that most 'possessions' did not involve a demon but rather 'an earthbound, possibly confused spirit who is attached to a person or place'.

Pearce-Higgins's ministry began as a result of his interest in parapsychology. When people asked him for exorcism he did not receive 'any help from the church as to how to deal with these requests', so he turned to Spiritualist mediums.[162] At first, Pearce-Higgins only exorcised with a medium's assistant but soon began receiving instructions in advance from his 'spirit guide' that allowed him to exorcise alone; the 'spirit guide' also prompted him to send a liturgy of exorcism he devised to clergy who asked for help. By 1971 Pearce-Higgins was working with a lay married couple, Roy and Joan Broster, who claimed to have received 'a charismatic gift for physical healing', and in an 18-month period in 1971–2 the team claimed to have dealt with '113 cases of genuine possession' out of 360 cases that were brought to them.[163] This statistic suggests that Pearce-Higgins did not share Petitpierre's view that possession was a vanishingly rare phenomenon.

The Brosters worked through the laying on of hands (something the York Report advised against out of fear of demonic contamination[164]) which resulted in the 'extrusion' of the possessing entity: 'Sometimes this produces various stretchings or contortions of the patient's body, but no words are spoken until the end, when I modify the prayer of "exorcism" into a thanksgiving that God has removed the entity'.[165] Pearce-Higgins defended his rejection of the language of demons by arguing that Jesus himself never spoke about demons, and he argued that belief in demons led to dualism. Pearce-Higgins traced his own approach back to the American Spiritualist Carl Wickland (1861–1945), who believed all spirits were capable of redemption. The most severe formula of exorcism Pearce-Higgins was prepared to use included the words 'In the authority of Christ, I command you to be taken hence and bound fast as with chains and cast into darkness, from which there is no return save through repentance'.[166]

Pearce-Higgins was critical of the Exeter Report, noting that there was 'little trace of a gentler approach' within it.[167] He believed exorcism would be more effective if exorcists relied more on the insights of mediums, and believed episcopal authorisation was not necessary to be an effective exorcist; laypeople could be just as successful.[168] Pearce-Higgins distinguished between 'good' and 'bad' Spiritualism, with the former offering 'genuine aid to the bereaved' while the latter was dabbling in the occult.[169] His reliance on Spiritualist techniques was the most distinctive aspect of his ministry but, if Pearce Higgins's own testimony is to be believed, the reason for this was the lack of guidance he received from the church. In the absence of an established tradition of exorcism, Pearce-Higgins may have felt that he had no choice but to turn to the practice of Spiritualists for inspiration. Stockwood's own belief in Spiritualism and the paranormal may have made him sympathetic to Pearce-Higgins as a diocesan exorcist.[170]

Like Pearce-Higgins, Christopher Neil-Smith (1920–95) deviated markedly in his beliefs and practices from the 'orthodox' approach to exorcism but nevertheless enjoyed episcopal approval, receiving a licence from the bishop of London, Robert Stopford, in 1972. Collins described Neil-Smith's approach as 'a hybrid of Sacramental exorcism and Charismatic deliverance with more than a nod in the direction of liberal theology and the popular culture of his day'.[171] Neil-Smith claimed to have performed 2,200 exorcisms since 1949, including one in front of television cameras for the BBC documentary *The Power of the Witch: Real or Imaginary?* (1971).[172] Neil-Smith claimed that evil was 'bad vibrations', and that he had the ability to detect these.[173] He declared that 'black magic' was 'rampant' and quoted Petitpierre's view that there were 'about four hundred Black Magic groups in this country and at least one in every university'.[174] Neil-Smith complained that 'the Church as a whole is far too reticent and reluctant to recognise its function to exorcise'.[175]

Describing how he entered the ministry of exorcism, Neil-Smith claimed to have been trained by Gilbert Shaw, in spite of the significant differences between Neil-Smith's and Shaw's approaches:

> I had been practising the Healing Ministry through the Laying on of Hands, and I was approached by a man who asked for healing. This man subsequently turned out to be an unfrocked priest, who had been practising Black Magic and as I tried to heal him, I felt the impact of an evil force come upon me. It affected me in various ways, like lack of concentration and also lack of sleep, and I went in this condition to the

late Gilbert Shaw, who, in fact, removed this oppressive force from me
by exorcism. It was then, that I was in fact 'saved to serve' and he
trained me subsequently to use exorcism for others.[176]

In addition to his unusual belief in 'vibrations', Neil-Smith's
eagerness to publicise his ministry was a far cry from Shaw's
reticence. He defended televised exorcisms, arguing that 'The Church
like the medical profession should have nothing to hide in an age
when openness is expected by the general public ... The Church can
often show its witness through exorcism on TV to people in their
homes who would never enter a church in the ordinary way'.[177] He
was dismissive of those who criticised him for sensationalism,
commenting 'I often wonder if such critics would have considered
Jesus sending devils into swine sensational'.[178]

Neil-Smith insisted that 'exorcism' was a term only properly
applied to 'the states of soul of living people molested by evil spirits
or evil forces', although he also exorcised places.[179] He defined
exorcism as 'a personal confrontation with the person and a
recognition of wrong – of sin if you like – in order that the evil
forces may be released'.[180] Unlike Petitpierre, Neil-Smith believed it
was the person rather than the demon that was exorcised, and this
may explain why Neil-Smith was so ready to exorcise. It was not
necessary for him to have any certainty of actual demonic possession
if all that was required was a vague awareness of 'evil forces'. Neil-
Smith followed Petitpierre in distinguishing between major and
minor exorcisms,[181] but differed from most other exorcists in
claiming that 'Exorcism is the removal of an actual force which can
be felt by impartial observers'. Neil-Smith was convinced that
the ejection of 'evil forces' could be physically felt and that it
produced violent movements on the part of both exorcist and
demoniac.[182]

Neil-Smith regarded the formula used for an exorcism as
unimportant, not even offering any advice on possible forms of
words, and he was critical of bishops who thought an exorcism 'can
be arranged like a marriage', noting that 'Naturally bishops who are
spiritually and pastorally minded recognise this'. He even recalled an
occasion when he performed an emergency exorcism in the presence
of a bishop.[183] Neil-Smith argued that, although anyone could

exorcise in an emergency, only a priest should perform a 'solemn exorcism', on the grounds that many possessions were caused by witches, who would only recognise a Christian priest as equivalent to them in status.[184] Neil-Smith was particularly preoccupied with the opening that 'kinky sex' offered to evil influences,[185] and reported that he had been called in to exorcise people in both hospitals and prisons.[186] He criticised the Exeter Report for its reluctance to use the term 'possession', insisting on the validity of the traditional demonological distinction between obsession and possession,[187] and was also critical of the report's failure to mention the charismatic movement.[188]

Neil-Smith dismissed concerns that exorcism might be damaging for the mentally ill, claiming that it was more dangerous *not* to exorcise some patients, since withholding exorcism increased the risk of suicide.[189] He claimed that people who became involved with witchcraft were liable to be possessed by the departed spirits of other witches, requiring an exorcism of the 'witch-force', often by violently physical means.[190] Neil-Smith was comfortable with the language of the 'new age', although he saw the 'new age' in Christian terms. He saw the upsurge of interest in the spiritual in the 1970s as a huge opportunity for the church, and argued that exorcism was one of the few ways in which the church could reach out in a very public way to bring about real change in people's lives.[191] His primary influences were Shaw and Michael Harper, but Neil-Smith's approach was characterised by his eagerness to exorcise anyone (or anything), his preoccupation with sex, and his practice of a highly physical form of exorcism accompanied by a hunger for publicity. It is easy to see why Neil-Smith was a controversial figure; he represented a new kind of proselytising exorcist who believed exorcism was a way of bringing people to faith.

CONCLUSION

The exorcists discussed in this chapter (Gilbert Shaw, Max Petitpierre, Donald Omand, John Richards, John Pearce-Higgins and Christopher Neil-Smith) were not the only Anglican priests involved in the ministry of exorcism in the post-war era. However, since these six exorcists all published books on the subject they established the parameters for other exorcists. It is clear that virtually all practice of exorcism in the modern Church of England can be traced back to Shaw, but without the 'moral panic' that followed social changes in the 1960s and 1970s it seems likely that exorcism would have remained an obscure and marginal practice. As it was, in the five years after the repeal of Canon 72 in 1969 exorcism rapidly became established in the Church of England.

The 1972 Exeter Report, which embodied an 'orthodox' approach to exorcism reinforced in the writings of Petitpierre and Richards, was the most influential document as far as the bishops were concerned, many of whom seem to have appointed diocesan exorcists in the wake of the report (in spite of its lack of official status). However, it is clear that several of these exorcists, such as Pearce-Higgins and Neil-Smith, held eccentric personal views on exorcism. Episcopal oversight meant little when many bishops had little understanding of the potential risks of permitting exorcists unfettered access to vulnerable people. Without any controls on exorcism, and a minority of the clergy determined to experiment freely with the newfound ministry, the Church of England was heading for a serious fall.

CHAPTER 5

Anglican Exorcism Normalised, 1975–2000

On 16 March 1974 William Friedkin's film *The Exorcist* was released in the UK. Although a debate on exorcism was already well underway in the Church of England at the time – clergy at the cinema even found themselves ministering to people distressed by the film[1] – the issue had not yet been resolved and clergy were essentially free to do whatever they chose. Christopher Neil-Smith noted that the film's release provoked an explosion of requests for exorcism,[2] to which many clergy responded all too willingly. However, the absence of regulation led to tragedy in October 1974 when one priest, Peter Vincent, exorcised a man who then returned home to murder his wife. The 'Barnsley case' produced a short-lived campaign by liberal theologians and churchmen for the Church of England to withdraw from the ministry of exorcism altogether, but a speech by Archbishop Donald Coggan in General Synod in 1975 reaffirmed the place of exorcism in the church and proposed a very basic set of guidelines to govern it.

Over the next 25 years exorcism became normalised as part of the practice of the Church of England, culminating in an extensive treatment of exorcism in a report on the ministry of healing approved by General Synod in 2000. Archbishop Coggan's guidelines, in an expanded form, remain in place to this day. This chapter describes the exorcism-related crisis that struck the Church of England in 1975 and the campaign against exorcism sparked by those events, led by Cambridge University's Regius Professor of Divinity, Geoffrey Lampe. The chapter assesses the reasons for the failure of that campaign and the church's eventual endorsement of exorcism, examining the development of the theory, practice and canonical status of exorcism in the established church for the remainder of the twentieth century.

THE BARNSLEY CASE

The brutal murder of Christine Taylor by her husband Michael following an exorcism in October 1974 (although the case did not become public until March 1975) initiated a period of soul-searching in the Church of England regarding a controversial ministry. *The Times* of 26 March 1975 summarised the account of the exorcism given by the counsel for the prosecution in Michael Taylor's murder trial, Geoffrey Baker:

> Mr Taylor and his wife had begun attending meetings of a local Christian fellowship group but one of the group was a satanist. Mr Taylor somehow became involved in witchcraft, which appeared to have had a profound effect. A week later he was still showing signs of instability, so a friend took him and his family to visit the Rev Peter Vincent of St Thomas's church, Gawber, Barnsley. Others were called in and they all came to the conclusion that Mr Taylor was demonically possessed.

Baker reported that, at midnight on 5–6 October Taylor was taken into the vestry at St Thomas' church: 'They laid him down on hassocks on the floor and at times they had to hold him down'. Vincent was accompanied by his wife, as well as a local Methodist minister and his wife, a Methodist lay preacher, and one other layman. Baker reported that the exorcists 'made a list of the spirits as they named themselves – incest, bestiality, blasphemy, heresy, lewdness, masochism', and burnt a wooden cross worn by Taylor. Harry Ognall, the counsel for the defence, claimed that Taylor 'was made to confess sins of which he was innocent and was subjected to indignities that defy comprehension', including 'having crosses being pushed into his mouth, and being sprinkled with water'.

Returning home to Ossett after the exorcism, Taylor murdered his wife, tearing out her eyes and tongue before strangling the family poodle. The police found him wandering the streets, naked and covered in blood, declaring 'It is the blood of Satan'. A psychiatrist who gave evidence at the trial suggested that the murder would not have occurred without the exorcism, which prompted Ognall to accuse the clergy involved of complicity in the murder:

> We say this: let those who truly are responsible for this killing stand up. We submit that Taylor is a mere cipher. The real guilt lies elsewhere. Religion was the key. Those laymen who have been referred to in evidence and those clerics, in particular, should be with [Taylor] in spirit now in this building and each day he is incarcerated in Broadmoor, and not least on the day when he must endure the bitterness of reunion with his five motherless children.

The judge in the case noted that he was unable to comment on a matter of religion, but hinted that the government might wish to pass laws restricting the practice of exorcism: 'those who care for us and govern us may well be concerned'. The jury found Taylor not guilty on the grounds of his being insane at the time of the murder, and he was committed to the secure psychiatric hospital at Broadmoor.[3] On the same day the bishop of Wakefield, Eric Treacy, met with Peter Vincent and issued a statement:

> I am bound to say that the attempts made at exorcism during the night before the murder were unwise. But I believe that the clergymen involved with it were actuated by good intent, and had a sincere desire to help Michael Taylor. Exorcism is a type of ministry which must be exercised with the greatest possible care.

Treacy wrote that no one in his diocese had his explicit permission to perform exorcisms, but noted that 'some clergymen will feel that it is a normal part of their pastoral ministry when occasion demands'. *The Times* reported that the 'current edition' of Vincent's parish newsletter (presumably produced since October 1974) made claims about 'wonderful healings and exorcisms' at services. The newspaper observed that Vincent had broken no rules, 'except perhaps for a canon dating from 1603 which forbids exorcism except by leave of the local bishop';[4] the journalist was evidently unaware of the discontinuation of Canon 72 in 1969.

In the aftermath of the Barnsley case Bishop Treacy appointed a commission to investigate exorcism. Treacy's decision not to authorise an exorcist in the diocese of Wakefield before 1974 is an indication that he either showed no interest in the Exeter Report, or else disagreed with it.[5] John Hargreaves describes Treacy as 'a liberal evangelical' and 'a cleric of middle ground views', although with essentially conservative instincts.[6] His statement on the Barnsley case seems to have been intended primarily to defend the freedom of the clergy to exorcise if they considered it necessary, and his criticism of Peter Vincent was muted. It is surprising that Treacy was not aware of the role an exorcism had played in Christine Taylor's murder until after the sentencing of Michael Taylor, and equally remarkable that Vincent apparently continued to perform exorcisms after October 1974.

While some were horrified by the Barnsley exorcism, such as the psychiatrist William Sargant,[7] others interpreted the behaviour of Michael Taylor as evidence for the reality of demonic possession. Enthusiasm for exorcism in the Church of England showed no sign of abating. In April 1975 Trevor Dearing, the charismatic vicar of St Paul's, Hainault, Essex performed a series of exorcisms on multiple individuals, inviting the press and even television cameras. John Linklater, writing in the *Spectator*, was critical of Archbishop Donald Coggan's televised statement on ITV's 'This Week' following the Barnsley case. Coggan stated that the church should 'move out of the realms of mumbo-jumbo', emphasised the importance of exorcists working with psychiatrists and suggested that when exorcisms were performed this should be 'never in the light of much publicity'.[8]

In Linklater's view, Coggan's statement 'discloses a veiled disapproval [of exorcism], coupled with some doubt about its reality and efficacy. It suggests that, if performed at all, exorcism should take place in respectable seclusion, without publicity, between consenting adults, so to speak'. Linklater rejected the idea that exorcism should be practised exclusively by trained professionals and criticised the church's reluctance to publicise the ministry:

> Having taken reasonable precautions, there would not seem to be any reason for low profile privacy. The cheerful witness and carefree faces of men and women from whom various demons had been exorcised by the

Reverend Trevor Dearing at Hainault, is surely something that should be publicised rather than hidden. Many of the patients had been treated medically, for years, without success.

Echoing the anti-Sadducists of the seventeenth century, Linklater suggested that denying the existence of the devil would only lead to denial of the existence of God:

> If Beelzebub has been replaced by a diffuse, generalised force of evil, then God has likewise been dispersed, and no longer exists. If exorcism is mumbo-jumbo, then so is prayer. A man who does not believe in demons cannot believe in the divinity of Christ, or in the New Testament. He cannot therefore be a Christian ... When doctors collude with the Church to bring gluttony, sloth, guilt and despair out of the reach of the exorcist, and into the surgery, they effectively strip mankind of personal dignity, individual choice and responsibility and reduce man to the status of a rather sick molecular joke.[9]

Linklater was convinced that scepticism about exorcism derived from a lack of belief in the existence of the devil, rather than from concerns about the ethical appropriateness of exorcising the mentally ill. Although Linklater expressed himself in more robust and colourful terms, many bishops may have shared his concern that the suppression of exorcism implied disbelief in the devil and therefore threatened the erosion of the Christian faith. It was not so much that senior clergy *supported* exorcism, but that they were more worried about the consequences of suppressing it than the consequences of permitting it.

Max Petitpierre, whose book *Exorcising Devils* was published in 1976, lamented that as a result of *The Exorcist* and the Barnsley killing, 'the entire concept [of exorcism] has been reduced to a source of controversy and misunderstanding'.[10] He claimed to have heard of only two other cases in which an exorcism had been followed swiftly by a death. An army padre had died shortly after being called in by a doctor to exorcise a man, and a 'possessed' man had left a church service declaring 'I must murder someone' in spite of being counselled by a priest. Petitpierre's conclusion was defiant: 'On the whole, the weight of the evidence is that there is more danger involved in *not* performing an exorcism at the right time, on the right person and under the right circumstances than in carrying one out'.[11]

THE CAMPAIGN AGAINST EXORCISM

Geoffrey Lampe (1912–80), who led the brief campaign against exorcism in 1975, was an ordained priest, a fellow of Gonville and Caius College, Cambridge and Cambridge University's Regius Professor of Divinity from 1970.[12] In late April 1975 Lampe, in conjunction with the dean of Emmanuel College, Don Cupitt, circulated a draft open letter to prominent theologians calling for the Church of England to withdraw from the ministry of exorcism, asking them to sign. The letter, which was published in *The Times* on 14 May 1975 with 65 signatories,[13] claimed that the Church of England was 'in danger of making a serious error of judgement':

> For some years now the practice of exorcism has been growing, with some encouragement from the authorities, in many English dioceses. Recent events have brought this fact to public notice, and the Church is at a disadvantage, because it has not yet openly debated the subject. Our fear is that, since exorcism has already come to be so widely practised, a compromise will be worked out. To control its excesses, exorcism will be regulated: but the effect of this will be to give it a more nearly official status in the Church than it has had since the old baptismal exorcism was abolished in 1552.[14]

Lampe and Cupitt proposed that 'exorcism should have no official status in the Church at all', offering five reasons. Firstly, they claimed that there was no historical evidence for a 'tradition' of exorcism in the Church of England. Secondly, they argued that encouraging belief in 'occult evil powers' could lead to dire social consequences. Thirdly, they lauded the demise of demonology and implied that exorcism was a kind of Christian magic on a par with 'occultist beliefs'. Fourthly, they claimed that 'the theology of redemption implied by the practice of exorcism' was incompatible 'with our Church's understanding of the Gospel'. Finally, the theologians turned to the New Testament, pointing out that Jesus' own beliefs 'need not be shared by all Christians at all times' and noting the absence of any mention of exorcism from John's Gospel and Paul's letters. Lampe and Cupitt further noted that the Eastern Orthodox churches did not adjure demons and that even 'the Roman Catholic Church is progressively abandoning exorcism'.

The theologians claimed that the Church of England's attempt to revive exorcism 'invites ridicule, not to mention the harm that may be done', and they concluded by urging 'all who hold high office in the Church to ensure that the practice of exorcism receives no official encouragement, and gains no official status in the Church'.[15] In a subsequent letter to the editor of the *Church Times* Lampe and Cupitt went into more detail about how they thought the church should manage the ministry of deliverance:

> It is true that people can become trapped in superstition and false belief, and a special ministry of deliverance may be needed. For this, perhaps, there might be a rite based on confession and absolution, the renewal of baptismal renunciations and vows, and perhaps sacramental healing. Are these not sufficient? The Church of England's faith has traditionally been sober, pure and orderly. We believe that we are trying to reassert a good old tradition, in which ideas of possession have no place. The *idea* of demon possession is dangerous, and we need to be delivered from it.[16]

Lampe and Cupitt also claimed that regularising exorcism in the Church of England would be damaging for other provinces of the Anglican Communion where clergy deliberately refrained from exorcising in an attempt to discourage belief in spirits in traditional societies. They argued that even regulating exorcism was theologically dubious: 'Criteria for the "right" use of exorcism must presuppose a God-of-the-gaps theology which introduces religious entities and operations at, and only at, the points where present scientific knowledge is incomplete'.[17]

Lampe and Cupitt acknowledged that it had been difficult to produce a form of words in the letter that everyone would agree with, and regarded it as imperfect – but they urged theologians to sign anyway.[18] Responses to Lampe and Cupitt's letter from the episcopate were mixed. The bishop of Oxford, Lampe's friend Kenneth Woollcombe (1924–2008), was largely supportive but offered some criticisms. Woollcombe had been tasked by Archbishop Coggan 'to investigate the rise in Black Magic, Satanism, Occultism etc', and insisted that Christians were genuinely delivering people 'from the evil of satanism', adding that 'they need to have some sort of guidance about the liturgical articulation of their ministry'.

However, Woollcombe also lamented the proliferation of 'clergy who have been bitten by the charismatic bug'. He reported that he had recently told the chaplain of an Oxford college 'that he must not exorcise without my consent, because I discovered that he had been monkeying about with one of my nuns'. Woollcombe reported that he received 'an average of two or three requests a week' for exorcism. He asked Lampe to provide him with a 'theological critique' of John Richards's *But Deliver Us From Evil* for the report he was preparing for Coggan. Unlike Richards, whose pastoral practice was unsupported by his theology, Woollcombe suggested that Lampe's theology was sound but that he needed to give more thought to 'the pastoral outcomes of your theology ... What I seek is a way of healing and restoring young people who have been injured by the evils of Satanism and of preventing charismatics from repeating the Wakefield crime'.[19]

Lampe duly sent Woollcombe an excoriating critique of Richards's 'lamentable book',[20] accusing Richards of the 'Pentecostal' error of conflating inspiration by the Holy Spirit with possession:

> Once one looks for the working of the Spirit in 'supernatural' manifestations at the sub-rational and sub-personal level, one is reducing the concept of 'yet not I, but Christ lives in me' to the level of the occultist notion of 'possession', and equating the occultist concept of the supernatural with the Christian understanding of communion with God.[21]

Lampe noted the haziness and inconsistency of Richards's presentation of demons.[22] Richards, who saw everything through the lens of demonology, provided little argument for his assertions, and according to Lampe 'In the few places where any argument is adduced to support the demonological interpretation of Richards' case-histories it amounts to nothing'.[23] Richards, in Lampe's view, was more concerned 'that Christian teaching should be fashionable' than with truth.[24] Lampe dismissed Richards's suggestion that exorcism could be justified by the help it appeared to offer patients:

> This is a very dangerous idea. No doubt a patient who believes himself to be possessed may be benefitted by being exorcised, and a minister who does not believe in demonic possession may be inclined to exorcise

him as an act of charitable 'accommodation'. But exorcism, if practised, is clearly a rite of the Church, administered by a priest or other representative of the Church, and a rite must express the faith of the Church. Moreover, the rite involves the solemn invocation of the name of God. It cannot be used like the bottle of coloured water which a doctor might give to a patient with a psychosomatic pain. A solemn rite cannot be performed with one's tongue in one's cheek as a placebo. Morally and theologically this kind of practice is quite unacceptable.[25]

Richards's case histories were 'derived from popular newspapers, gossip retailed by books published in the "charismatic underworld", and other suspect sources', revealing him to be 'a man of limitless credulity'. Lampe was disappointed that the Queen's Foundation, Birmingham had sponsored 'this assortment of superstitious journalism'. Lampe also provided Bishop Woollcombe with a critique of the York Report, which he described as 'a dangerous encouragement to popular occultism'.[26] Lampe concluded his critique by laying out what he thought 'deliverance ministry' should look like:

> Surely what is needed is a firm refusal by the Church authorities to give any encouragement whatever to exorcism in any circumstances, and a corresponding emphasis on spiritual healing. The latter seems a ministry that helps everyone, and especially the psychologically disturbed, to open themselves up to the healing love and compassion and care of God, so as to be 'made whole'. With this the 'scientific' doctors and psychiatrists can, or should, fully co-operate. I think that for those who have been entangled with Satanism and so forth spiritual healing should take special forms; but with all the resources available to us of prayer, renewal of baptismal vows (and renunciations), Communion, laying on of hands, unction, and confession and absolution, we should be able to provide what they need without selling out to occultism and thereby reinforcing their false presuppositions which were the root of their troubles ... The vitally important thing in these services of deliverance is that everything that is said, otherwise than to the congregation or the 'patient' should be addressed to *God*. No form of *exorcism*, addressing a supposed demon ('I command you', 'I bind you') is tolerable. An address in these terms confers a substantial reality on the 'spirit of evil' and therefore can only confirm congregation and patient alike in a false belief. This is playing on the occultists' wicket.[27]

Lampe seems to have been baffled that the Church of England, which until so recently had eschewed any form of imperative exorcism, was now embarking on a path more extreme even than the Roman Catholic church, which was moving away from exorcism.[28] Yet he was in no doubt that 'the damage done by the Exeter Report in encouraging this sort of thing' was behind the sudden shift.[29]

Woollcombe received Lampe's critique of Richards's book at the same time as a long letter from Richards himself. Woollcombe thought Richards was 'becoming a little paranoid, and is not helping his own case'.[30] Woollcombe promised to do what he could to represent Lampe's concerns to the House of Bishops; he was doubtful that they would accept the argument of the open letter, but thought they might agree with Lampe's suggestion that exorcism, and especially imperative exorcisms directed at the devil, dangerously reinforced harmful beliefs.[31]

Lampe received supportive responses to the open letter from the dean of Norwich, Alan Webster,[32] and Michael Wilson, an ordained medical doctor who lectured in pastoral theology at the University of Birmingham.[33] In November 1974 Wilson had delivered a paper to the clergy of the diocese of Birmingham that was published in July 1975.[34] Wilson had reached the same conclusion as Lampe and Cupitt – that Christians were not obliged to believe everything that Jesus believed.[35] He regarded the use of the language of possession and exorcism as a matter of interpretation,[36] and condemned the facile approach to evil ('getting rid of the bad') implied by exorcism.[37] Exorcism sought to 'clinicalise' evil, delegating its expulsion to experts, when the real challenge was 'promoting health … by withstanding evil as Jesus did on the Cross, using it, as it were, as fuel for growth together towards holiness'.[38]

The bishop of St Albans, Robert Runcie (who would become archbishop of Canterbury five years later) was supportive of Lampe's letter and was one of the few bishops to actually sign it. Although he admitted to entrusting exorcism-related matters to Max Petitpierre, Runcie confessed that he was becoming 'increasingly uncomfortable about it all':

> I think that exorcism attempts short cuts. It is my reading of the New Testament that our Lord's temptations are a reflection on His whole ministry. Thus there is a sense in which miracle and the power of

supernatural ministry are rejected in the way of the Cross; there are, as St Paul reminds us, no short cuts in the long haul of loving.[39]

The bishop of Kingston, Hugh Montefiore (1920–2005), was less enthusiastic about Lampe's open letter. He criticised Lampe's reading of Anglican tradition: 'If authority to control exorcism persisted until new canons were promulgated in 1964 and 1969, on what grounds can exorcism be called "at variance with the entire history and tradition of the Church of England"?' Montefiore also pointed out that many immigrants came from other parts of the Anglican Communion where exorcism was commonplace, and therefore exorcism was not alien to their tradition. He accused Lampe of being 'unscientific' by dismissing out of hand the possibility that people might be 'hindered by the effects of disturbed spirits'. He compared exorcism to private confession, suggesting a need for 'regulations for a personal proclamation of Christ's lordship for those still burdened by feelings of evil influence or domination'.[40]

Montefiore's criticism of Lampe's interpretation of Canon 72 was echoed by a letter from T. M. Parker published in *The Times* on 17 May, which contended that Canon 72 'admit[ted] and regulate[d] the practice of exorcism'. Lampe replied that 'exorcisms did take place, but so very rarely and in such an obscure fashion as to justify our contention that exorcism "is alien to the whole tradition of our Church" … [Canon 72's] purpose is not to commend licensed exorcism but merely to forbid unlicensed'.[41] The ambiguity of Canon 72 was causing problems once again.

The bishop of Peterborough, Douglas Feaver (1914–97) criticised Lampe for different reasons. He felt that sending an open letter to the press simply inflamed an unhealthy public interest in exorcism:

> I have found in this diocese that by refraining from appointing an 'expert' on exorcism, and by reserving all cases of alleged possession to myself, that what might possibly have become a fashionable interest by one or two priests has been restrained within bounds of sanctified common sense. And I can see no reason whatsoever why all Bishops could not quietly and firmly do this, and do it without theorising or dogmatising about it.

Feaver told Lampe that he could not subscribe to his letter, since he had come across 'two or three people who seemed to be dominated by a more precise power than evil, more like "an evil one"', but he rejected the need for a '"form of exorcism" issued under ecclesiastical authority' and agreed with Lampe that exorcism should not be given any official status:

> I agree with you wholeheartedly that regulations drawn up by General Synod or put into a canon, would be to give exorcism unwarranted importance. No such regulation would diminish disorderly zeal by some priests. I think that the Bishops have enough pastoral influence to ensure that such disorderliness dies the death.[42]

Woollcombe's observation that John Richards was becoming 'paranoid' was borne out by a letter Richards sent Lampe on 9 July, in which he accused Lampe of being 'a high level mason', adding that 'If I don't hear back a denial within a reasonable time, I shall deduce that it is true'.[43] Richards seems to have been implying that Lampe's hostility to Christian demonology was due to his being a Freemason – an ironic accusation, given that Bishop John Phillips of Portsmouth, who openly supported the exorcistic ministry of Donald Omand, was a Masonic Provincial Grand Master.[44]

Lampe received both critical and supportive letters from ordinary members of the public, some of whom reported that relatives had been at the receiving end of abusive exorcisms and wished Lampe success in his efforts to suppress the ministry. Lampe took the trouble to reply personally to these correspondents. However, Lampe and Cupitt's lightning campaign against exorcism seems to have had no impact whatsoever on the Church of England's developing position on the subject, in spite of the publicity given to the open letter and the senior figures who signed it. The hastily drafted letter and the speed of the campaign may have had something to do with this, as well as lack of public interest in the pronouncements of theologians.

Maurice Wiles (Lampe's counterpart as Regius Professor of Divinity at Oxford), who was a signatory of the original letter, cautioned Lampe that the letter might come across as complacent to those who accepted the reality of demonic phenomena, since it made no suggestions for how the church might minister to those who believed themselves to be under demonic influence.[45] Another Oxford theologian who signed the letter, Peter Baelz, expressed similar misgivings. Baelz pointed out that people really fell under the influence of 'satanists' and experienced real oppression, and suggested that the church might modify its approach to pray to God for deliverance rather than abandoning the field of deliverance altogether.[46] John Macquarrie, another signatory, warned Lampe that the letter 'said too much' and was therefore too open to criticism.[47]

Archbishop Coggan seems to have ignored the letter entirely, in spite of the fact that Lampe warned him in advance of the letter's imminent publication. Lampe and Cupitt may have miscalculated, making their letter too much like a theological critique; it was simultaneously too complex for the average layperson to understand, and too open to criticism from other theologians. However, Bishop Feaver of Peterborough's comment to Lampe is perhaps the most reflective of the views of the House of Bishops; the bishops feared the publicity that would arise from enacting a canon regulating exorcism, and believed their 'pastoral influence' was enough to control wayward clergy.

Petitpierre's reaction to the open letter was to accuse its signatories of being out of step with the worldview of the 1970s:

> I am struck not only by the fact that I myself have seen the healing qualities of the practice and so can vouch for its usefulness – a view reinforced by many psychiatrists who have also witnessed its effects – but by the extraordinarily old-fashioned, conservative nature of the views the theologians largely express. Their so-called 'rational' approach, their emphasis on the 'scientific' approach, appears to me to be wholly bedded in nineteenth-century thought. They see no room at all for the concept of a 'nonhuman' mind ... Their objections to angels, devils and so on lies four-square with the scientific attitude to hypnosis and telepathy in the last century. They seem blissfully unaware that there is a whole field of human activity not covered by the scientific-humanist approach.[48]

Petitpierre may have been right, at least to the extent that the sort of sober scepticism advocated by Lampe and Cupitt was hardly in fashion. However, Petitpierre also seized on another vulnerability of the signatories: he knew that none of them had any practical experience of exorcism. Petitpierre accused them of being mere theorists and suggested that their outlook might have been quite different if they had received the opportunity to encounter demonic phenomena first-hand.[49] Exorcists and practical demonologists are always able to fall back on this 'experiential' defence, hinting at their own superior knowledge in the field.

ARCHBISHOP COGGAN'S 'FACTORS'

During the summer 1975 sitting of General Synod it became clear that the Church of England was not going to adopt any of the views of the signatories of Lampe's letter. On 30 June 1975, by prior arrangement, Prebendary Henry Cooper (a priest with a particular interest in exorcism and demonology) formally asked Archbishop Donald Coggan, Chairman of the House of Bishops: 'In the light of recent events connected with exorcism, what advice does the House of Bishops propose to give to the Church?' The archbishop replied: 'I have talked to the bishops about this, and as a result report that many of them have in the exercise of their diocesan duties already given much advice and issued certain directions and regulations. They intend to continue to do this, especially in view of much current perplexity'.

Coggan went on to outline 'the wisest approach', asserting that exorcism had a place in the church: 'The Christian ministry is a ministry of deliverance and healing. Jesus Christ exercised such a ministry and has commended its continuance to His Church. There are many men and women so within the grip of the power of evil that they need the aid of the Christian Church in delivering them from it'. Coggan went on to list five 'factors [that] should be borne in mind' regarding exorcism:

(1) It should be done in collaboration with the resources of medicine.
(2) It should be done in the context of prayer and sacrament.
(3) It should be done with a minimum of publicity.
(4) It should be done by experienced persons authorised by the diocesan bishop.
(5) It should be followed up by continuing pastoral care.[50]

The fact that Coggan made this pronouncement as Chairman of the House of Bishops, rather than just as archbishop of Canterbury, gave it a little more authority; he could claim to be speaking on behalf of the episcopate as a whole. However, Coggan's minimalistic 'factors' were not voted on (or even 'taken note of') by General Synod, nor did they result in any amendment to the canons. Coggan issued some very basic guidelines on the use of exorcism, but left the matter entirely to the discretion of individual bishops – which was exactly how matters had stood before 1975. All that Coggan added was a strong reaffirmation of the ministry, something it had never received before from an archbishop of Canterbury. Coggan's guidelines were even less specific than those offered by the Church of England's 1958 report on healing, yet his pronouncement in General Synod was supposed to be the last word on the ministry of exorcism. He addressed barely any of the concerns raised in Lampe and Cupitt's open letter, and said nothing of the form that exorcism should take. The implication was that the Exeter Report, in spite of its unofficial status, remained normative.

EXORCISM AT BAPTISM

In addition to Archbishop Coggan's guidelines, another indication of changing attitudes towards exorcism in the Church of England was the inclusion of a deprecative exorcism preceding baptism in the baptismal liturgy contained within the *Alternative Service Book* of 1980. The proposed revised *Book of Common Prayer* of 1928, by contrast, did not deviate from the original 1662 liturgy in this respect. The short deprecative exorcism of the *ASB*, 'May almighty God deliver you from the powers of darkness, and lead you in the light and obedience of Christ'[51] subsequently passed into *Common Worship* and is used in most Anglican baptismal liturgies in England today. Although it is not imperative, the formula is close in form to an exorcism since it directly addresses the candidates (unlike the old oblique prayer beginning 'O merciful God, grant that the old Adam in this Child may be so buried …')

David Holeton observed that 'the recovery of baptismal ceremonies which disappeared in either 1549 or 1552' was a feature of the 1980 liturgy, which 'reflects a post-Christendom Church'. In Holeton's view 'these "dark and dumb ceremonies" now speak clearly not only to the community gathered but also to the baptismal candidates who are, as often as not, adults'.[52] The return of pre-baptismal exorcism may owe more to liturgists' preference for the shape of the pre-Reformation Catholic rite than to concerns about the demise of Christendom, however. It is unlikely that any contemporary Anglican would regard candidates for baptism as *needing* exorcism, except perhaps in the sense of purification and consecration to God. It is not obvious why the exorcistic language of the *ASB* speaks more clearly to a post-Christian culture than the non-exorcistic language of the *Book of Common Prayer*, and many who attend services of baptism will not recognise the words as an exorcism at all.

MICHAEL PERRY, DOMINIC WALKER AND MARTIN ISRAEL

The Church of England's stance on exorcism remained essentially unchanged and unelaborated from Coggan's five 'factors' throughout the 1980s and 1990s. In the 1980s the Australian biblical scholar Graham Twelftree's work on the significance of exorcism in Jesus' ministry sparked a renewed debate on the compatibility of spiritual and medical explanations for 'possession' phenomena. In Neal Milner's view, Anglicans adopted a *via media*; they 'accepted the possibility that Satan is actually present in a person, but emphasized other explanations of evil, including physical or psychological ones'.[53] However, it remained the case that a 'rather proper and mainstream set of beliefs' could be distorted to enable abuse. For example, Andrew Arbuthnot, an Anglican priest, was accused in 1994 of inserting his fingers in women's vaginas to make the sign of the cross during exorcisms at the London Healing Mission. Although the Church of England disavowed Arbuthnot, whose permission to officiate had been revoked a year earlier,[54] in the absence of a canon regulating exorcism or recognising it as a rite of the Church of England, it is far from clear that Arbuthnot was prohibited from exorcising when his permission to officiate was removed.

Milner suggested that the press coverage and attention from anti-cult organisations attendant on the Arbuthnot case profoundly disconcerted the Church of England, which values its mainstream, established status so much.[55] Exorcism, Milner has argued, is a threat to the church because it 'can lead to abuse, violence, unrestrained theology and practice, and even criminal activity'. Furthermore, 'Exorcism can cause trouble by forcing the Church to become involved with the law and by threatening the Church's own internal discipline and control'.[56] In other words, it is in the church's interest to bring exorcism under control.

The 1980s saw the emergence in America of claims by psychotherapists and social workers to have uncovered memories of 'Satanic Ritual Abuse' through questioning children and adults. In the late 1980s and early 1990s cases of this kind began to be reported in the United Kingdom.[57] Although the concept of Satanic Ritual Abuse has since been discredited as the product of leading questioning by social workers and psychotherapists, the extensive media publicity given to it at the time served to legitimate the agenda of demonologists and exorcists in the Church of England and other churches.

Another key shift that occurred in the 1980s was the Church of England's transition to the euphemism 'deliverance ministry' to refer to exorcism, in contrast to the willingness of clergy to use the term 'exorcism' in the 1960s and 1970s. The change in terminology was formalised when the Christian Exorcism Study Group (CESG), the continuation of the committee that drew up the Exeter Report in 1972, changed its name to the Christian *Deliverance* Study Group (CDSG) in 1987. Richards had already argued in the 1970s that exorcism was a small part of a much broader practice called 'deliverance', and by using this term 'the Church tries to reduce the likelihood that the most frightening and bizarre part of its healing processes will be used'.[58]

In 1987 the archdeacon of Durham, Michael Perry (1933–2015), a member of the CDSG, edited a book that embodied much of the work of the group since the Exeter Report, entitled *Deliverance: Psychic Disturbances and Occult Involvement*. The book was reprinted in 1996 and again in 2012 as part of SPCK's 'Classics' series, thereby highlighting the extent to which Perry's *Deliverance* has become accepted as an authoritative guide to the subject. Like John Richards before him, Perry is as much interested in diagnosing the demonic potential of the New Age and occultism as he is in the practice of exorcism itself. Thomas Waters has highlighted Perry's ambivalence towards witchcraft; Perry considers it down to the minister to assess the reality of such claims.[59] Collins described Perry as the 'least enthusiastic' of twentieth-century Anglican exorcists and demonologists, since he was the least inclined to give much weight to experience.[60]

Perry summarises the canonical position of the rite of exorcism within the Church of England[61] and describes the normative working of diocesan deliverance teams. Perry notes that, whereas in the aftermath of the Exeter Report many bishops appointed one priest to deal with exorcism-related matters, it was now more common for a team to be available to give advice to parish clergy.[62] Perry does not seem to have envisaged the possibility that deliverance teams would take such matters out of the hands of parish clergy altogether, which has since become the norm in some dioceses. According to Perry's model, only in the case of a 'major exorcism' would the team seek permission from the bishop, and thereby presumably act apart from parish clergy.[63] Perry recommends that a deliverance team should consist of several priests, at least one woman (who, after 1994, might be one of the priests) and a psychiatrist. The psychiatrist need not be a Christian, but needs to be someone 'sufficiently in sympathy with the aims and methods of the group not to be a destructive force within it'.[64]

According to Perry, a member of the parish clergy concerned that someone is in need of the ministry of deliverance should approach the appropriate contact person, who might be the rural dean or the bishop's chaplain, who would then put him or her in touch with a member of the diocesan deliverance team. That team member should advise the member of the clergy over the telephone and take notes. Many cases may be resolved this way, but if appropriate the team might ask 'an experienced' priest to visit the person or place that is a cause for concern. If that priest considers that there is a case for exorcism, at least two members of the team, accompanied by a member of the parish clergy, should visit the 'client' in his or her own home so that a 'provisional diagnosis' can be made.[65]

In most cases some action other than exorcism will be appropriate. However, if the team decides on an exorcism of the place this should proceed immediately. If, however, the team decides on a 'major exorcism' of a person, 'this should never be carried out until a competent psychiatric opinion has been obtained and the express permission of the bishop has been granted'. Assuming that the bishop gives permission for a 'major exorcism' to go ahead, a detailed report should be submitted to the bishop on the exorcism immediately.[66]

Perry distinguishes between three approaches to the exorcism of places, namely a blessing, 'lesser exorcism' and 'greater exorcism'. The distinction between minor and major exorcism is, according to Perry, the difference between deprecative and imperative exorcism, and a major exorcism (even of a place) should take place only 'with the direct and express permission and knowledge of the diocesan bishop'.[67] Perry advised that a priest called in to deal with a 'disturbance' should never leave without performing some 'ritual act', if only because doing so would assuage the anxieties of the 'client'.[68] Indeed, Perry goes further than advocating exorcism as a form of therapy, claiming that someone could act as an exorcist (and presumably *should* so act) even if he or she lacks a belief in demons as personal entities, because it is Christ who exorcises and not the exorcist: 'the agnostic can therefore act "as if"'.[69] Perry gives the impression that the overwhelming imperative is to exorcise, whether or not the exorcist believes real demonic activity is present and whether or not the exorcist even believes in exorcism.

Perry holds back from describing what a major exorcism of a person would be like, noting that such a rite will be a rare event. He directs readers to the CDSG for more information.[70] However, since Perry writes 'As with places, so with people', we can presume that Perry envisages a major exorcism of a person as having the same basic features as a major exorcism of a place:

> Exorcize immediately, using an imperative form of words ... There should be a second priest ready to take over at once if the first is prevented in any way. It is advisable to have the words of the formula written out in the exorcist's hand, to prevent the evil spirit from so

confusing the exorcist that he finds it impossible to remember the
words he is intent on using. The exorcism must continue whatever
happens or appears to happen, and whomever or whatever is
threatened, until all opposition of any kind has ceased.[71]

Perry seems to presume that a major exorcism will always be required
as a result of someone dabbling in the occult, and requires a
renunciation from all involved 'of all Satanic or occult worship'.
Needless to say, the idea that any involvement in the occult amounts
to 'worship' implies a very particular theology. Any 'occult' books or
manuscripts should also be burnt.[72]

Although Perry's *Deliverance* proved an influential text, it still did
not have the status of an official Church of England document on
exorcism. In 2000, the church finally produced and approved such a
document, in the context of the broader healing ministry. The report
A Time to Heal was debated in General Synod in July 2000. Synod
voted to 'take note' of the report, and a copy was sent to all clergy in
order to enable diocesan and deanery synods and parish church
councils to discuss the report.[73] One of the figures behind the report
was the then bishop of Reading (later bishop of Monmouth),
Dominic Walker, whose book *The Ministry of Deliverance* (1997) is
considered by many Anglicans a modern classic on the subject.
Walker's cautious approach influenced *A Time to Heal*, especially his
insistence on using the term 'deliverance', wherever possible, as a
euphemism for exorcism. Walker justifies his reluctance to speak of
exorcism on the grounds of its rarity:

> [W]hilst exorcism is a perfectly good New Testament word, it implies a
> rite to deliver someone from demonic possession. Such a rite is rarely
> appropriate even though a person may feel under some evil influence.
> The term 'deliverance ministry' is much wider and includes counselling,
> confession, anointing and Holy Communion as means of ministering to
> those who seek freedom from evil.[74]

Walker largely endorses Michael Wilson's view that it is not necessary
for Christians to believe everything Jesus believed, and qualifies the
importance of exorcism in the New Testament by noting that neither
John nor Paul made reference to the practice. He suggests that 'the
attitude to exorcism in the early Church depended much on the
influence of the local leader'.[75] Like Perry, Walker emphasises the

extreme rarity of demonic possession and argues that people sometimes display the apparent symptoms of possession because they are acting out the evil being projected on them by others.[76]

Walker goes on to claim that theologians speaking of 'demonic possession' and psychiatrists speaking of 'possession syndrome' are talking about the same thing, and he argues that exorcism might provide helpful psychological relief for sufferers if priests and doctors work together.[77] He also acknowledges the potential damage exorcism might cause, arguing for a more holistic approach to 'deliverance':

> [W]hen exorcism is carried out in an over-zealous way, it often only ministers to the spiritual nature of the person and ignores their psychological and physical needs. It can encourage them to deny responsibility for their own conduct, and if unsuccessful, leave them with the feeling that they are evil and that God can't or doesn't want to help them.[78]

On one interpretation, Walker's intention is to minimise the possibility that a priest of the Church of England would actually diagnose someone as demonically possessed and exorcise him or her for that reason. Walker provides an alternative interpretation for virtually every case of apparent demonic possession, while not at any point denying the reality and possibility of actual demonic possession. Yet at the same time, Walker seems more interested in discouraging diagnoses of possession than in discouraging the practice of exorcism; indeed, his suggestion that priests and doctors work together to provide therapeutic exorcisms regardless of whether a person is really possessed suggests that Walker believes exorcism serves an important pastoral function.

Walker reflects a broader trend in the Church of England towards epistemic minimalism and liturgical maximalism when it comes to exorcism; priests should be almost infinitely sceptical of claims of demonic possession, to the point where literal possession is hedged about with an indefinite number of qualifications, but at the same time priests are encouraged to make use of 'dark and dumb ceremonies' if these may be beneficial to the faithful. Clearly, this approach is open to criticism – from theological conservatives because it appears to make it impossible to perform a traditional exorcism, and from liberals because Walker refuses to question the real existence of demonic possession as distinct from mental illness. Lampe's critical comments on those who peddle exorcism 'like the bottle of coloured water' are also apposite.

While authors such as Perry and Walker reflect a convergence in the late twentieth-century Church of England towards an approach to exorcism largely modelled on the practice of Petitpierre and influenced by the Exeter Report, eccentric outliers continued to exist. Martin Israel (1927–2007), an Anglican priest who acted as an exorcist in the Diocese of London, published *Exorcism: The Removal of Evil Influences* in the same year as Walker's *Ministry of Deliverance* (1997). Israel's eccentric distinction between exorcism and deliverance sets the tone for the book: 'Exorcism entails the ejection of an undesirable psychic entity from a person or a locality, whereas deliverance is concerned more with the handing over of the entity to God's care'.[79]

Israel was unusual among Anglican exorcists in allying the rites of the church with Spiritualism, arguing that the divine authority of the exorcist 'transcends any purely psychic power without in any way denying that power'.[80] Israel defended the tossing of a 'blessed coin' to diagnose possession as 'sacred lots' and advocated remote exorcisms, even claiming to have conducted a requiem mass over the telephone.[81] Israel's early exorcisms were performed with the assistance of a psychic medium named Geraldine ('Geral'), with whom Israel continued to work as a disembodied spirit after her death. He described the standard procedure he would use in an exorcism:

> These are the words I use: 'In the name of God the Creator, God Most High, God the Father, God the Son and God the Holy Spirit, Geral and I command you demonic spirit to leave here, and proceed to that place in the life beyond death which God has prepared for your reception and healing.' After a brief period, I repeat the formula, this time bidding the demonic spirit to leave here 'and this earthbound plane' instead of simply 'here' as in the first command. After a few more seconds I repeat the formula a third time, bidding the demonic spirit to leave here 'and proceed to that place in the life beyond death that God has prepared for your reception and healing, there to do the work for which you were created'. I end each command with the instruction, 'Go in the name of

God the Father, God the Son, and God the Holy Spirit'. After the third command I remain absolutely quiet for a short time, and then I free the spirit (no longer demonic) from all obedience to evil humanity.[82]

Israel's conviction that 'demonic spirits' could be redeemed was rooted in the optimistic, universalist theology of Spiritualism. Although several twentieth-century exorcists acknowledged their own psychic gifts and were even prepared to use them on occasion in the diagnosis of cases, Israel was alone among British Anglicans in advocating a synthesis of Christian and Spiritualist approaches. Israel's practice demonstrates that considerable room for idiosyncratic ministries of exorcism still existed in the Church of England in the 1990s.

Collins described Israel as 'the end of the line in terms of the pseudo-spiritualist, Anglican sacramental exorcism', characterising his approach as 'altogether aberrant'.[83] Collins may have been right that Israel's methods, which conjure up images of 1930s parlour séances, were dated by the late 1990s. Israel's hostility to the charismatic tradition, when the tendency of Anglican 'sacramental' exorcists has been to assimilate and accommodate it, also set him apart from the mainstream. It is hard to imagine any contemporary Anglican exorcist deciding to draw on the resources of Spiritualism, which is generally demonised by charismatics.

'A TIME TO HEAL'

The Church of England's report on the ministry of healing, *A Time to Heal* (2000) was compiled by a committee that included at least two individuals with experience of the ministry of deliverance, Bishop Dominic Walker and Michael Selman, the bishop of Exeter's advisor on healing and deliverance.[84] The report provides thorough overviews of the place of exorcism in the Bible,[85] exorcism in the early church,[86] and the range of contemporary theological views on the subject.[87] Although strongly influenced by Walker's approach, the report goes further than Walker by not only advocating the use of the term 'deliverance' but also claiming that 'deliverance' is a more accurate term than exorcism, on the grounds that the latter word is never used in the New Testament for the ministry of Jesus and the apostles. However, the report's recognition that exorcism is an 'emotive' term is a more honest assessment of the main reason for the shift in vocabulary.[88]

The report is clear that the ministry of deliverance has 'a place in the modern Church', but cautions against both underestimating and overestimating 'the power of spiritual evil'.[89] *A Time to Heal* highlights the importance of the Exeter Report, tracing the practice of appointing 'a suitable person to undertake this ministry in each diocese'[90] to that document, and endorsing the Exeter Report's distinction between major and minor exorcism (derived from Petitpierre's approach).[91] *A Time to Heal* points to three developments since 1972 that have raised awareness of deliverance ministry – namely, the growth of the charismatic renewal, 'growing public interest in the occult and the paranormal which tends to sensationalise the subject', and the presence of 'ethnic groups from countries among whom the power of spiritual evil is regarded as a hazard of everyday life'.[92]

> [I]f we believe that spiritual influences are at work for evil as well as good, then some form of deliverance ministry may be appropriate ... Some will be able to accept and work with the biblical model, language and imagery. Others will prefer to demythologize some of the biblical language but nevertheless accept the underlying belief that there can be objective evil forces at work in people and in society, and that with the right professional safeguards the Church has a unique contribution to offer.[93]

A Time to Heal follows Walker's practice in describing a range of psychological symptoms that might be misinterpreted as demonic possession, without ever making clear what the definitive signs of demonic possession would be.[94] However, the report also asserts that 'the ... limitations of medical science must be recognised',[95] without making clear whether these limitations are absolute or contingent on the current state of psychiatric knowledge. Like the Exeter Report, *A Time to Heal* appears to accept uncritically the reality of the paranormal,[96] but it condemns other beliefs as 'unorthodox teachings'. These include the idea that demons have 'physical as well as spiritual properties which enable them to enter a person through bodily orifices and they are then expelled physically', and the idea that possession is 'due to the influence of witchcraft in previous generations'.[97]

Although the report notes that such beliefs often lead to abusive behaviour towards the 'possessed', it offers no explanation as to why these are 'unorthodox teachings'. The report's observation that people turn to 'mainstream churches' (including the Church of England) because they have been damaged by deliverance ministry in other denominations glosses over the fact that some Anglicans hold the beliefs condemned in the report as 'unorthodox'. It is unclear whether the report is condemning *any* form of belief in witchcraft (a belief Perry was content to countenance in *Deliverance*) or just a belief in the generational effect of curses. *A Time to Heal* does not censure the more bizarre beliefs advocated in the Exeter Report or by influential figures such as John Richards and Max Petitpierre. Ultimately, *A Time to Heal* is clear that some form of exorcism must be practised in the Church of England:

> [W]e do not wish to reduce or explain away evil oppression or possession simply in medical or psychological terms. We recognize that there are evil forces at work which cannot be psychologically integrated and where the resources of medicine and psychology are only partial solutions. Prayers of deliverance or exorcism, with all the necessary safeguards, may in some cases be appropriate and beneficial.[98]

The report does not prescribe a particular liturgical form for exorcism, instead recommending that

> the service itself should be simple and may include the ministry of absolution, Holy Communion, anointing and the laying on of hands. The welfare of the subject is paramount and as far as possible the service should not be emotionally charged. The service is one of authority and love, not magic or manipulation. It sets people free from fear and false belief and brings them to truth and freedom.[99]

Overall, *A Time to Heal*'s guidance on exorcism of possessed persons is ambiguous and confusing – perhaps deliberately, in an effort to simultaneously affirm the necessity of the ministry of deliverance and discourage anyone from performing the rite of major exorcism.

LITURGICAL DEVELOPMENTS

The absence of any authorised liturgy for exorcism, apart from the suggested liturgical material appended to the 1972 Exeter Report, led clergy to devise inventive solutions to the Church of England's lack of anything resembling a rite of exorcism in its official liturgical books, *The Book of Common Prayer* and (from 1980) the *Alternative Service Book*. The overtly imperative material in the Exeter Report was clearly inappropriate for many pastoral contexts. Perry evidently did not consider the Church of England's liturgical resources sufficient for deliverance ministry, since his book on exorcism included material taken from a 1983 draft report of the Liturgical Committee of the Church of South Africa. Perry omitted the text of the rite of major exorcism, directing enquirers to the CDSG. The rite of major exorcism Perry declined to disclose was probably the one appended to the Exeter Report. From the South African church, Perry supplied a rite for the blessing of a house, Holy Communion at the blessing of a house, a rite of exorcism of a home or other place, a blessing of holy water, and a rite of deliverance or minor exorcism.[100]

One widely used unofficial manual of pastoral prayers, which carried a foreword by the bishop of Salisbury, David Stancliffe, was reprinted five times and included a variety of formulae of exorcism. These included imperative formulae closely based on those recommended by the Exeter Report.[101] Although the manual directs the reader to the writings of Michael Perry and John Richards, it does not share Perry's reticence to provide liturgical material for a 'major exorcism'. Indeed, the manual does not make any obvious distinction between 'major' and 'minor' exorcism, nor does it inform the reader that a major exorcism should be performed only by a priest specifically authorised by a bishop to do so, merely advising that 'No ministry should be undertaken unless proper preparation has been made and professional advice has been sought'.[102] The omission of any mention of episcopal authorisation may indicate that the editors were unaware of Archbishop Coggan's guidelines; alternatively, it may reflect a prevailing reality of ministry in which parish clergy seek advice from the diocesan deliverance team but nevertheless use imperative formulae of exorcism without explicit authorisation.

In 2000, the same year as *A Time to Heal*, the Church of England produced its revised liturgy, *Common Worship*. This included 'Prayers for Protection and Peace', consisting of a series of prayers for 'those suffering from a sense of disturbance or unrest'. These are not exorcisms, and the rubrics of *Common Worship* warn that 'The ministry of exorcism and deliverance may only be exercized by priests authorized by the bishop, who normally requires that permission be obtained from him [*sic.*] for each specific exercise of such a ministry', adding that 'On occasions when exorcism and deliverance are administered, it is for the bishop to determine the nature of the rite and what form of words should be used'.[103]

These rubrics are in line with the Exeter Report and *A Time to Heal*, but they are at odds with Perry's insistence that the role of a diocesan deliverance team should be primarily advisory to parish clergy.[104] Clearly, views on the role of the deliverance team shifted significantly between 1987 and 2000. The change was probably down to concerns about insurance; the handbook issued to accompany *A Time to Heal* warns that, although deliverance teams may be insured on a diocesan level, a parish's insurance does not extend to the ministry of deliverance as a parochial ministry.[105] It is worth noting that the word 'exorcism' is used in *Common Worship* alongside the euphemism 'deliverance', presumably in order to clarify what is meant by the latter term. However, since both Perry and *A Time to Heal* make clear that not every member of a diocesan deliverance team will be ordained, *Common Worship*'s stipulation that the ministry of deliverance in general (as opposed to exorcism in particular) should only be exercised by a priest is puzzling.[106]

THE 'BUREAUCRATISATION' OF EXORCISM?

Neal Milner has argued that exorcism in the Church of England brings with it a 'combination of eroticism and supervision, belief and danger'. He situates the revival of exorcism within the context of the church's role in the establishment, arguing that 'worries about the excess manifestations of uncontrolled spirituality' produced exorcism as a reaction. For Milner, the church is primarily concerned about the 'uncontrolled spirituality' of Pentecostals and charismatics, whose spirituality the Church of England is influenced by but seeks to control 'through beliefs and mechanisms that normalize and medicalize demon possession, bureaucratize exorcism procedures, and encourage norms of self-restraint'.[107] Milner goes on to argue that 'Exorcism, as the Church of England tries to practise it, is a means of maintaining the Church's control and autonomy', whilst noting that such 'control' is always under threat in exorcism because of its risky and unpredictable nature.[108]

The attitude of charismatic Anglicans towards exorcism may be more sophisticated than Milner suggests. Graham Smith argues that two models of spiritual warfare, 'power encounter' and 'truth encounter' exist in charismatic Anglican theology. While 'power encounter' envisages the casting out of evil spirits, 'truth encounter' means 'aligning a person's life with gospel truth which in itself has the power to set them free'.[109] 'Truth encounter' requires renunciation of involvement in the occult (which may explain why such renunciation is recommended in most recent Anglican literature on deliverance ministry), and it is easy to see why this alternative, non-exorcistic approach to dealing with spiritual evil is preferred by charismatics in light of the difficulty of obtaining episcopal permission for exorcisms. On the other hand, Stephen Hunt has argued, on the basis of empirical fieldwork conducted in Anglican charismatic churches in the UK, that 'teachings on "signs and wonders", especially in terms of healing and deliverance' makes charismatic Christianity appealing to its target congregation. Hunt describes this target group as 'the largely affluent middle-classes',[110] but he does not explain why deliverance ministry might appeal to this group.

According to Milner, the Church of England attempts to 'normalise' exorcism in three ways:

> Firstly, the doctrine places the practice securely in a healing context, so that exorcism is an infrequent way of healing. Secondly, the doctrine medicalizes both the problems associated with Satanic possession as well as the procedures used to dealing with them. Finally, rules and guidelines for exorcism stress the need not simply to get rid of the devil, but to make the afflicted person whole by affirming his/her relationship with God and with the broader community.[111]

By imposing categories on supernatural phenomena the church manages 'to nuance responses, to minimize the use of exorcism, and to maximize the participation of doctors and therapists'. Milner identified six such categories: ghosts and poltergeists, place memories, unrested souls, temptation, obsession and possession. Exorcism is only suitable for the last of these, with possession becoming a 'last ditch diagnosis' if no naturalistic or non-demonic paranormal explanation can be found.[112] Furthermore, exorcists' adoption of paranormal explanations allows them to deal with these issues by psychotherapy rather than exorcism – for instance, the idea that poltergeist activity is best stopped by encouraging people to 'own' the destructive feelings that have supposedly produced a psychic projection.

In Milner's view, 'The blurring of boundaries between spiritual and psychological and between normal and paranormal explanations' is characteristic of contemporary Anglican exorcistic practice. The CDSG emphasises 'the complementarity of epistemologies, explanations, and methods' rather than imposing a single demonological view, and privileges practical effectiveness over theoretical consistency. Psychological and parapsychological explanations act as what Milner describes as 'gatekeepers' for the Church of England, potentially preventing the need for introducing supernatural entities into the equation.[113]

The Church of England's 'bureaucratisation' of exorcism takes the form of a set of guidelines and requirements for those involved in 'deliverance', advising them to work in teams, keep case notes and discuss cases with the rest of the team. Furthermore, in the case of exorcisms of persons, the requirement to obtain specific permission from the bishop and to file a report to the bishop afterwards further 'bureaucratises' the process. Milner sees the CDSG as 'a group that carries the imprimatur of the Church hierarchy' and argues that its guidelines are 'more like rules when exorcism is involved'.[114]

Although Milner acknowledged that the Church of England's controls on exorcism could fail,[115] his argument that the church is deeply preoccupied with controlling exorcism is not altogether unproblematic. While Milner may be right that the Church of England has taken steps to regulate exorcism via the subtle means he outlines, the question remains as to why the church does not employ more stringent – and more conventional – means of regulating the practice. Milner does not offer an explanation for why the Church of England has failed to produce a canon on exorcism, for instance.

CONCLUSION

The normalisation of exorcism as a ministry of the Church of England (albeit a ministry that parish clergy are not supposed to engage in without permission and advice) proceeded in the 1970s in spite of scandal and opposition. The Ossett murder case had the potential to discredit the ministry of exorcism altogether, as did Geoffrey Lampe's campaign against exorcism among influential churchmen and theologians. However, the consensus of the bishops, shared by Archbishop Coggan, was that outlawing exorcism was more problematic than permitting it, and the media and public were divided on whether the horrors of the 'Barnsley case' proved the reality of demonic possession or the unacceptability of exorcism. A growing fear of the occult overcame the Church of England's traditional stance of scepticism, and the sketchy nature of the advice provided by Coggan lent an inflated importance to the Exeter Report, whose recommendations were still being cited as late as 2000 in the General Synod report *A Time to Heal*. By the turn of the millennium exorcism was entrenched both in documents of General Synod and in the rubrics of *Common Worship*, in spite of the fact that the rite remained without any canonical foundation in the church.

CHAPTER 6

Anglican Exorcism in the Twenty-First Century

The position of exorcism in the contemporary Church of England is largely unchanged since the millennium, when the General Synod report *A Time to Heal* (2000) and the rubric in *Common Worship* (2000) lent a certain degree of official status to the rite. However, although the 1975 guidelines of the House of Bishops remain in force, in 2012 these were expanded and clarified, largely in response to the Church of England's obligations under legislation regarding the safeguarding of children and vulnerable adults. The contemporary church's laudable commitment to safeguarding, which is informed by notable failures in the past, exists in tension with an ongoing doctrinal commitment to the possibility of exorcism, which has the potential to be easily defined as a form of spiritual abuse. This chapter assesses the compatibility of exorcism with the church's commitment to safeguarding and examines the thought-world of contemporary Anglican exorcists and practical demonologists, concluding with an examination of whether a 'tradition' of exorcism is discernible in the history of the Church of England.

DEVELOPMENTS SINCE 2000

A Time to Heal and the cautious approach to exorcism it embodied was not without its critics. In 2003, one of the most thoroughgoing defences of the church's ministry of deliverance was provided by the then bishop of Carlisle, Graham Dow, who described the amusement of a visiting Chinese clergyman when Dow explained that many Anglican clergy did not believe in evil spirits. For Dow, accepting the reality of an evil spiritual realm meant respecting the beliefs of the majority of Christians worldwide:

> We should be open to the possibility that the rest of the world is right in its perception of the way things are ... the New Testament view of reality should at least be considered without prejudice. We should simply see whether or not it makes better sense of what we experience today than the interpretative models commonly used in our society.[1]

Dow was critical of the Church of England for being too cautious in its approach to exorcism, arguing that obtaining an explicit licence from the bishop for every exorcism 'is impractical if spirits are widespread and mostly not very powerful'. Dow rejects Perry's distinction between deprecative minor exorcisms and major imperative exorcisms requiring episcopal permission: 'This seems unsatisfactory, if Jesus is our model, since he dealt with all spirits by command'. Dow advised practitioners of deliverance ministry to reach agreement with their bishops to work without consulting them regularly, so that they would consult with the bishop only 'over any case which looks serious and has the feel of a major deliverance about it'.[2] Dow was an unusual dissenting voice among bishops, but his reluctance to constrain exorcism by excessive bureaucracy is typical of evangelicals.

The retired bishop of Birmingham, Hugh Montefiore, who had been critical of Geoffrey Lampe's open letter against exorcism in 1975, expressed his ongoing support for the ministry in a book about the paranormal published in 2002. Montefiore condemned 'profligate use of exorcism' among charismatics,[3] but defended the use of exorcism in general. He recalled the Ossett exorcism case and the open letter it led to:

> Although the signatories of the Open Letter were mostly my friends, and some were former colleagues, I personally regarded them as gravely mistaken in their views. *Abusus non tollit usum*: Abuse of anything does not invalidate its right use. It seemed to me that these academics were remote from the pastoral realities of life. I was then a bishop in South London, and there were quite a few cases of paranormal disturbance,

especially among West Indian Christians. Mostly, these were of the poltergeist type. The diocese [of Southwark] had appointed an experienced parish priest (who had served in the rural areas of South Africa) as its 'diocesan exorcist' ... This priest's task was not to go around exorcising right, left and centre, but to deal sensitively with those who had been shaken by paranormal phenomena and who had been referred to him by their parish priests. Usually, all that was needed was some counselling and the ministry of reassurance, but occasionally more was required. When I went to the See of Birmingham, I appointed four experienced parish priests to carry out similar duties. I found that other parish priests called them in when they were faced with situations with which they could not easily deal. I wonder how the signatories of the Open Letter would have dealt with them in these circumstances. If people are terrified by paranormal phenomena, it only makes them worse to tell them that they are simply being superstitious.[4]

Montefiore interviewed Dominic Walker for his book, who explained the work of the CDSG. Walker compared deliverance ministry to 'extended communion or the marriage of divorced people: it's something that happens so it has to be controlled!'[5] Walker reported that he had blessed places 'where there have been black arts ... [and] Satanic sacrifices have taken place', but did not exorcise because 'I don't find any scriptural authority for exorcising a place'.[6] Walker reported that he had only encountered demonic possession 'in two or three cases', and recounted an exorcism he had performed on a girl in Fiji. He cautioned that people in different cultures 'act out' possession very differently, but insisted that possession was still an objective phenomenon.[7]

Ken Gardiner, an exorcist in the diocese of Rochester, published a short account of his experiences in 2002 in which he made clear his disagreements with the CDSG, most notably over the distinction between major and minor exorcisms. Gardiner advocated the use of imperative commands in the 'cleansing' of places, even in the absence of episcopal permission for a 'major exorcism', arguing that the spirits who infest places are not as powerful as those who possess human beings. Gardiner also argued (against the CDSG's advice) that poltergeists should be adjured.[8] In spite of *A Time to Heal's* unambiguous condemnation of belief in ancestral curses and the physical ejection of spirits from bodily orifices, Gardiner subscribes to both notions.[9] In contrast to Walker, Gardiner portrays the imperative exorcism of demoniacs as a fairly frequent occurrence in his 30 years of ministry as an exorcist. Gardiner follows no set liturgy of exorcism but his adjuration would typically take the form:

> I take authority over every spirit contrary to the Holy Spirit, and I cut you off from any and every source of power. I set the name (blood, victory) of Jesus between you and the powers of darkness. You are on your own now; your time has come to leave this person, be subject to the Lord Jesus, and never again enter any living being. You are to come out now.[10]

In July 2005 the bishop of Blackburn, Nicholas Reade, noted that General Synod had not approved any services of deliverance, 'these falling within the purview of individual diocesan bishops', but he also observed that General Synod had 'endorsed' the 1975 guidelines by taking note of *A Time to Heal*. Reade 'judged that these guidelines still held good in the light of pastoral experience since the 1970s' and stated that 'The key to this is the application of good practice within dioceses based on the tried and tested guidelines'.[11] The bishop of Chelmsford, responding to a suggestion that the guidelines on deliverance ministry should be updated in the light of 'recent adverse publicity', said that he hoped dioceses would work 'to ensure good practice ... in this crucial area of ministry' through regular training for clergy.[12]

In 2007 Beatrice Brandon, the principal author of *A Time to Heal*, was appointed the Archbishops' Advisor for the Healing Ministry. In 2009 Brandon began researching deliverance ministry across the Church of England, producing a report in 2010 that was reviewed by the bishops of Winchester, Southwell and Tonbridge. The review group then issued an expanded set of guidelines, still based on Archbishop Coggan's, on behalf of the House of Bishops. The 2012 guidelines consist of a series of points expanding each one of Coggan's five 'factors', beginning with Coggan's advice that the ministry should be performed 'by experienced persons authorised by the diocesan bishop'. The 2012 guidelines interpret this as meaning that the ministry should *only* be performed by an episcopally authorised priest, although they allow that the priest may be accompanied by a 'lay minister of mature pastoral experience who is similarly authorized', which presumably restricts such assistance to lay ministers holding the bishop's licence, such as Readers. The guidelines propose regular training, and that priests with this responsibility should understand 'the deliverance practices of other churches'. They also insist that each diocese should ensure that priests performing deliverance ministry are covered by diocesan insurance.

Interpreting Coggan's advice that deliverance 'should be done in the context of prayer and sacrament', the 2012 guidelines require that 'If an exorcism is to be performed, permission for it must be received under the authority of a diocesan bishop, for each specific exercise of such a ministry', although the local incumbent would normally be consulted and involved. Oddly, the guidelines state that 'Suitable resources from The Book of Common Prayer, Common Worship or any other approved source should normally be used' for exorcism, when in fact neither *The Book of Common Prayer* nor *Common Worship* contains anything resembling an exorcism. It is unclear what would count as 'any other approved source', but it presumably means anything the bishop decides on. The guidelines recommend that 'The recipient(s) should be made aware that what is offered is a specific ministry of the Church', and, setting the ministry within the context of safeguarding policy, counsel that 'Recipients should be made aware of how the ministry is to be exercised and no one should receive ministry against their will'.

When Coggan advised that deliverance 'should be done with the minimum of publicity' it seems likely that he had in mind public and televised exorcisms. The 2012 guidelines interpret this statement as referring to confidentiality only, advising that 'Any limitations to confidentiality should be explained in advance and any disclosure should be restricted to relevant information, which should be conveyed only to appropriate persons, normally with consent and again, within the constraints of the Data Protection Act'.[13] Presumably, therefore, the 2012 guidelines do not rule out a public exorcism if someone gave their consent for this to take place. Perhaps the authors of the guidelines considered that it went without saying that a public or broadcast exorcism was unthinkable.

In 2012 Beatrice Brandon revealed some of her own views on exorcism in an article for the newsletter of the Spirituality and Psychiatry Special Interest Group of the Royal College of Psychiatrists.[14] Brandon portrayed ghosts as 'psychologically projected apparitions of dead people', but accepted the reality of poltergeists as 'actual paranormal phenomena'. Brandon is ambivalent concerning the reality of demons as personal entities, speaking instead of situations 'where a disturbed person appears, or claims to be afflicted by a power of evil or evil spirit'. She notes that 'some individuals do experience a strong sense of evil, either within a location or in connection with themselves'. On the other hand, Brandon claims that 'true demonic possession is extremely rare' – which implies that it does, nevertheless, exist. Brandon goes on to define exorcism:

> Christian exorcism could be defined as the rite of casting out evil spirits, based on the example of Christ and the apostles. It is the specific act of binding and releasing, performed on a person who is believed to be possessed by a non-human malevolent spirit … Minor or lesser exorcism is a supplicatory form of exorcistic prayer, in which the exorcist or authorized priest prays supplicatory prayers to God asking God to remove the spiritual or demonic influence on or around the client. Supplicatory exorcistic prayers are used when the exorcist or authorized priest believes that there is some spiritual or demonic force oppressing the client, but not actually possessing the body of the client.

Brandon states that major exorcism should take place 'if the exorcist and bishop are convinced beyond moral doubt that the client's body is demonically possessed and the bishop has given his authorization for the exorcism'. In the vast majority of cases, Brandon insists, deliverance ministry will not involve something so drastic. Instead, she emphasises the importance of a 'multi-disciplinary' approach towards people who believe themselves to be under demonic attack, who must be questioned carefully to establish whether they have attempted to 'self-diagnose' their predicament, often within a misconceived framework of occultism or popular culture. In Brandon's view, Anglican deliverance ministry should be 'prayerful and pastoral, gently forensic and multi-disciplinary, taking care to avoid collusion and the labelling as diabolical of that which cannot yet be explained scientifically'. Brandon also distances herself from Perry's view that exorcism may provide psychological relief: 'this would devalue true exorcism, reducing it to a psychiatric tool to be used as a mental healthcare response'.

The 42 dioceses of the Church of England differ significantly in the ways in which they describe and present their ministry of deliverance to the public. A search of the websites of the dioceses in August 2017 revealed that nine dioceses make no public mention of the ministry at all. Four dioceses mention the ministry only in their diocesan safeguarding policies, warning against the potential danger of 'intrusive deliverance ministries'. Seven dioceses simply identify the diocesan advisor on deliverance ministry and inform clergy that continuing ministerial education (CME) is available in this area. The diocese of Chelmsford reports the appointment of area healing and deliverance advisors in the diocesan magazine. Seven dioceses (Birmingham, Ely, Gloucester, Guildford, Lichfield, London and St Albans) provide a brief explanation of what deliverance ministry is, the circumstances in which someone might ask for it and the procedure to be followed in requesting it. Only four dioceses (Canterbury, Exeter, Hereford and Southwell) make the detailed guidance issued to clergy publicly available on their websites. Newcastle and Worcester provide fairly detailed advice for the laity and suggest possible prayers. All dioceses presumably provide advice to clergy that they do not choose to make public.

The diocese of Canterbury's guidelines to clergy on deliverance include likely indications of the need for deliverance for places and persons, although they caution that 'apparent place phenomena can be person related and apparent person phenomena can be place related'. In the case of exorcism, the guidelines advise that 'a prayer restraining evil' may be appropriate, in order to allow an 'opportunity for proper prayerful discernment'. The guidelines require that exorcism should take place during daylight hours, should be performed in pairs, and should involve 'liturgical or informal prayers of authority in the name of Christ commanding the evil presence to depart', thereby excluding the possibility of deprecative exorcisms.[15] The diocese of Exeter's guidelines advise that the bishop's advisor on deliverance ministry need not be involved in concerns regarding places, but should always be called upon when a 'living creature' (presumably including animals as well as humans) is involved. Exeter theoretically permits parish clergy to exorcise, but only with the explicit permission of the bishop and the advisor on deliverance (although it is unclear whether this means the advisor could veto an exorcism already authorised by the bishop).[16]

The fact that the term 'deliverance' is used simultaneously as a euphemism for exorcism and a more holistic term for pastoral aid to people in 'spiritual crisis' creates a paradoxical situation. For example, in a July 2014 letter to his clergy the then acting bishop of Southwell and Nottingham, Richard Inwood, wrote that 'The Ministry of Deliverance should only be carried out by persons authorised by the Bishop, who have been trained nationally and are insured for this specific ministry'. However, in the same letter the bishop insisted that 'Deliverance Ministry ... should not be separated from the wider context of the Church's ministry to those who are ill'; something difficult to do, if the ministry is the preserve of trained specialists. The bishop continued that 'Ministries of Deliverance are part of the wider healing and pastoral ministry', but instructed clergy to consult an advisor: 'In particular, whilst initial consultation, groundwork, prayer and support may be carried out by the local ministers, no exorcism should be attempted without such consultation and only ever with Episcopal authorization'.[17]

Inwood's statement implies that the exorcist need not be the bishop's advisor on deliverance, and raises the question of what 'deliverance ministry' actually is; does it include the 'initial consultation, groundwork, prayer and support'? Or is it, in fact, just imperative exorcism? The problem seems to be that the rubric in *Common Worship* uses the term 'deliverance' as a synonym for exorcism and therefore restricts the ministry to 'priests authorized by the bishop' (which implies trained diocesan advisors), while *A Time to Heal* takes a more holistic view of what deliverance is and sees it as part of the total ministry of the clergy as a whole, with bishop's advisors in an advisory role to the parish clergy in all but the most serious cases. The Church of England's failure to produce a clear definition of what deliverance is (as well as its reluctance to speak openly of exorcism as a particular kind of deliverance ministry) makes for a confused picture and ambiguous advice.

In an interview published in the *Church Times* in February 2017, Brandon defined the paranormal as those phenomena 'not within the sphere of widely accepted scientific knowledge', but denied that it was the church's role to research the paranormal: 'Our priority is the spiritual care of people'. Brandon rejected 'reductionist' approaches to deliverance, since 'we need to be ... willing to be alongside people and help them in their faith journey'. Brandon made clear her opposition to publicising cases of exorcism (even when personal details are anonymised) but advocated greater public knowledge of the Church of England's deliverance ministry in general terms: 'I would like deliverance ministry not to be tucked away in a dark corner'.[18]

Anglican demonologist John Woolmer, writing in the same newspaper, similarly advocated the church 'bearing witness to the powerful ministry of deliverance' now that a climate of scepticism no longer prevailed. Woolmer disagreed with Dominic Walker's suggestion to Hugh Montefiore that demonic possession was acted out, to some extent, according to cultural norms: 'I want to assert strongly that these matters are not cultural. Exactly the same phenomena occur in sophisticated Oxford, rural Somerset, and inner-city Leicester as are exhibited in ... faraway places'. Nevertheless, Woolmer reported that concern about 'disturbances in buildings' was something typical of England. Woolmer suggested that 'an attraction to and repulsion from Jesus; speaking in strange voices; inordinate strength; and self-harm' are diagnostic of demonic possession, although 'there are no litmus-paper tests'. In spite of *A Time to Heal*'s rejection of the notion of ancestral curses, Woolmer asserted his belief that 'people inherit spiritual problems',[19] an indication that clergy involved in deliverance ministry (as Woolmer is) retain their own idiosyncratic views and do not necessarily adhere to the views expressed in church documents. Woolmer is adamant that some people need exorcism, and in such cases no other diagnosis can explain away the symptoms, and no other help will do.[20]

EXORCISM AND CANON LAW

In 1964 and 1969 all of the canons of 1604 were formally superseded (with the exception of Canon 113), including Canon 72. No canon regulating exorcism took the place of Canon 72. In his brief comment on exorcism in the standard textbook of canon law, Mark Hill notes the provisions of Canon 72 and refers to Archbishop Coggan's 1975 statement in General Synod, adding that 'Diocesan regulations or norms generally make appropriate provision'.[21] In other words, exorcism is regulated by bishops' instructions in each diocese, produced on the basis of Coggan's guidelines (as updated by the House of Bishops in 2012). Bishops' instructions and documents produced by the House of Bishops are examples of what Hill describes as 'quasi-legislation', 'interstitial in their nature, filling legislative lacunae, supplementing, clarifying and interpreting formal law'. Although statements from the House of Bishops are not law and do not have the force of statute, they are considered to have 'great moral force' and may be relied upon by a consistory court.[22]

According to Daniel Stevick, the Church of England's ecclesiastical laws 'continue in effect except where later legislation has occupied the field', and 'when new legislation is adopted, the old law is seldom expressly revoked'.[23] Since no canon has taken the place of Canon 72, the Canon might be presumed still to apply (as *The Times* thought in 1975), but this is far from clear. Even without the old Canon, it is doubtful that any member of the clergy could be successfully disciplined for performing an exorcism without episcopal permission. The Clergy Discipline Measure 2003 states that disciplinary proceedings may be initiated against a member of the clergy who acts 'in contravention of the laws ecclesiastical', but there are no laws ecclesiastical (in the strict sense) governing exorcism.

Furthermore, there is not (as Michael Perry claimed) a 'strict code of practice required of the priest … enshrined in Canon Law' regarding confidentiality when it comes to exorcisms.[24] As guidelines on the conduct of the clergy issued in 2015 make clear, the absolute duty of confidentiality imposed by Canon 113 of 1604 applies only to something revealed in confession; confidentiality in other matters, including exorcism, is a moral rather than a canonical imperative.[25] There is therefore no legal impediment, strictly speaking, to members of diocesan deliverance teams publicising their activities and even naming individuals who have undergone exorcism.

A member of the clergy who disobeyed his or her bishop by performing an exorcism, or who never sought episcopal permission in the first place, might be accused of 'conduct unbecoming to the office and work of a clerk in Holy Orders'.[26] However, it is unlikely that such an accusation would lead to successful disciplinary proceedings, since a member of the clergy could make the case that exorcism is part of 'the office and work of a clerk in Holy Orders'. Since no canon obliges a member of the clergy to seek episcopal permission for exorcisms, exorcising without episcopal permission breaches the rubrics of *Common Worship* and bishops' instructions only.

An exorcist might also be exposed to the accusation of using rites not authorised by canon, but Canon B5(2) permits a minister to use forms of service 'for which no provision is made in the *Book of Common Prayer* or by the General Synod ... considered suitable by him for those occasions'.[27] Since there is no authorised rite of exorcism, the rite of exorcism recommended by the CDSG presumably falls under the provisions of Canon B5(2), as would any rite of exorcism used by any member of the clergy. Even if the bishop's instructions in a diocese specifically authorised a particular rite of exorcism and specified that this was to be used only with the bishop's permission, it is not certain that these instructions would be legally enforceable.

Under Canon C18(4) the bishop possesses the right 'of conducting, ordering, controlling, and authorising all services in churches, chapels, churchyards and consecrated burial grounds'.[28] An exorcist might therefore be challenged for performing a rite of exorcism not authorised by the bishop. However, it is not clear that exorcism constitutes a 'service' (since there is no authorised rite) and, in any case, if an exorcism were performed somewhere other than a church it would be outside the scope of Canon C18(4). It would seem, therefore, that although a bishop could initiate disciplinary proceedings against a rogue exorcist, there are several reasons why those proceedings might not succeed in a consistory court. It would be easier, in fact, to report a rogue exorcist to the civil authorities for assault or some other offence than it would be to impose ecclesiastical discipline on such an individual.

EXORCISM, ETHICS AND SAFEGUARDING

In his influential book *But Deliver Us From Evil* (1974) John Richards wrote that, during an exorcism, 'it is normal … to have feelings of tenderness for the *person* eclipsed by righteous anger at the cruelty and suffering caused by the *demonic*'.[29] More recently, Ken Gardiner insisted that 'although it is the person who *exhibits* the distress [during an exorcism], it is actually the evil spirit within them that causes it'.[30] The ethical danger inherent in statements such as these should be obvious. If a particular demonology predisposes someone to see the 'demoniac' primarily in terms of the infinitely evil demonic personality that supposedly dominates him or her, thereby legitimating anger against the demoniac – or at least indifference to the demoniac's suffering – it is a short step to physical violence against the supposedly possessed person. The potential for physical, psychological, emotional, sexual and spiritual abuse in the practice of exorcism is amply testified in the historical record, as well as in contemporary British cases (many of them associated with African Pentecostal churches).

The Church of England, to its credit, recognises exorcism's abusive potential. As part of its recommendations for good practice, the General Synod's 2006 report *Promoting a Safe Church* recommended that 'Church workers should recognize their limits and not undertake any ministry that is beyond their competence or role', giving deliverance ministry as one example. The report suggested that 'In such instances the person should be referred to another person or agency with appropriate expertise'.[31] According to the report, the category of spiritual abuse might include 'intrusive healing and deliverance ministries, which may result in vulnerable people experiencing physical, emotional or sexual harm'. The report noted that 'If such inappropriate behaviour becomes harmful it should be referred for investigation in the usual way', and promised that 'Careful supervision and mentoring of those entrusted with the pastoral care of adults should help to prevent harm occurring in this way'.[32]

It is important to note that the best practice guidelines in *Promoting a Safe Church* are non-binding and do not actually restrict exorcism to specialists. No definition is given of what would count as 'intrusive' deliverance ministry, nor how deliverance ministry might cause 'harm' or constitute spiritual abuse. There is no description of what an exorcism that is *not* spiritual abuse would look like. The report might have the effect of deterring would-be clerical exorcists from performing exorcisms for fear of referral for investigation by a safeguarding officer. However, *Promoting a Safe Church* does not specify what 'careful supervision and mentoring' of exorcists would look like.

The handbook issued to accompany *A Time to Heal* explains the procedure for safeguarding concerns about deliverance teams, and notes that 'within the ministries of healing and deliverance, there is scope for unwilling and even deliberate abuse, and ministers who are self-aware will know of the temptations and dangers which can arise'.[33] The handbook advises that a diocese's insurance cover can be extended 'to cover professional diocesan roles such as the authorized diocesan deliverance team'. The handbook also warns that 'some approaches' to exorcism 'might be misconstrued as assault if carried out without clear ongoing consent', although insurance might cover an exorcist's legal expenses if such an accusation were made.[34]

It is possible that an exorcist might be acting within the law if he or she received 'clear ongoing consent' for an exorcism involving physical contact or restraint. However, since any subject of a 'major exorcism' would be, in the eyes of at least some medical professionals, mentally ill, it is doubtful whether that person would be capable of giving informed consent under the law. The insistence of the 2012 guidelines that no one should be exorcised 'against their will' skirts the issue of informed consent. How is someone expected to express his or her opposition to being exorcised if one of the symptoms of demonic possession commonly recognised by demonologists is abhorrence of sacred things and words and hostility to the exorcist? Exorcists may even interpret hostility and reluctance as confirmation of demonic activity and, therefore, as evidence for the need for exorcism.

When the theology of possession is taken into consideration as well, it is clear that a possessed person is (by definition) without the capacity for consent; to require a possessed person's consent for a major exorcism is a theological nonsense, since he or she is not in control of his or her personality. Furthermore, a person manifesting the symptoms of possession (however those are interpreted) must surely be considered a vulnerable adult. Beatrice Brandon has noted that 'In deliverance ministry, greater awareness is emerging of ... the need to respect the individual's free will and responsibility for self', and she emphasises the importance of 'getting everyone's informed consent'.[35] Yet if, as Brandon believes, demonic possession is possible (and saying that it is extremely rare does not eliminate the problem), a demonically possessed person (or a person who believes him or herself to be demonically possessed) cannot give informed consent. On these grounds alone, it is puzzling that the Church of England is prepared to contemplate the possibility of major exorcism. The question is not so much whether exorcism is ever necessary or justified; the question the Church of England must confront is whether the very structural characteristics of exorcism mean that it has no place (even theoretically) in a church that takes seriously the safeguarding of children and vulnerable adults.

A Time to Heal takes pains to emphasise the importance of safeguarding in the ministry of deliverance, but fails to offer any reflection on the question of whether safeguarding requirements make exorcism practically impossible. The focus of the report's accompanying handbook is on protecting deliverance teams from accusations rather than protecting vulnerable individuals from spiritual abuse. Although the dangers and temptations of the ministry are noted, there is no evidence of reflection in the report on whether these dangers and temptations make the ministry too risky in the first place. A common response by demonologists and exorcists to concerns about the ethics of exorcism is to emphasise the reality of demonic phenomena, as if this somehow justifies a suspension of ethical norms and the depersonalisation of allegedly possessed persons. Yet debates about the reality of the devil and demons, the possibility of demonic possession and the literal 'efficacy' of exorcism in casting out demons are only tangentially relevant to the question of whether an exorcism should ever be performed.

It is perfectly possible to believe that the devil is real and active in the world, whilst at the same time believing that exorcism is an ethically unacceptable practice that violates norms of safeguarding by victimising the vulnerable, as well as exposing the church to unacceptable legal risks. Writers on exorcism and demonology, such as Graham Dow, often pass from arguments about the reality of a demonic realm to the necessity of the practice of exorcism without comment, as if it is obvious that the latter follows from the former. This transition from 'is' to 'ought' ('There really *is* a demonic realm, so the church *ought* to exorcise') not only assumes that none of the opponents of exorcism believe in the reality of spiritual evil; it also skips over historically significant debates within Protestant Christianity about the propriety of imperative exorcism and disregards ethical and safeguarding considerations. As Graham Smith observes, exorcists who draw a comparison between their experiences and the exorcisms of Jesus and the apostles described in the New Testament are adopting a particular analogical reading of the Bible, often without being conscious that they are doing so.[36]

None of the Church of England's literature on exorcism and deliverance ministry shows any sign of engagement with historical scholarship on exorcism, which is extensive and draws attention to the historic use of the rite to victimise marginalised people, especially women, children, indigenous people and ethnic minorities. Open theological discussion on the appropriateness of exorcism in the contemporary Church of England is hampered by the fact that knowledge of deliverance ministry is almost entirely confined to members of deliverance teams who are selected for their 'expertise', and are therefore committed to the continuance of their ministry in spite of the significant ethical and legal concerns associated with it.

The absence of any canon governing exorcism means that it is a matter under the discretion of diocesan bishops. This was not the intention of the church's 1958 report on exorcism, which envisaged a central advisory panel, but the church's failure to implement these recommendations meant that bishops took matters into their own hands – most notably Robert Mortimer of Exeter, by commissioning his own report. However, episcopal control of exorcism is not necessarily a guarantee of safety. Some bishops, such as Graham Dow, have held views on exorcism at odds with the church's official policy. Other bishops may not be sufficiently interested in the ministry to regulate it properly; in the 1970s, Robert Runcie chose to entrust the ministry of exorcism entirely to one individual and, owing to his embarrassment regarding the ministry, left his diocesan exorcist largely to his own devices.

Other bishops may appoint a priest as a diocesan advisor because he or she is particularly interested in the paranormal and occult. A number of twentieth-century diocesan exorcists, such as John Pearce-Higgins and Martin Israel, held profoundly eccentric views, and there is little evidence that an episcopal licence acted as any sort of brake on the behaviour of Donald Omand. Even more recent exorcists, such as Woolmer and Gardiner, have publicly dissented from official policy, and the writings of Anglican exorcists often give the impression that the ministry of exorcism was (and perhaps still is) as much an outlet for clergy fascinated by the paranormal and the occult as a pastoral response. Gardiner suggests that almost all the members of the CDSG believe themselves to possess psychic powers.

Even recent books by Anglican exorcists contain controversial claims that might be considered inappropriate, offensive and discriminatory. Gardiner claims to have exorcised 'a spirit of autism',[37] and attributed one man's psychic gifts to inherited influence from his Romany ancestry. Clearly, there is a danger of racism in associating inherited spiritual influences with specific ethnic identities. The taking of 'detailed case histories' in deliverance ministry may also turn into intrusive questioning about people's medical history; on one occasion Gardiner reports that he succeeded in making a woman admit to having an abortion.[38] Those Anglican exorcists who have written about their practice, such as Woolmer and Gardiner, are notable for their readiness to dissent from the Church of England's 'official' line rather than for their support for it. In one way this is hardly surprising; historically, exorcism has been a charismatic ministry based on ideas of spiritual discernment, and attempts to impose a particular shape on it by rules have only ever been partially successful.

The light touch of a church that prides itself on unity in diversity may become a cause for concern when no truly rigorous means exist of regulating a ministry that can so easily become spiritually abusive. Only if exorcism were governed by canon could clergy be formally disciplined for misusing it. A canon regulating exorcism would need to pass through General Synod, attracting considerable media attention, and this is probably the reason why the Church of England has avoided taking this path. The difficulty of defining exactly what counts as exorcism and deliverance may also have hindered a more rigorous approach; the 'ministry of deliverance' is such a broad term that it covers everything from counselling and pastoral prayer to full-blown imperative exorcism.

THE THOUGHT-WORLD OF THE EXORCIST

From the sixteenth century to the present day, the idea that exorcists are battling human agents working on behalf of the devil has served to legitimate and validate their work. In the twentieth and twenty-first centuries, those human agents are not imagined to be the solitary witches encountered in lonely places by sixteenth-century victims of possession;[39] rather, they are 'black magic groups', 'witches' covens' or 'Satanist groups' who supposedly collaborate with the forces of darkness. However, exorcists are only ever able to supply anecdotal evidence of the supposed spiritual harm caused by 'dabbling in the occult'; anecdotal evidence obtained, in the vast majority of cases, from those disturbed individuals who have approached the church for exorcism in the first place. Clearly, these individuals cannot be considered reliable sources, and a view of occultism constructed from the reports of those who believe themselves to be under harmful occult influence is unlikely to reflect the reality of the beliefs and practices of what the Church of England calls 'New Religious Movements' (NRMs).

It is clear from the writings and reported practices of contemporary exorcists in the Church of England that they often *expect* to find evidence of involvement in the occult when paranormal phenomena are reported, and question people with this expectation in mind. It is scarcely surprising that leading questioning of individuals often produces the stories of Satanic initiation that exorcists are expecting, especially if some of those individuals are mentally ill. One particularly persistent preoccupation of Christian demonologists is the existence of large, secretive and organised networks of Satanists.

This reflects the roots of modern demonology in sixteenth-century paranoia about imaginary devil-worshipping cults of witches, which were believed to be hierarchically organised as a satanic mirror-image of the church. Witchcraft was thus defined and represented as an 'inversion' of all that was good, right and wholesome.[40] In spite of presenting themselves as authorities on the subject of this (largely imaginative) world of sinister organised occultism, demonologists typically discourage further exploration of the subject by their readers. John Richards, for example, declared that his account of occultism was 'not written to encourage readers to study it more deeply, but rather to save them having to look elsewhere'.[41]

While exorcists and demonologists may sincerely believe that further study of the occult is dangerous, by discouraging it they ensure their readers are unlikely ever to encounter counterarguments to the demonisation of the religious and spiritual beliefs of NRMs. In this way, the 'myth of the occult' spun by demonologists is perpetuated indefinitely, and the thought-world of the exorcist becomes a closed system, supported by the testimony of alleged victims of occult involvement who, under leading questioning from the exorcist, confess their entanglement in the occult and therefore legitimate the reality of demonic agency and the need for exorcism. Any opposition to exorcism is further evidence of the reach of Satan's conspiracy – as John Richards clearly thought when he accused Geoffrey Lampe of being a Freemason. Exorcists and demonologists have a tendency to respond to scepticism with a barrage of anecdotal evidence from their own experience rather than replying in any substantive way to their critics. This is no accident, since exorcism is an inherently charismatic ministry where experience and intuition are much more significant than set rules of behaviour. Exorcists are unassailable specialists, since they alone have the knowledge from experience that justifies their practice. Alternatively, exorcists may accuse critics of holding an overly sensationalised view of exorcism, or of failing to understand what priests really do in deliverance ministry. Yet such responses fail to address legitimate concerns about the church's practice.

The 'intuitive' and 'experiential' approach of exorcists can open them up to ridicule when some of their claims and assumptions are more closely investigated. Perry recounts one case in which an exorcism was conducted to relieve a negative atmosphere in a church which, 'research revealed', was in the vicinity of 'numerous sites ... which could have been used for pagan and cult worship'. Parishioners concluded that the church was probably built on such a site too. The idea that most ancient churches were deliberately built on pre-existing pagan sacred sites was widely believed from the early twentieth century and became strongly associated with ley line hunters, but there is no convincing archaeological or historical evidence to support it.[42] Furthermore, virtually every rural church in England is close to some prehistoric landscape feature, but the belief that human sacrifice was practised at megalithic sites is an out-dated assumption largely unsupported by archaeological evidence; it is possible that the Neolithic and Bronze Age builders of megalithic monuments did not practise human sacrifice at all.[43] Perry reported that the strongest 'opposition' was felt when the exorcist approached an Anglo-Saxon cross which 'had pagan carvings and no suggestion of Christian symbolism' (apart from, presumably, the fact that it was cross-shaped).[44] It is not possible to claim that any Anglo-Saxon carving is 'pagan', since we do not know enough about pre-Christian Anglo-Saxon religion to reliably identify pagan themes, nor is there any evidence that pagan worship survived in England beyond the later decades of the seventh century (and most surviving Anglo-Saxon sculpture dates from a later period).

If exorcists and demonologists remain attached to a 'myth of the occult' based on shaky evidence, and perhaps informed by popular culture, they are equally committed to a controversial belief in the reality of paranormal phenomena. Paranormal explanations are important to exorcists because they provide a crucial way of 'explaining away' claimed phenomena that might otherwise be interpreted as demonic, without the need to dig deeper for naturalistic or psychological explanations. According to Beatrice Brandon, 'Deliverance ministry involves ... discerning what is paranormal, that is to say, beyond generally accepted and scientifically proven phenomena'.[45] This raises the question of why clergy, rather than scientists, are attempting to 'discern' phenomena not yet known to science. Furthermore, if paranormal phenomena are not 'generally accepted', it is unclear why the Church of England should accept them. Paranormal phenomena are not, by the exorcists' own admission, spiritual in nature. They do not therefore fall within the purview of exorcists, and it is not obvious why exorcists continue to claim expertise in 'discernment' of the paranormal. The entanglement of Anglican exorcists with parapsychology is especially problematic in light of the view taken by the majority of scientists that parapsychological claims are founded on pseudo-science.[46] For as long as deliverance teams continue to 'discern' supposed parapsychological phenomena such as telepathy and telekinesis, they endorse the reality of parapsychological claims and potentially bring the Church of England into disrepute as credulous, anti-scientific, or both.

EXORCISM: AN ANGLICAN TRADITION?

From the beginning, 'tradition' has been accorded some significance in the Church of England's self-understanding, so the existence or non-existence of a tradition of exorcism in the church's past matters a great deal to the future of the practice. In general terms, exorcism is without doubt part of the religious tradition of the western church as a whole, with a history of unbroken practice in Roman Catholicism. For Catholic-minded Anglicans, this fact alone may be enough to justify the practice of exorcism within a Church of England that they see as part of the one, holy, catholic and apostolic church. Similarly, Anglicans in the evangelical and charismatic traditions may have scant regard for tradition, regarding biblical precedents and the practice of other denominations as sufficient justification for exorcism. Other Anglicans may appeal to the practice of exorcism in other provinces of the Anglican Communion as evidence for the existence of a global Anglican tradition. However, this begs the question of whether the prominence of exorcism in the Anglican churches of the developing world has anything to do with the fact they are Anglican, or whether it is simply a result of the cultural context in which churches have developed.

Based on the evidence presented in this book, it is difficult to offer an unequivocal verdict on whether a tradition of exorcism exists in the Church of England. On the one hand, exorcism in the true, imperative sense was not practised by clergy of the established church in England after 1559, and even the 'dispossession' that replaced exorcism was effectively outlawed by canon in 1604. Virtually every clergyman and theologian of the Church of England between the 1600s and the 1970s would have rejected (and probably deplored) the kind of imperative exorcism authorised by the church today. On the other hand, there is evidence that some dispossessions took place after 1604. The ban on dispossessions was not total, and sporadic cases can be discovered in the historical record during the seventeenth, eighteenth and nineteenth centuries. Whether these are enough to claim that a 'tradition' existed, however, is questionable. Perhaps the one practice that can lay claim to some measure of continuity is the dispossession of haunted houses by clergy of the established church, although even here it can be difficult to disentangle folklore from reality. Milner has described exorcism as a 'dormant' practice in the Church of England until the 1960s,[47] but this is a somewhat laden term that implies exorcism was accorded some legitimacy before 1958, when the practice was first mentioned in an official document.

The practice of exorcism proper – that is to say, the imperative exorcism of persons believed to be under demonic influence – is a very recent innovation in the Church of England. Gilbert Shaw's 1943 exorcism at St Anne's, Soho, was probably the first formal exorcism performed in England since the exorcism of George Lukins in 1788. Exorcism was not mentioned in a church document until 1958 and did not become widely accepted as a normative practice until the 1970s. Furthermore, the Church of England's adoption of the practice was largely the result of the work of one man – Shaw himself. Rarely does the Church of England change its official attitude on a subject so quickly, with so little debate, and under the influence of such a tiny number of individuals. No debate in General Synod preceded or followed the introduction of Archbishop Coggan's 'guidelines' in 1975, because they were presented to Synod merely as advice from the House of Bishops. Anglican opponents of exorcism were forced to take to the press instead, to no avail.

The very recent recrudescence of exorcism and the unusual manner in which this ministry came to be adopted may give some

Anglicans pause for thought about its future. In a few decades the Church of England moved from extreme reticence regarding the rite of exorcism to Michael Perry's confident assertion that an exorcist should never depart a house without performing some rite as a form of psychological reassurance. Yet Geoffrey Lampe's objection that exorcism is 'at variance with the entire history and tradition of the Church of England' (at least after 1604) has yet to be answered satisfactorily by contemporary Anglican demonologists and others who advocate the continuing legitimacy and necessity of exorcism in the Church of England.

It is undeniable that there is a continuing demand for exorcism. If possession phenomena and exorcism are seen as anthropological constants which the church must negotiate in every age, then liturgical precedents are less important than finding the least satisfactory way to deal with popular belief in possession, fulfilling a pastoral need whilst simultaneously avoiding scandalising secular society. On this interpretation, the Church of England's mission to be 'a Christian presence in every community' may also include being present for those who believe themselves to be demonically possessed. If Anglicans opt for this line of defence of exorcism, then they must be prepared to admit that exorcism as practised in the contemporary Church of England is essentially a twentieth-century invention whose use the church must justify without recourse to spurious precedents.

It is surely no accident that exorcism emerged as a major ministry of the Church of England in the early 1970s, at the same period when the Roman Catholic church was retreating from this ministry, although it is unclear whether the Church of England was responding unwittingly to a demand no longer met by Roman Catholic priests or whether it was actively moving into a pastoral space vacated by Rome. While the Church of England has produced several documents on exorcism since World War II at national and diocesan level, as well as a considerable literature by practising Anglican exorcists, the Roman Catholic church in England and Wales has produced no documents on exorcism in the same period, no Roman Catholic diocese makes anything public about this ministry, and only one practising Roman Catholic exorcist in Britain has ever written anything on the subject.[48] Furthermore, in its revised rite of exorcism published in 1999, the Roman Catholic church withdrew from imperative exorcism, recommending deprecative forms.[49] This trend has not been followed by the Church of England, whose approach to exorcism is now more 'traditional' than that of the Roman Catholic church.

The Church of England's long-time stance of practical cessation-ism (at least officially) regarding miracles and demonic possession, adopted by some bishops as early as the 1580s, was significantly eroded in the twentieth century. During this period Anglo-Catholicism and charismatic evangelicalism both took their place within the broad comprehensiveness of the Church of England, and both strands of belief presume the continuance of miracles. On the other hand, the practical cessationism and suspicion of preternatural phenomena which in many ways differentiated committed adherents of England's established church from Roman Catholics and puritans in the sixteenth and seventeenth centuries still survive as an integral part of the Anglican tradition for many. Given the Church of England's historic stance, and the continued adherence of many Anglicans to this stance, it is problematic for bishops to expect clergy to accept the reality of any preternatural phenomenon or to approve of the practice of exorcism. No canon obliges any member of the clergy to engage in or facilitate an exorcism, but the existence of established procedures of referral within dioceses potentially puts clergy who might conscientiously object to any involvement in exorcism in a difficult position. Furthermore, the existence of deliverance ministry in every diocese could mean that opposition to any form of exorcism might be an obstacle to someone being chosen as a bishop.

Anglicans who do not share a belief in possession and exorcism are excluded, by definition, from participation in a ministry that might benefit from their sceptical insights and willingness to provide alternative interpretations. Perry acknowledged this, noting that doctors should be assured that 'although there is a wide variety of opinion among the clergy [on exorcism], there is in nearly every diocese a team of persons who have the expertise, who have been appointed to this ministry by the bishop, and who may be called upon for advice'.[50] Yet to assert that there is such a thing as 'expertise' in dealing with preternatural phenomena is to pre-judge the question of whether such phenomena are real. Since only clergy with 'expertise' will be appointed to diocesan deliverance teams, only clergy who believe implicitly in the reality of demonic and paranormal phenomena will be part of those teams, and clergy with different views will be side-lined as a matter of course.

CONCLUSION: EXORCISM PRESENT AND FUTURE

It is by no means obvious that clergy and others who reject the idea of exorcism or disbelieve in demonic possession have nothing to contribute to the ministry of deliverance. Deliverance teams could be trained to recognise potential natural causes for alleged paranormal phenomena, thereby providing much needed reassurance to anxious occupants of 'haunted houses'; they could also be trained to provide counselling for people troubled by 'paranormal' phenomena without in any way endorsing belief in the paranormal or demonic. 'Deliverance teams' can and do pray with and for people who believe themselves to be affected by 'paranormal' phenomena without committing themselves to the reality of those manifestations. However, while the Church of England continues to countenance the theoretical possibility of exorcism (however unlikely), 'deliverance teams' are liable to be perceived as exorcists by the public at large.

The most thorough recent attempt to explain the continuing significance of exorcism in the Church of England was research conducted in the first decade of the twenty-first century by psychologist Gerard Leavey. Leavey portrayed debates about demonic possession and exorcism in the Church of England as part of a wider confrontation between 'the liberal leadership of the Church of England' and 'increasingly muscular evangelicalism', strengthened by African Christianity with its 'entrenched dualistic beliefs on Satan, witchcraft, and possession'.[51] Leavey noted 'a widespread repugnance among mainstream Christians concerning the notion of the demonic', quoting one Anglican priest who declared 'I don't think it's an appropriate thing for me or any other Christian – in coming across someone who is mentally ill – to try to drive out the illness by addressing a sin'.[52] However, another priest described the services of deliverance teams as 'a back-up', suggesting that even generally sceptical clergy were reluctant to reject altogether the possibility that exorcism might be required.

One priest interviewed by Leavey admitted to the collusion that was inevitably involved in offering people 'the spooky magic' of exorcism rather than directing them towards a psychiatrist.[53] Other priests, such as the London clergyman whom Leavey called 'Reverend Rollins', were less ambivalent about exorcism. Rollins, who had been a trained psychiatrist before ordination, was not the only minister in his parish to be experienced in diagnostic demonology. He reported dealing personally with a woman who used blasphemous language and showed strength 'equivalent to six men', even though 'in the Church of England we have an official Exorcist to deal with difficult cases'.[54] Rollins emphasised the importance of 'taking a clinical history' of a person he suspected of being possessed, apparently with the aim of discovering some involvement with the occult.[55]

Leavey's analysis showed that, although Anglican priests tended to construe mental illness in terms of 'biopsychosocial determinants', they were also frequently reluctant to countenance 'the total elimination of the supernatural as an explanation for suffering'. Leavey observed 'a degree of cognitive strain' experienced by most clergy between their knowledge of science and medicine and their demonological beliefs, although even some medically-trained clergy were still prepared to accept unhesitatingly the need for exorcism. The group of clergy who displayed the greatest 'cognitive strain' were those 'who reject both any concrete linkage between sin and misfortune and also the reality of demonic intervention but feel compelled to validate the reality of positive spiritual forces'.[56] In other words, advocates of prayer and spiritual healing felt themselves compelled to accept the possibility of some sort of demonic influence to be prayed against or removed by healing.

Leavey noted that the Church of England's reports on exorcism 'strongly strain to show a degree of theological equipoise towards evangelical and liberal perspectives', and observed among clergy 'deep concern that medicine and psychiatry may fail to discern the demonic and may also obstruct legitimate religious intervention'.[57] Furthermore, Leavey thought that clergy could not reject supernatural belief out of hand because such beliefs were sometimes cherished by their congregations, especially in areas where 'western-trained, Enlightenment-inculcated priests preside over congregations containing people rooted in African culture'.[58] Ultimately, Leavey concluded that religion might provide an overarching interpretative 'canopy' under which both psychiatric and theological vocabulary could be included.[59]

Leavey's analysis sought to explain the continued acceptance of exorcism even by liberal clergy in the Church of England, for which he adduced four main factors: attachment to practices (such as spiritual healing) that seem to imply some need to engage with demonology; concern about psychiatry's refusal to recognise a spiritual dimension to mental health; a fear of offending cultural sensibilities within ethnically diverse congregations; and a desire for 'theological authenticity'.[60] In addition, Leavey argued that 'there remains a vestigial, often private and inchoate, acceptance and attachment to occult spirituality within seemingly secular societies'.[61] The 13 per cent of British people who claimed to believe in 'witchcraft' in a 2005 poll cannot simply be explained as those influenced by African spirituality,[62] and the emotional appeal of belief in witchcraft cannot be dismissed in purely functional terms.[63] A shortcoming of Leavey's analysis is his simplistic tendency to set 'liberal' and 'evangelical' Anglicanism in opposition to one another, neglecting the fact that it was the conservative Anglo-Catholicism of Gilbert Shaw and Max Petitpierre that actually played the most decisive role in the twentieth-century revival of exorcism.

If exorcism was not truly part of the Anglican tradition before the 1970s, it has certainly become so since then. The widespread (albeit sometimes reluctant) acceptance from all wings of the Church of England that exorcism forms part of the church's ministry is an indication that the ministry is no longer the preserve of a minority of clergy at the fringe. Anglican deliverance ministers have become part of modern English culture. Phil Rickman's crime-solving Anglican exorcist Merrily Watkins, a fictional deliverance advisor in the diocese of Hereford, is the subject of 14 novels and an ITV drama series.[64]

The Anglican priest and media personality Richard Coles, using the language of the *Harry Potter* books, describes diocesan deliverance advisors as 'C of E Aurors'.[65] However, the lack of any meaningful debate on the place of exorcism within the Church of England should be a cause for concern to Anglicans, especially in the light of a strong tradition of opposition to exorcism within historic Anglicanism. Should the Church of England still accommodate scepticism within its tradition, or should Anglicans be expected to reject opposition to imperative exorcism as outmoded and wrongheaded? The criticisms raised by opponents of exorcism in the Church of England in 1975 still remain largely unanswered, primarily because the church has circumvented extensive public debate on the issue by confining its instructions on exorcism to non-binding 'guidelines'.

Perhaps exorcism – a service that the Church of England is able to offer to anyone in the country – is one way in which the church is enabled to enact its relevance in wider society, reassuring itself of its continued importance. As Gardiner puts it, 'if the church, and particularly the established church of the land, is unwilling to offer help to those oppressed ... where can they go, other than to spiritists and witches?'[66] In other words, if the Church of England does not provide exorcism, someone else will – thereby further marginalising the church in the nation at large. It is unlikely that the Church of England, fearful of losing its privileged place in the life of the nation, will withdraw from the market for exorcism any time soon.

APPENDIX

Accessory Material for the *Book of Common Prayer* taken from the Danish Church (1711)

'Offices out of several Protestant Liturgies, &c. which are not in the Liturgy of the Church of England', in William Nicholls, *A Supplement to the Commentary on the Book of Common Prayer* (London, 1711), pp. 9–10

[Out of the Danish Ritual:] Of Possessed Persons, and those who are vexed by the Devil, or any of his wicked Spirits.

If the Minister be called to any one who is possessed or otherways vexed by the Devil, he must not deny his Assistance to them who send for him; but having prayed for him, as he is in ordinary Duty bound, he shall then set himself to enquire into the State and condition of the indisposed Person.

But if he shall not be called, and he credibly informed that there is such a Person among his Flock, he ought then to come of his own accord, accompanied, if he pleases, with his Co-adjutors, or some other pious Persons of the same Church.

But let him take care that he does not judge rashly in this Matter, or make Fault either in the Excess or the Defect: For tho' (God be thanked) Examples of this kind in this Age are very rare in the Christian World, since the Strong Man is overcome by the stronger than he, and the Lion of Judah has obtained Victory, and since the

Angel from Heaven, Christ Jesus, has trodden upon the great Serpent, shewing his Power over Satan, has *bound him in chains, that he should deceive the Nations no more*, Rev. XX. I. However, all things which are related of this kind among us, are not to be esteemed as Fables, Dreams, melancholy Illusions and Dotages of a disturbed Mind; neither must we think that we are now altogether free from the Insults of Satan, as if he had no Place among Christians; for he is not so tyed to the bottomless Pit, but that every day he still *walks about like a roaring Lion, seeking whom he may devour*, I Pet. v. 8. And why should he not at present walk among Christians, as well as he formerly did among the Ephesians and Philippians, where the Doctrine of Christ was taught as truly among us? *Acts* xvi. 16. and xix. 15. If he was present in Paradise, and did not spare the Inhabitants thereof in their unlapsed State, *Gen.* iii. 1, 13. If he was present in the holy Temple, and did not spare God's own, and only begotten Son, *Mat.* iv. 5. What Peace can we expect from him, whilst we continue in this militant State of the Church? And now, to our Grief, we find many Instances among Christians upon whom he exercises his Craft and Cruelty, both inwardly and outwardly, and those very pious and innocent Persons.

Neither must the Minister unwarily credit all the common People's Talk about these Matters: But being serious and grave, let him know how to distinguish what are the Works of the Devil, and not taking one thing for another, judge that Person to be possessed, who experiences only the outward Assaults of the Devil, or is reduced to that Condition by Poison or other evil Arts, or being under a natural Disease looks as if he were possessed; for there are several Diseases found which in all respects look like Possessions; as those of Lunaticks, Mad Men, Epilepticks and the like.

Therefore when a Minister visits a Person so afflicted, he ought first of all to consider the State and the Passions of the afflicted, accurately examining by what means his Affliction came upon him. Which when he has found out, he ought to give notice thereof to his Bishop, with all the Circumstances attending it; in the mean time being diligent in Prayer, using all his Endeavours to afford comfortable Advice to the afflicted Person, taking daily notice of what occurs, for his fuller Information concerning the Nature of his Distemper.

After this, let the Bishop assign certain Ministers in the Neighbourhood, who together with the Minister of the Place, may pray and read in their turns before the affected Person.

Let these several times meet, in the Presence of some Physicians, at the afflicted Person's, and consult among themselves whether it be a natural Disease or otherwise. If it be not Natural, whether it be a Diabolical Illusion, by which the Devil oftentimes blinds Men, and so perverts their Senses, that they oftentimes seem to see that with their Eyes, which are plainly nothing at all; whether he may truly be esteemed to be corporally possessed by the Devil, so that he has got the Mastery over his whole Body, and all its Members, Senses, Reason, and all the Faculties of his Soul; or only has gained Possession of one or two Members of his Body, and there chiefly exerts his Power, as he did over the dumb Man in the Gospel, *Luke* xi. 14.

If the affected Person by his own Crimes has brought this Judgment and Affliction upon himself, or having tied himself by any Pacts with the Devil, has voluntarily made himself a Slave to him, or by any other Wickedness, has given Occasion to the Devil to exercise his Tyranny over him, let the Minister admonish him out of the Word of God, how grievously he has offended therein against his Lord and God, shewing how great a Power the Devil has over those who despise God, *Job* i. 8. *Tob.* vi. 17. *Eph.* ii. 2. How ill he treats his Servants, and how miserable a Reward they must expect for their Service to him. Let him also admonish him, that he acknowledge his Sin for which he is so miserably vexed, offering to him yet in the Name of God, Pardon and Salvation, if from the Bottom of his Soul, he detest his wicked Manners, bidding adieu to Satan, and, tho' his Tongue be bound, he breathe out of his Breast fervent and devout Prayers, and at length with a true Faith fly to the infinite and precious Merits of his dear Saviour Jesus Christ, for whose sake, relying upon the Divine Mercy, he may, according to the Fatherly Will of God, expect a certain Deliverance from these snares of the Devil, that being disengag'd from these he may sing eternal and immortal Praises to God.

But if he be a pious Person, who having lived a godly and Christian Life, so that it can be objected by no one, that he has brought upon himself this great Affliction by his own Fault, as a Sign of the Divine

Anger, as a just Punishment for any horrid or Diabolical Wickedness; let the Minister, bringing Comforts out of the Word of God, shew him that God does for just Reasons permit even honest and pious Persons some short Time to be afflicted by the Devil, as *Paul*, 2 *Cor.* xii. and before him holy *Job*, chap. i.12 and ii.16. altho' God gave Testimony in his behalf, and said, *There is none like him in the Earth, a perfect and an upright man, one that feareth God and escheweth evil*; and in these things we must say with *David*, a Child of God, *Righteous is the Lord, and true are his judgements*, Psal. cxix.137. For *we know that all things work together for good to them that love God*, Rom. viii.28. He should exhort him, not to have that regard to Satan and his Instruments, to think that they have this Power from themselves, or that they can torment the Children of God at their Pleasure. No; but let him have regard to God alone, from whom both *good things* and *evil things* proceed, *Job* ii.10. *Deut.* xxviii.59. That *a hair of our head cannot fall without his pleasure*, Mat. x.30. And when he saith to Satan, *Behold he is in thy hand*, before that Time Satan does not dare to lay his Hand upon any pious Person, nor is he able to torment him any longer than God permits him, as the History of *Job* does clearly represent to us. Neither let the Sinner who is under this Tryal, think immediately that he is deserted by God and delivered over to the Tyranny of the Devil, because he suffers him to be exposed to the outward Insults of a wicked Spirit; but interpreting this Misfortune to be only God's Fatherly Correction he should return to himself, and cry out with the People of God in the Prophet, *I will bear the indignation of the Lord because I have sinned against him*, Mic. vii.9. Let him therefore consider and weigh in his Mind, that perhaps God would by this Tryal prove the constancy of his Faith, what Hope and Patience he has in him worthy of a Christian, whether God and Christ be of that account with him, that for his honour he can patiently bear the troubles of this World without dejection of Mind; but in all things like to constant *Job*, he can say with a strong and confirmed Mind, *Tho' God kill me I will yet trust in him*, Job xiii.15. Being conscious that God is merciful to him in the midst of his greatest Anguishes, and that *he will not suffer him to be tempted above what he is able*, I Cor. x.13. And that he will not allow Satan to have a Power over his Soul, but that he will find ways to preserve it to the

Day of our Lord Jesus. *For there is no condemnation to them that are in Christ Jesus*, Rom. viii.1. Neither can Satan, let him do what he can, be ever able to separate a Child of God *from that Love which is in Christ Jesus*, Rom. viii.39.

And if the Minister find the tempted Person thus disposed, *viz.* full of Love towards God, patient under the burden of his Cross, resolutely bent to oppose our common Enemy the Devil, and desirous to partake of the most holy Body and Blood of our Saviour Christ, let him deliver it to him in his most holy Name, in the Intervalls between the Devil's Temptations, and when he is judged to be in the best condition fitly to receive this holy Rite. At which time he shall briefly admonish him of the Vow which he has bound himself by in Baptism, to renounce the Devil and all his Works, to fight valiantly against his and God's sworn Enemy as a good Soldier of Christ, that holding a good Conscience to the end he may with joy see and feel the force of the Death of Christ, by which he has deprived the Devil of all Power against those who love and fear him.

Then the Minister shall conclude all with the Lord's Prayer, and the solemn Form of Blessing pronounced over the tempted Person, which he must always make use of when he departs from him.

Abbreviations

Almond, *Darling*   *The most wonderful and true story of a certain Witch named Alice Gooderige of Stapen Hill, who was arraigned and convicted at Derby at the Assizes there. As also a true report of the strange torments of Thomas Darling, a boy of thirteen years of age, that was possessed by the Devil* (London, 1597), reprinted in P. Almond (ed.), *Demonic Possession and Exorcism in Early Modern England* (Cambridge: Cambridge University Press, 2004), pp. 155–91

Almond, *Disclosing*   *The Disclosing of a late counterfeited Possession by the devil in two maidens within the City of London* (London, 1574), reprinted in Almond, P. (ed.), *Demonic Possession and Exorcism in Early Modern England* (Cambridge: Cambridge University Press, 2004), pp. 62–70

Almond, *Glover*   J. Swan, *A true and brief report, of Mary Glovers vexation, and of her deliverance by the means of fasting and prayer* (London, 1603), reprinted in P. Almond (ed.), *Demonic Possession and Exorcism in Early Modern England* (Cambridge: Cambridge University Press, 2004), pp. 291–330

Almond, *Lancashire*	G. More, *A true Discourse concerning the certain possession and dispossession of seven persons in one family in Lancashire* (London, 1600), reprinted in P. Almond (ed.), *Demonic Possession and Exorcism in Early Modern England* (Cambridge: Cambridge University Press, 2004), pp. 197–239
Almond, *Nyndge*	E. Nyndge, *A true and fearful vexation of one Alexander Nyndge* (London, 1615), reprinted in P. Almond (ed.), *Demonic Possession and Exorcism in Early Modern England* (Cambridge: Cambridge University Press, 2004), pp. 46–57
ATTH	B. Brandon and J. Gunstone (eds), *A Time to Heal: A Report for the House of Bishops on the Healing Ministry*, GS 1378 (London: Church House Publishing, 2000)
ATTH Handbook	B. Brandon and J. Gunstone (eds), *A Time to Heal: The Development of Good Practice in the Healing Ministry: A Handbook*, GS Misc 607 (London: Church House Publishing, 2000)
CCEd	Clergy of the Church of England database
CDSG/CESG	Christian Deliverance Study Group (before 1987 the Christian Exorcism Study Group)
CUL	Cambridge University Library, Cambridge
First and Second Prayer Books	*The First and Second Prayer Books of Edward VI*, ed. E. C. S. Gibson (London: J. M. Dent, 1910)
LPL	Lambeth Palace Library, London
ODNB	*The Oxford Dictionary of National Biography* (Oxford: Oxford University Press, 2004), 60 vols
Wesley, *Journal*	J. Wesley (ed. N. Curnock), *The Journal of the Rev. John Wesley, A.M.* (London: Charles H. Kelly, 1909–16), 8 vols

Notes

INTRODUCTION

1. For the most detailed discussion of the etymology of the word see A. Nicolotti, *Esorcismo Cristiano e Possessione Diabolica tra II e III Secolo* (Turnhout: Brepols, 2011), pp. 33–8.
2. For detailed discussions of exorcisms in the New Testament and early Christianity see E. Sorensen, *Possession and Exorcism in the New Testament and Early Christianity* (Tübingen: Mohr Siebeck, 2002); G. H. Twelftree, *In the Name of Jesus: Exorcism among the Early Christians* (Grand Rapids, MN: Baker Academic, 2007).
3. F. Young, *A History of Exorcism in Catholic Christianity* (London: Palgrave MacMillan, 2016a), pp. 30–8.
4. Ibid., pp. 40–4.
5. Ibid., p. 64.
6. On exorcism in medieval England see ibid., pp. 80–97.
7. For discussions of how to interpret demoniac behaviour see M. MacDonald, *Mystical Bedlam: Madness, Anxiety and Healing in Seventeenth-Century England* (Cambridge: Cambridge University Press, 1981), p. xl; B. P. Levack, *The Devil Within: Possession and Exorcism in the Christian West* (New Haven, CT: Yale University Press, 2013), pp. 29–31; M. Sluhovsky, *Believe Not Every Spirit: Possession, Mysticism and Discernment in Early Modern Catholicism* (Chicago, IL: University of Chicago Press, 2007), pp. 2–6.
8. See Nicolotti (2011), p. 31.
9. Recent historical treatments of exorcism include Sluhovsky (2007); Levack (2013); Young (2016a).
10. D. Hempton, *The Religion of the People: Methodism and Popular Religion c.1750–1900* (London: Routledge, 1996), pp. 23–34; P. Elmer, '"Saints or Sorcerers": Quakerism, Demonology and the Decline of Witchcraft in Seventeenth-Century England', in J. Barry, M. Hester and G. Roberts (eds), *Witchcraft in Early Modern Europe: Studies in Culture and Belief*

(Cambridge: Cambridge University Press, 1996), pp. 145–82; O. Davies, 'Methodism, the Clergy, and the Popular Belief in Witchcraft and Magic', *History* 82 (1997), pp. 252–65; F. Young, 'Catholic Exorcism in Early Modern England: Polemic, Propaganda and Folklore', *Recusant History* 29 (2009), pp. 487–507; F. Young, *English Catholics and the Supernatural, 1553–1829* (Farnham: Ashgate, 2013), pp. 189–230; F. Young, 'Bishop William Poynter and Exorcism in Regency England', *British Catholic History* 33 (2016b), pp. 278–97.

11. F. W. Brownlow, *Shakespeare, Harsnett and the Devils of Denham* (Newark, NJ: University of Delaware Press, 1993); T. S. Freeman, 'Demons, Deviance and Defiance: John Darrell and the Politics of Exorcism in late Elizabethan England', in P. Lake and M. Questier (eds), *Conformity and Orthodoxy in the English Church, c.1560–1660* (Woodbridge: Boydell, 2000), pp. 34–63; P. Almond (ed.), *Demonic Possession and Exorcism in Early Modern England* (Cambridge: Cambridge University Press, 2004); K. R. Sands, *Demon Possession in Elizabethan England* (Westport, CT: Praeger, 2004); M. Gibson, *Possession, Puritanism and Print: Darrell, Harsnett, Shakespeare and the Elizabethan Exorcism Controversy* (London: Pickering and Chatto, 2006); A. Cambers, 'Demonic Possession, Literacy and "Superstition" in Early Modern England', *Past and Present* 202 (2009), pp. 3–35; M. Harmes, 'The Devil and Bishops in Post-Reformation England', in M. Harmes and V. Bladen (eds), *Supernatural and Secular Power in Early Modern England* (Farnham: Ashgate, 2015), pp. 185–206.

12. See O. Davies, *Witchcraft, Magic and Culture 1736–1951* (Manchester: Manchester University Press, 1999); Davies (1997); O. Davies, *Popular Magic: Cunning Folk in English History*, 2nd edn (London: Continuum, 2007a); O. Davies, *The Haunted: A Social History of Ghosts* (London: Palgrave MacMillan, 2007b); J. Barry, *Witchcraft and Demonology in South-West England, 1640–1789* (London: Palgrave MacMillan, 2012).

13. T. Waters, 'Magic and the British Middle Classes, 1750–1900', *Journal of British Studies* 54 (2015b), pp. 632–53.

14. J. Oppenheim, *The Other World: Spiritualism and Psychical Research in England, 1850–1914* (Cambridge: Cambridge University Press, 1986); G. Byrne, *Modern Spiritualism and the Church of England, 1850–1939* (Woodbridge: Boydell and Brewer, 2010).

15. R. D. Hacking, *Such a Long Journey: A Biography of Gilbert Shaw, Priest* (London: Mowbray, 1988).

16. J. M. Collins, *Exorcism and Deliverance Ministry in the Twentieth Century: An Analysis of the Practice and Theology of Exorcism in Modern Western Christianity* (Bletchley: Paternoster, 2009).

17. G. R. Smith, *The Church Militant: Spiritual Warfare in the Anglican Charismatic Renewal* (Eugene, OR: Pickwick, 2016).

18. See N. Milner, 'Giving the Devil His Due Process: Exorcism in the Church of England', *Journal of Contemporary Religion* 15 (2000), pp. 247–72;

G. Leavey, 'The Appreciation of the Spiritual in Mental Illness: A Quantitative Study of Beliefs Among Clergy in the UK', *Transcultural Psychiatry* 47 (2010), pp. 571–90.

CHAPTER 1   THE CHURCH OF ENGLAND AND THE REFORMATION OF EXORCISM, 1549–1603

1. Freeman (2000), p. 43.
2. K. Thomas, *Religion and the Decline of Magic: Studies in Popular Beliefs in Sixteenth- and Seventeenth-Century England*, 4th edn (London: Penguin, 1991), p. 574.
3. G. Parry, *The Arch-Conjurer of England: John Dee* (New Haven, CT: Yale University Press, 2011), p. 257 inaccurately describes John Darrell as a 'Presbyterian minister'.
4. Freeman (2000), p. 38.
5. For a recent discussion of difficulties associated with defining 'puritanism' see R. J. Pederson, *Unity in Diversity: English Puritans and the Puritan Reformation, 1603–1689* (Leiden: Brill, 2014), pp. 284–309.
6. See R. Poole (ed.), *The Lancashire Witches: Histories and Stories* (Manchester: Manchester University Press, 2002), p. 66.
7. P. Elmer, *Witchcraft, Witch-Hunting and Politics in Early Modern England* (Oxford: Oxford University Press, 2016), p. 34.
8. Harmes (2015), pp. 192–3.
9. N. Johnstone, *The Devil and Demonism in Early Modern England* (Cambridge: Cambridge University Press, 2006), pp. 102–3.
10. Ibid., p. 104.
11. See Young (2016a), pp. 80–97.
12. A. Goddu, 'The Failure of Exorcism in the Middle Ages', in A. Zimmerman (ed.), *Soziale Ordnungen im Selbstverständnis des Mittelalters*, Miscellanea Mediaevalia 12/2 (Berlin: Walter de Gruyter, 1980), pp. 540–57; Young (2016a), pp. 62–3.
13. Young (2016a), pp. 88, 94–5.
14. D. Oldridge, *The Devil in Tudor and Stuart England*, 2nd edn (Stroud: History Press, 2010), pp. 33–5.
15. Young (2016a), p. 96.
16. Ibid., p. 90.
17. Ibid., pp. 91–2.
18. Ibid., pp. 92–3.
19. Ibid., p. 95n.
20. O. Williams, 'Exorcising Madness in Late Elizabethan England: "The Seduction of Arthington" and the Criminal Culpability of Demoniacs', *Journal of British Studies* 47 (2008), pp. 30–52, at p. 43.
21. Young (2016a), p. 90. On exorcism of revenants see also N. M. Caciola, *Afterlives: The Return of the Dead in the Middle Ages* (Ithaca and London: Cornell University Press, 2016), p. 327.

22. P. Marshall, *Beliefs and the Dead in Early Modern England* (Oxford: Oxford University Press, 2002), p. 234.
23. Oldridge (2010), p. 157.
24. Young (2013), pp. 203–9.
25. See ibid., pp. 197–201.
26. Ibid., pp. 18, 146.
27. E. Duffy, *The Stripping of the Altars: Traditional Religion in England, 1400–1580* (New Haven, CT: Yale University Press, 1992), p. 473.
28. *First and Second Prayer Books*, p. 238.
29. Ibid., p. 327.
30. Ibid., p. 241.
31. D. R. Holeton, 'Initiation', in S. Sykes, J. Booty and J. Knight (eds), *The Study of Anglicanism*, 2nd edn (London: SPCK, 1998), pp. 293–307, at pp. 294–6.
32. Johnstone (2006), p. 61.
33. Ibid., p. 60.
34. Ibid., pp. 64–5.
35. Ibid., p. 66.
36. Holeton (1998), p. 296.
37. *First and Second Prayer Books*, pp. 397–8.
38. Ibid., p. 398.
39. Duffy (1992), p. 473.
40. Johnstone (2006), pp. 64–5.
41. Oldridge (2010), p. 150.
42. Thomas (1991), pp. 40–1.
43. Young (2016a), pp. 89–90.
44. Ibid., pp. 31–2.
45. Ibid., p. 37.
46. Thomas (1991), p. 571.
47. Ibid., p. 62.
48. Ibid., p. 582.
49. Levack (2013), pp. 68–70.
50. E. Cameron, *Enchanted Europe: Superstition, Reason, and Religion, 1250–1750* (Oxford: Oxford University Press, 2010), pp. 205–8.
51. Ibid., p. 207.
52. Oldridge (2010), p. 138.
53. J. Jewel (ed. J. Ayre), *The Works of John Jewel* (Cambridge: Parker Society, 1848), vol. 3, pp. 273–4.
54. Ibid., vol. 1, p. 328.
55. J. F[isher], *The Copy of a Letter Describing the Wonderful Woorke of God in Delivering a Mayden within the City of Chester* (London, 1565), unpaginated.
56. Thomas (1991), p. 575n.
57. CCEd 31115 (Lane); 31543 (Rogers), accessed 28 February 2017.
58. R. Scot, *The Discovery of Witchcraft*, 2nd edn (London, 1665), p. 74.
59. Almond, *Nyndge*, p. 50.
60. Ibid., p. 51.

61. Ibid., pp. 51–2.
62. Ibid., pp. 55–6.
63. Ibid., p. 51.
64. On the Nyndge case see Almond (2004), pp. 43–5; Cambers (2009), pp. 3–35.
65. Thomas (1991), pp. 574–5; T. S. Freeman, 'Foxe, John', in *ODNB*, vol. 20, pp. 695–709, at p. 704.
66. Almond, *Disclosing*, p. 68.
67. Ibid., p. 65.
68. Ibid.
69. Ibid., p. 63.
70. Freeman, 'Foxe', in *ODNB*, vol. 20, p. 704.
71. Almond, *Disclosing*, pp. 66–7.
72. Young (2013), p. 153.
73. Young (2016a), pp. 68–9.
74. Scot (1665), pp. 71–3. On the puritan context of the Westwell exorcism see Elmer (2016), p. 21.
75. Freeman (2000), p. 39.
76. H. Robinson (ed.), *The Zurich Letters* (Cambridge: Parker Society, 1842–45), vol. 1, p. 303.
77. On Norwich's stranger community see F. Williamson, *Social Relations and Urban Space: Norwich, 1600–1700* (Woodbridge: Boydell, 2014), pp. 93–124.
78. G. R. Elton, *Policy and Police: The Enforcement of the Reformation in the Age of Thomas Cromwell* (Cambridge: Cambridge University Press, 1972), pp. 57–8.
79. P. Collinson, *From Cranmer to Sancroft* (London: Continuum, 2006), p. 151.
80. Ibid.
81. Parry (2011), pp. 209–10.
82. F. Young, *Magic as a Political Crime in Medieval and Early Modern England: A History of Sorcery and Treason* (London: I.B.Tauris, 2017), pp. 124–9.
83. R. J. Roberts and A. G. Watson (eds), *John Dee's Library Catalogue* (London: Bibliographical Society, 1990), D14.
84. Young (2013), p. 39.
85. Ibid., p. 160.
86. On Dee's involvement in the Lancashire exorcisms see S. Bowd, 'John Dee and the Seven in Lancashire: Possession, Exorcism, and Apocalypse in Elizabethan England', *Northern History* 47 (2010), 233–46.
87. J. Dee (ed. E. Fenton), *The Diaries of John Dee* (London: Day Books, 1998), p. 249.
88. *First and Second Prayer Books*, pp. 264–5.
89. Ibid., pp. 249–50.
90. Ibid., p. 250.
91. Almond (2004), p. 192.
92. Parry (2011), pp. 212–13 notes that a coroner's report on Frank's death would have revealed Dee's exorcism and angered Archbishop Whitgift, but this is speculation.

93. Ibid., p. 264.
94. S. Harsnett, *A Discouery of the Fraudulent Practises of Iohn Darrel* (London, 1599), p. 226.
95. T. S. Freeman, 'Darrell, John', in *ODNB*, vol. 15, pp. 166–7.
96. Almond, *Darling*, pp. 159–60.
97. Ibid., p. 177.
98. Ibid., p. 183.
99. On the demoniac as the primary agent of exorcism see Johnstone (2006), pp. 103–4.
100. Almond, *Darling*, pp. 187–91.
101. Almond (2004), pp. 192–3.
102. Parry (2011), p. 259.
103. Ibid., p. 261.
104. Ibid., pp. 261–2.
105. Almond, *Lancashire*, p. 233.
106. Ibid., pp. 218–20.
107. Ibid., p. 217.
108. D. Frankfurter, 'Where the Spirits Dwell: Possession, Christianization and Saints' Shrines in Late Antiquity', *Harvard Theological Review* 103 (2010), pp. 27–46, at p. 41.
109. Almond, *Sommers*, p. 268.
110. Oldridge (2010), p. 157.
111. Almond (2004), pp. 240–1.
112. Almond, *Sommers*, pp. 247–8.
113. Freeman, 'Darrell', in *ODNB*, vol. 15, p. 167.
114. Almond (2004), p. 287. For detailed studies of the controversial literature produced by the late Elizabethan exorcism controversy see Brownlow (1993); Gibson (2006).
115. Freeman (2000), p. 60n.
116. W. Hinde, *A Faithfull Remonstrance of the Holy Life and Happy Death of Iohn Bruen of Bruen-Stapleford, in the County of Chester, Esquire* (London, 1641), p. 151.
117. Ibid., p. 152.
118. Harmes (2015), p. 202.
119. Sands (2004), p. 195.
120. Elmer (2016), pp. 46–7.
121. Almond (2004), p. 287.
122. Ibid., p. 17.
123. Ibid., pp. 288–9.
124. Ibid., pp. 292–5.
125. Freeman (2000), p. 59.
126. On James's evolving views on witchcraft and possession see P. G. Maxwell-Stuart, 'King James's Experience of Witches, and the English Witchcraft Act of 1604', in J. Newton and J. Bath (eds), *Witchcraft and the Act of 1604* (Leiden: Brill, 2008), pp. 31–46, at pp. 42–4; P. G. Maxwell-

Stuart, *The British Witch: The Biography* (Stroud: Amberley, 2014), p. 198; Harmes (2015), p. 194.
127. Almond, *Glover*, p. 324.
128. Ibid., pp. 323–4.
129. Harmes (2015), p. 189.
130. Freeman (2000), pp. 57–8.
131. Ibid., p. 58.
132. Almond, *Glover*, pp. 321–2.
133. Harmes (2015), pp. 197–8.
134. Collinson (2006), p. 165.
135. Ibid., p. 137.
136. Almond, *Glover*, p. 330.
137. Almond (2004), p. 290.
138. Almond, *Lancashire*, p. 199.
139. Almond, *Glover*, p. 305.
140. Ibid., p. 313.
141. Oldridge (2010), p. 138.
142. Freeman (2000), p. 43.
143. Ibid., p. 38.
144. Young (2016a), p. 5.
145. Ibid., pp. 116–20 (on the 1614 liturgy), 162–5 (on the suppression of other liturgies).
146. Oldridge (2010), pp. 157–8.
147. Young (2016a), p. 6.
148. Harmes (2015), p. 204.
149. Ibid., p. 205.
150. Freeman (2000), p. 63.
151. Ibid., p. 55.
152. Ibid., p. 54.
153. Johnstone (2006), p. 106.

CHAPTER 2   EXORCISM MARGINALISED, 1604–1852

1. Davies (1999), p. 27.
2. Ibid., p. 28.
3. Davies (2001), p. 109.
4. N. W. S. Cranfield, 'Bancroft, Richard', in *ODNB*, vol. 3, pp. 647–55, at p. 652.
5. On earlier attempts at revision see P. Ayris, 'Canon Law Studies', in P. Ayris and D. Selwyn (eds), *Thomas Cranmer: Churchman and Scholar* (Woodbridge: Boydell, 1993), pp. 316–24.
6. Quoted in M. MacDonald (ed.), *Witchcraft and Hysteria in Elizabethan London: Edward Jorden and the Mary Glover Case* (London: Routledge, 1991), p. li.
7. Freeman (2000), p. 60.

8. G. L. Bray, *The Anglican Canons, 1529–1947* (Woodbridge: Boydell, 1998), pp. 362–5.
9. See A.-F. Morel, 'Church Consecration in England 1549–1715: An Unestablished Ceremony', in M. Delbeke and M. Schraven (eds), *Foundation, Dedication and Consecration in Early Modern Europe* (Leiden: Brill, 2012), pp. 297–314.
10. Harmes (2015), p. 187.
11. M. Hill, *Ecclesiastical Law*, 3rd edn (Oxford: Oxford University Press, 2007), p. 10.
12. Collinson (2006), p. 151.
13. Freeman (2000), p. 43.
14. J. Sharpe, *The Bewitching of Anne Gunter: A Horrible and True Story of Deception, Witchcraft, Murder, and the King of England* (London: Routledge, 2000), p. xii.
15. Thomas (1991), p. 579.
16. Freeman (2000), p. 62.
17. J. Hall (ed. J. Pratt), *The Works of the Right Reverend Father in God Joseph Hall, D.D.* (London, 1808), vol. 1, p. xxix.
18. Davies (2007a), p. 172.
19. Ibid., p. 36.
20. M. MacDonald, *Mystical Bedlam: Madness, Anxiety and Healing in Seventeenth-Century England* (Cambridge: Cambridge University Press, 1981), p. 216.
21. Young (2013), pp. 204–6.
22. For example, the puritan vicar of West Ham, Robert Jennings, attempted the unlicensed exorcism of a young woman in 1621 (Elmer (2016), p. 39).
23. MacDonald (1981), p. 9. On Nonconformist exorcisms and exorcisms during the Interregnum see Thomas (1991), pp. 580–1.
24. J. Hall (ed. P. Wynter), *The Works of the Right Reverend Joseph Hall, D.D.* (Oxford: Oxford University Press, 1863), vol. 7, p. 326.
25. Ibid., p. 328.
26. Ibid., pp. 328–9.
27. [R. Baddeley], *The Boy of Bilson: Or, a True Discovery of the Late Notorious Impostures of Certain Romish Priests in their Pretended Exorcism* (London, 1622), reprinted in Almond (2004), pp. 334–57, at pp. 346–7.
28. *The Most Strange and Admirable Discovery of the Witches of Warboys* (London, 1593) reprinted in Almond (2004), pp. 75–149, at pp. 122–3.
29. Thomas (1991), p. 580n.
30. J. Andrews, 'Napier, Richard', in *ODNB*, vol. 40, pp. 181–3.
31. Quoted in MacDonald (1981), p. 215.
32. Ibid.
33. Napier met Dee in July 1604 (Parry (2011), p. 267).
34. Davies (2007a), pp. 79–80.
35. J. Blagrave, *Blagraves Astrological Practice of Physick* (London, 1671), p. 169. According to a variant version of Blagrave's account, *The Evil Spirit Cast-Out* (London, 1691), p. 4: 'I councelled her Father to go to some Pious Divine, to make an Essay in the matter, and to see what his Devotion could do, he

answer'd me, That he had done it already, but to no purpose; for one Doctor – – – – the Minister of the Parish, a Learned, Judicious, and Pious Man, had spent some time in attempting to do it, yet could not prevail, but was forced to desist, and advised their seeking Remedy of some body else, whom God might give Strength and Faith to perform so great a Work'.

36. CCEd 96691, accessed 27 March 2017.
37. Cameron (2010), pp. 258–60.
38. Ibid., p. 276.
39. R. Clarke, *A Natural History of Ghosts: 500 Years of Hunting for Proof*, 2nd edn (London: Penguin, 2013), p. 29.
40. J. Glanvill, *Saducismus triumphatus* (London, 1681), pp. 28–9.
41. Ibid., p. 83.
42. Barry (2012), p. 115.
43. Quoted in ibid., p. 114.
44. T. J[ollie], *A Vindication of the Surey Demoniack* (London, 1698), pp. 25–6.
45. Ibid., p. 26.
46. J. Taylor (ed. R. Heber and C. P. Eden), *The Whole Works of the Right Rev. Jeremy Taylor, D.D.* (London: Longman, Brown, Green and Longmans, 1852), vol. 6, p. 266.
47. Waters (2015b), pp. 637–8.
48. Ibid., p. 647.
49. T. Brown, *The Fate of the Dead: A Study of Folk Eschatology in the West Country after the Reformation* (London: Folklore Society, 1979), p. 48.
50. Ibid., pp. 18–19.
51. Davies (2007b), p. 75.
52. Brown (1979), p. 49.
53. Ibid., p. 50.
54. Ibid., pp. 55–7.
55. Ibid., pp. 57–8.
56. Ibid., p. 58.
57. Ibid., p. 59.
58. Ibid., p. 61.
59. Ibid., p. 60.
60. For an example see E. M. Leather, *The Folk-lore of Herefordshire* (Hereford: Jakeman and Carver, 1912), pp. 29–31.
61. Davies (2007b), p. 75.
62. Ibid., p. 76.
63. Ibid.
64. Ibid., p. 75.
65. Brown (1979), p. 62.
66. J. Westwood and J. Simpson, *The Lore of the Land: A Guide to England's Legends, from Spring-Heeled Jack to the Witches of Warboys* (London: Penguin, 2005), p. 398.
67. Ibid., p. 399.
68. Davies (2007b), p. 77.

69. Ibid., p. 79.

70. Ibid., pp. 76–7.

71. Ibid., p. 74.

72. Brown (1979), p. 49.

73. J. Venn, *Biographical History of Gonville and Caius College 1349–1897* (Cambridge: Cambridge University Press, 1897), vol. 1, pp. 390–1.

74. Ibid., p. 21.

75. Ibid., pp. 20–1. For the elaboration of the legend see C. Hole, *English Folklore* (London: Batsford, 1940), pp. 162–4.

76. H. Bourne, *Antiquitates vulgares* (Newcastle, 1725), pp. 91–112. On Polidori see Sluhovsky (2007), pp. 85–6.

77. Bourne (1725), p. 90.

78. Ibid., p. 114.

79. P. K. Monod, *Solomon's Secret Arts: The Occult in the Age of Enlightenment* (New Haven, CT: Yale University Press, 2013), p. 191.

80. Davies (2007a), p. 77.

81. J. F. Chanter, 'Parson Joe and his Book', *Devon and Cornwall Notes and Queries* 8 (1914–15), pp. 87–8.

82. Brown (1979), pp. 51–2.

83. Davies (2007b), p. 81.

84. Ibid., p. 82.

85. Ibid.

86. Davies (2001), p. 108.

87. On this dispute see R. Davies, *Bishop Nathaniel Spinckes and the Non-Juring Church* (London: Royal Stuart Society, 2007), pp. 16–20.

88. Ibid., p. 18.

89. T. Deacon, *A Compleat Collection of Devotions* (London, 1734), vol. 1, p. 158.

90. T. Deacon, *A Full, True and Comprehensive View of Christianity* (London, 1748), p. 227.

91. Ibid., p. 68.

92. Ibid., p. 70. Exorcism was also mentioned in the lesson on the sign of the cross, p. 87.

93. Ibid., p. 71.

94. Deacon (1734), vol. 1, pp. 86–7.

95. Ibid., pp. 87–8.

96. Ibid., p. 228.

97. W. Nicholls, *A Supplement to the Commentary on the Book of Common Prayer* (London, 1711), title page.

98. Ibid., p. 9. The complete text is reproduced as an appendix to this book.

99. Ibid., p. 10. The text of 'the solemn Form of Blessing' is not given by Nicholls.

100. Davies (1999), p. 2.

101. R. Porter, 'Witchcraft and Magic in Enlightenment, Romantic and Liberal Thought', in M. Gijswit-Hofstra and R. Porter (eds), *Witchcraft and Magic in Europe: The Eighteenth and Nineteenth Centuries* (London: Athlone Press, 1999), pp. 191–254, at p. 210.

102. Barry (2012), p. 165.
103. G. Hammond, *John Wesley in America: Restoring Primitive Christianity* (Oxford: Oxford University Press, 2014), pp. 38–9.
104. Ibid., p. 71n.
105. J. Telford, *The Life of the Rev. Charles Wesley, M.A.* (London: Methodist Book Room, 1900), p. 104.
106. Wesley, *Journal*, vol. 5, p. 32.
107. CCEd 166218, accessed 3 April 2017.
108. Wesley, *Journal*, vol. 5, p. 33.
109. Ibid.
110. Ibid., p. 34.
111. Ibid., p. 35.
112. R. Webster, '"Did God Do That?"': Common and Separating Factors of Eighteenth-Century Methodism and Contemporary Pentecostal and Charismatic Renewal', in R. Webster (ed.), *Perfecting Perfection: Essays in Honour of Henry D. Rack* (Cambridge: James Clarke and Co., 2016), pp. 208–32, at p. 219.
113. Barry (2012), p. 223.
114. Ibid., p. 166.
115. Monod (2013), p. 307.
116. S. Mandelbrote, 'Hutchinson, John', in *ODNB*, vol. 29, pp. 14–15.
117. W. Jones, *A Course of Lectures on the Figurative Language of the Holy Scripture* (London: SPCK, 1864), pp. 226–7.
118. Barry (2012), p. 184.
119. Ibid., p. 188.
120. Ibid., p. 177.
121. Ibid., pp. 236–7.
122. Ibid., p. 208.
123. Ibid., p. 209.
124. J. Easterbrook, *An Appeal to the Public Respecting George Lukins* (Bristol, 1788), p. 7.
125. Ibid., p. 14.
126. Ibid., p. 16.
127. Ibid., p. 17.
128. Barry (2012), pp. 210–11.
129. Ibid., p. 236.
130. Ibid., p. 239.
131. Ibid., p. 241.
132. Ibid., p. 242.
133. Davies (2001), p. 107.
134. C. H. Davis (ed.), *The English Church Canons of 1604* (London: H. Sweet, 1869), p. 72.
135. Barry (2012), p. 253.
136. Davies (1999), p. 27.

CHAPTER 3 SPIRITUALISM AND THE RETURN OF EXORCISM, 1852–1939

1. J. Oppenheim, *The Other World: Spiritualism and Psychical Research in England, 1850–1914* (Cambridge: Cambridge University Press, 1986), p. 68.
2. Young (2016a), pp. 203–6.
3. The so-called 'Confederation Riots' of April 1876 in response to a British proposal to unite Barbados and the Windward Isles.
4. John Mitchinson to Archibald Campbell Tait, 10 September 1877, LPL MS Tait 234, fols 83r–v.
5. Ibid., fol. 83v.
6. See Young (2016a), pp. 172–4.
7. Archibald Campbell Tait to John Mitchinson, 1 October 1877, LPL MS Tait 234, fols 84r–85r.
8. Hill (2007), p. 10.
9. G. Byrne, *Modern Spiritualism and the Church of England, 1850–1939* (Woodbridge: Boydell and Brewer, 2010), p. 157.
10. A. Hastings, *A History of English Christianity, 1920–2000*, 4th edn (London: SCM Press, 2001), p. 68.
11. Byrne (2010), p. 145.
12. Waters (2015b), p. 644.
13. Byrne (2010), p. 150.
14. Ibid., On Raupert, who later converted to Roman Catholicism, see Young (2016a), p. 205.
15. Oppenheim (1985), p. 409n.
16. 'E. W. Barnes on "Evil Spirits"', *Church Times*, 2 March 1917 (reprinted in *Church Times*, 3 March 2017, p. 14).
17. On Davies's career see Byrne (2010), pp. 165–9.
18. Charles Maurice Davies to Archibald Campbell Tait, undated [1881], LPL MS Tait 270, fol. 15r.
19. Ibid., fol. 10r.
20. Ibid., fol. 17r.
21. Byrne (2010), pp. 50–1.
22. W. T. Stead to Edward White Benson, 15 June 1893, LPL MS Benson 116, fol. 235r.
23. D. M. Image to Edward White Benson, 24 June 1893, LPL MS Benson 116, fols 236r–37r.
24. D. M. Image to Edward White Benson, 28 June 1893, LPL MS Benson 116, fols 238r–39v.
25. Randall Davidson to Edward White Benson, 29 June 1893, LPL MS Benson 116, fols 240r–41r.
26. 'The Response to the Appeal. From Prelates, Pundits and Persons of Distinction', *Borderland* 1 (July 1893), pp. 10–11.
27. Byrne (2010), pp. 144–5.

28. Quoted in ibid., p. 147.
29. Charles Bousfield Hulleatt to Frederick Temple, 22 May 1902, LPL MS F. Temple 54, fols 179v–180v.
30. Ibid., fols 181r–v.
31. Ibid., fol. 190r.
32. Ibid., fols 182v–183v.
33. Ibid., fol. 184r.
34. Ibid., fols 184r–v.
35. Ibid., fols 187v–188r.
36. Ibid., fol. 185v.
37. Ibid., fol. 186r.
38. Ibid., fols 181v–182r.
39. Ibid., fols 179r–v, 186r–v.
40. Ibid., fol. 182r.
41. R. C. Trench, *Notes on the Miracles of Our Lord* (London: John W. Parker, 1846), p. 167.
42. R. C. Trench, *Notes on the Miracles of Our Lord*, 5th edn (London: John W. Parker, 1856), p. 161.
43. Ibid., p. 64.
44. Ibid., p. 65.
45. On witchcraft belief in the nineteenth century and beyond see Davies (1999); W. De Blécourt, 'The witch, her victim, the unwitcher and the researcher: the continued existence of traditional witchcraft', in W. de Blécourt, R. Hutton and J. de la Fontaine (eds), *Witchcraft and Magic in Europe: The Twentieth Century* (London: Athlone Press, 1999), pp. 141–219; O. Davies, 'Magic in Common and Legal Perspectives', in D. J. Collins (ed.), *The Cambridge History of Magic and Witchcraft in the West: From Antiquity to the Present* (Cambridge: Cambridge University Press, 2015), pp. 521–46.
46. Charles Bousfield Hulleatt to Frederick Temple, 22 May 1902, LPL MS F. Temple 54, fol. 185v.
47. Frederick Temple to Charles Bousfield Hulleatt, 27 May 1902, LPL MS F. Temple 54, fol. 191r.
48. Byrne (2010), p. 151.
49. Ibid., pp. 149–50.
50. Ibid., pp. 151–3.
51. K. Gardiner, *The Reluctant Exorcist: A Biblical Approach in an Age of Scepticism*, 2nd edn (Watford: Instant Apostle, 2015), p. 63.
52. R. Petitpierre, *Exorcising Devils* (London: Hale, 1976), pp. 115–25.
53. Byrne (2010), p. 156.
54. Petitpierre (1976), pp. 123–4.
55. Byrne (2010), p. 163.
56. Ibid., p. 178.
57. Ibid., p. 180.
58. Ibid., pp. 163–4.

59. One of the signatories, Archibald Webling, rector of Risby, Suffolk, was made an honorary canon of St Edmundsbury Cathedral in spite of publishing a book that explicitly denied the Christian doctrine of the afterlife (See A. Webling, *The Two Brothers* (Leicester: Edmund Ward, 1948), pp. 213–21).

60. Byrne (2010), p. 181.

61. Oppenheim (1985), p. 69.

62. Byrne (2010), pp. 190–220.

63. G. R. Smith, *The Church Militant: Spiritual Warfare in the Anglican Charismatic Renewal* (Eugene, OR: Pickwick, 2016), p. 28.

64. J. Robinson, *Divine Healing: The Holiness-Pentecostal Transition Years, 1890–1906* (Eugene, OR: Pickwick, 2013), pp. 106–7.

65. Smith (2016), pp. 29–30.

66. Quoted in J. Robinson, *Divine Healing: The Years of Expansion, 1906–1930* (Eugene, OR: Pickwick, 2014), p. 88.

67. On Bethshan see C. W. Nienkirchen, *A. B. Simpson and the Pentecostal Movement: A Study in Continuity, Crisis, and Change* (Eugene, OR: Wipf and Stock, 2010), pp. 15–19; Robinson (2013), pp. 166–82.

68. C. Williams, *The Treatment of Insanity by Exorcism* (London: Ambrose, 1908), p. 6.

69. Robinson (2014), pp. 85–6.

70. Ibid., p. 87.

71. Ibid., p. 86.

72. Quoted in ibid.

73. Ibid., pp. 87–8.

74. R. M. Woolley, *Exorcism and the Healing of the Sick* (London: SPCK, 1932), p. vii.

75. Ibid., pp. 7–8.

76. Ibid., p. 8.

77. Ibid., p. 68.

78. 'I exorcise you, creature of oil …'

79. On Dorothy Kerin's ministry see Robinson (2014), pp. 92–6.

80. Petitpierre (1976), pp. 19–22.

81. Archbishop Lang.

82. Philip Worsley to Alan Campbell Don, 15 May 1937, LPL MS Lang 156, fols 272r–v.

83. Alan Campbell Don to Philip Worsley, 24 May 1937, LPL MS Lang 156, fols 273–4.

84. Philip Worsley to Alan Campbell Don, 15 May 1937, LPL MS Lang 156, fol. 275.

85. Hacking (1988), pp. 14–15.

86. Ibid., p. 19.

87. Ibid., p. 23.

88. Petitpierre (1976), p. 12.

89. Ibid., pp. 147–8.

90. Hacking (1988), pp. 24–5.
91. Ibid., p. 27.
92. Ibid., pp. 12–13.
93. 'Appendix: The Exorcism of Haunted Houses', in H. Thurston (ed. J. H. Crehan), *Ghosts and Poltergeists* (London: Burns and Oates, 1953), pp. 204–8 (an English translation of a Spanish rite from 1631).
94. On Leo XIII's exorcism see Young (2016a), pp. 188–91.
95. Petitpierre (1976), p. 13.
96. Hacking (1988), p. 29.
97. Ibid., pp. 13–15.
98. Ibid., p. 17.
99. Ibid., pp. 17–18. The tumulus was probably Cock Hill, an Anglo-Saxon burial mound located southwest of the church of St Peter and St Paul.
100. See S. Newton, 'The Forgotten History of St Botwulf (Botolph)', *Proceedings of the Suffolk Institute of Archaeology and History* 43 (2016), pp. 521–50. 'Exorcism' of indigenous religious sites was also a technique deployed by Catholic missionaries in South America in the sixteenth and seventeenth centuries (see Young (2016a), pp. 143–6).
101. Gilbert Shaw to E. G. Jay, 18 March 1954, LPL MS Fisher 135, fol. 90.
102. Waters (2015a), pp. 101–2.
103. Ibid., p. 111.
104. Ibid., p. 113.
105. Ibid., p. 116.
106. M. Summers, *Witchcraft and Black Magic* (Rider and Co: London, 1946), p. 32.
107. Waters (2015a), p. 116.
108. Hacking (1988), pp. 75–8, 81–3.
109. Young (2016a), pp. 191–2.
110. Ibid., pp. 188–91.

CHAPTER 4   THE RISE OF THE ANGLICAN EXORCISTS, 1939–1974

1. Hill (2007), p. 10.
2. R. D. Hacking, 'Shaw, Gilbert Shuldham', in ODNB, vol. 50, pp. 97–8.
3. Hacking (1988), p. 77.
4. Petitpierre (1976), pp. 26–7.
5. Ibid., p. 27.
6. Hacking (1988), pp. 84–5.
7. Ibid., p. 85.
8. Ibid., p. 86.
9. Ibid., p. 87.
10. Quoted in ibid., p. 73.
11. Ibid., p. 86.
12. Ibid., p. 79.
13. Ibid., p. 92.

14. Ibid., p. 90.
15. Ibid., pp. 93–4.
16. Ibid., p. 84.
17. Ibid., p. 89.
18. E. G. Jay to Gilbert Shaw, 23 October 1953, LPL MS Fisher 119, fol. 129.
19. Gilbert Shaw to E. G. Jay, 26 October 1953, LPL MS Fisher 119, fol. 130.
20. Ibid., fols 131–2.
21. Ibid., fol. 136. Nashdom Abbey closed in 1987 and the community moved to Speen near Newbury and then Sarum College in Salisbury.
22. Ibid., fol. 137.
23. Hacking (1988), p. 86.
24. LPL MS Fisher 119, fol. 137.
25. Gilbert Shaw to E. G. Jay, 17 November 1953, LPL MS Fisher 119, fol. 140.
26. Gilbert Shaw to E. G. Jay, 18 March 1954, LPL MS Fisher 135, fol. 90.
27. E. G. Jay to Gilbert Shaw, 23 November 1954, LPL MS Fisher 135, fol. 93.
28. E. G. Jay to A. Hiam, 22 November 1954, LPL MS Fisher 135, fol. 92.
29. Waters (2015a), pp. 101–6.
30. *The Power of the Witch: Real or Imaginary?* (1971), youtube.com/watch?v=wi9pZEhNQvQ, accessed 9 May 2017.
31. Quoted in J. Richards, *But Deliver Us From Evil: An Introduction to the Demonic Dimension of Pastoral Care* (London: Darton, Longman and Todd, 1974), p. 177.
32. Quoted in ibid., p. 184.
33. Hacking (1988), pp. 87–8.
34. *The Church's Ministry of Healing: Report of the Archbishops' Commission* (London: The Church Information Board, 1958), p. 77.
35. Ibid.
36. Ibid., p. 78.
37. Ibid.
38. Hacking (1988), p. 89.
39. Ibid., p. 87.
40. On these theological debates see Young (2016a), pp. 213–16.
41. Waters (2015a), p. 113.
42. LPL MS BM 15/1.
43. LPL MS BM 16/14–15.
44. LPL MS BM 17/1.
45. LPL MS BM 17/61.
46. LPL MS BM 18/203.
47. M. Alexander, *To Anger the Devil: An Account of the Work of Exorcist Extraordinary the Reverend Dr Donald Omand* (St Helier: Neville Spearman, 1978), pp. 33–6.
48. Ibid., pp. 37–40.
49. Ibid., p. 41.
50. Ibid., p. 15.
51. Ibid., p. 27.

52. Ibid., p. 25.
53. Ibid., pp. 28–30.
54. Ibid., pp. 85, 157–74 (on Omand's exorcism of the Bermuda Triangle).
55. Richards (1974), p. 165.
56. Alexander (1978), pp. 175–6.
57. D. Omand, *Experiences of a Present Day Exorcist* (London: Kimber, 1970), p. 9.
58. Alexander (1978), p. 19.
59. Collins (2009), p. 185.
60. Gardiner (2015), p. 12.
61. Richards (1974), p. x.
62. Petitpierre (1976), p. 34.
63. Ibid., p. 37.
64. Ibid., pp. 73–4.
65. Ibid., pp. 123–4.
66. Ibid., pp. 97–8.
67. Ibid., p. 107.
68. Robert Runcie to Geoffrey Lampe, 2 May 1975, CUL MS Add. 9349/3/5/39.
69. A. Anderson, *An Introduction to Pentecostalism: Global Charismatic Christianity* (Cambridge: Cambridge University Press, 2004), pp. 153–4.
70. Smith (2016), pp. 54–5.
71. Ibid., p. 57.
72. Ibid.
73. Ibid., p. 59.
74. Ibid., p. 71.
75. Ibid.
76. See A. G. Walker, 'The Devil You Think You Know: Demonology and the Charismatic Movement', in T. Smail, A. G. Walker and N. G. Wright (eds), *Charismatic Renewal: The Search for a Theology* (London: SPCK, 1995), pp. 86–105, at pp. 88–96.
77. Smith (2016), p. 121.
78. Collins (2009), p. 177.
79. R. Hutton, *The Triumph of the Moon: A History of Modern Pagan Witchcraft* (Oxford: Oxford University Press, 1999), pp. 257–61.
80. Ibid., p. 268.
81. B. Ellis, *Raising the Devil: Satanism, New Religions, and the Media* (Lexington, KY: University Press of Kentucky, 2000), pp. 214–15.
82. On the development of demonological discourse of witchcraft and black magic in twentieth-century Britain see Waters (2015a), pp. 99–122.
83. M. Perry (ed.), *Deliverance: Psychic Disturbances and Occult Involvement* (London: SPCK, 1987), pp. 91–2.
84. Smith (2016), p. 63.
85. R. Petitpierre (ed.), *Exorcism: The Report of a Committee Convened by the Bishop of Exeter* (London: SPCK, 1972), p. 9. On the Exeter Report see L. Malia, 'A Fresh Look at a Remarkable Document: Exorcism: The Report

of a Commission Convened by the Bishop of Exeter', *Anglican Theological Review* 83 (2001), pp. 65–88.

86. D. J. Hamblin, 'Those Mad, Merry Vicars of England', *Life* 58:4 (29 January 1965), pp. 76–83, at p. 77.
87. Smith (2016), p. 41. This interpretation seems unlikely, since the Exeter Report does not once mention the charismatic movement.
88. Ibid., p. 9.
89. H. J. A. Sire, *Father Martin D'Arcy: Philosopher of Christian Love* (Leominster: Gracewing, 1997), p. 179. Crehan was responsible for editing his fellow Jesuit Herbert Thurston's writings about the paranormal.
90. Hacking (1988), p. 73.
91. Ibid., p. 84.
92. Petitpierre (1972), pp. 11–15.
93. Ibid., p. 16.
94. Ibid., p. 18.
95. Ibid., p. 23.
96. Ibid., pp. 19–20.
97. Ibid., pp. 29–30.
98. Ibid., p. 20.
99. Ibid., p. 37.
100. Ibid., p. 45.
101. Hacking (1988), p. 89.
102. Petitpierre (1972), p. 26.
103. Ibid., p. 23.
104. Ibid., p. 25.
105. Young (2016a), pp. 211–13.
106. See ibid., pp. 216–19.
107. Petitpierre (1972), p. 26.
108. Ibid., pp. 21–2.
109. Tumuli in the English landscape are either Bronze Age or Anglo-Saxon in origin, while stone circles are Neolithic. None of these landscape features is therefore 'Celtic' (a controversial term typically applied to the British Iron Age). The idea that prehistoric shrines were linked by 'snake paths' was first advocated by the eighteenth-century antiquary William Stukeley (1687–1765) and has long since been dismissed by archaeologists (see R. Sweet, *Antiquaries: The Discovery of the Past in Eighteenth-Century Britain* (London: Hambledon and London, 2004), pp. 132–3).
110. Richards (1974), p. 124.
111. The report even provided a liturgy for the licensing of lay exorcists by the bishop or his representative (M. Maddocks (ed.), *The Christian Ministry of Deliverance and Healing: A Report from the York Group* (York, 1974), p. 15).
112. Ibid., p. 11.
113. Ibid., p. 10.
114. Ibid., p. 13.

115. Ibid., p. 11.
116. Ibid., p. 17.
117. Ibid., p. 16.
118. Collins (2009), p. 76.
119. Richards (1974), pp. 1–18.
120. Ibid., pp. 19–37.
121. Ibid., pp. 38–90.
122. Ibid., pp. 91–118.
123. Ibid., pp. 119–54.
124. Ibid., pp. 155–91.
125. Ibid., pp. 192–214.
126. Ibid., p. vii.
127. Ibid., pp. 17–18.
128. Ibid., p. 18.
129. Ibid., p. 119.
130. Ibid., p. 122.
131. Ibid., p. 120.
132. Ibid., p. 121.
133. Ibid., pp. 121–2.
134. Ibid., p. 124.
135. Ibid., p. 126.
136. Ibid., p. 132.
137. Ibid., p. 123.
138. Ibid., p. 176.
139. Ibid., p. 161
140. Ibid., p. 163.
141. Ibid., p. 164.
142. Ibid., p. 165.
143. Ibid., p. 166.
144. Ibid., p. 167.
145. Ibid., pp. 181–2.
146. Ibid., pp. 167–8.
147. Ibid., pp. 169–70.
148. Ibid., p. 171.
149. Ibid., p. 174.
150. Ibid., p. 176.
151. Ibid., p. 121.
152. Quoted in ibid., p. 179.
153. Ibid. Richards recognised that there would always be a role for the specialist 'to bring his experience to difficult and very acute cases' (ibid., p. 183).
154. Ibid., p. 180.
155. Ibid., p. 186.
156. Ibid., p. 187.
157. Ibid., p. 152.

158. Ibid., p. 153.
159. Ibid., p. 190.
160. Ibid., pp. 222–5.
161. M. Ebon, *Exorcism Past and Present* (London: Cassell, 1975), pp. 213–14.
162. Ibid., p. 200.
163. Ibid., p. 201.
164. Maddocks (1974), p. 17.
165. Ebon (1975), p. 202.
166. Ibid., pp. 203–5.
167. Ibid., p. 206.
168. Ibid., pp. 208–10.
169. Ibid., p. 212.
170. See C. Neil-Smith, *The Exorcist and the Possessed: The Truth about Exorcism* (St Ives: James Pike, 1974), p. 26.
171. Collins (2009), p. 179.
172. Neil-Smith (1974), pp. 9–10.
173. Ibid., p. 13.
174. Ibid., p. 14.
175. Ibid., p. 15.
176. Ibid., pp. 15–16.
177. Ibid., p. 19.
178. Ibid., pp. 95–6.
179. Ibid., p. 27.
180. Ibid., p. 30.
181. Ibid., pp. 31–2.
182. Ibid., pp. 35–6.
183. Ibid., pp. 38–9.
184. Ibid., pp. 66–7.
185. Ibid., pp. 39–42.
186. Ibid., pp. 42–4.
187. Ibid., pp. 47–8.
188. Ibid., p. 97.
189. Ibid., pp. 64–5.
190. Ibid., pp. 67–70.
191. Ibid., p. 116.

CHAPTER 5   ANGLICAN EXORCISM NORMALISED, 1975–2000

1. Smith (2016), p. 41.
2. Neil-Smith (1974), p. 96.
3. 'Exorcism turned man into brutal killer', *The Times*, 26 March 1975.
4. C. Longley, 'Exorcism for man who later killed wife was unwise, bishop says as church bodies seek full report', *The Times*, 27 March 1975.
5. Treacy later commissioned his own report on exorcism (see LPL MS 3575, fols 47–156).

6. J. A. Hargreaves, 'Treacy, Eric', in *ODNB*, vol. 55, pp. 243–5.
7. W. Sargant, 'Dangers of amateurs dabbling in exorcism', *The Times*, 27 March 1975.
8. LPL MS Coggan 6, fol. 205.
9. J. Linklater, 'Bell, book and stethoscope', *Spectator* 7662 (2 May 1975), p. 546.
10. Petitpierre (1976), p. 52.
11. Ibid., pp. 52–3.
12. M. Wiles, 'Lampe, Geoffrey William Hugo', in *ODNB*, vol. 32, pp. 347–8.
13. Four theologians teaching at University of Wales, Lampeter, later added their support on 15 May, CUL MS Add. 9349/3/5/47.
14. 'An open letter to the archbishops, the bishops and the members of the General Synod of the Church of England', CUL MS Add. 9349/3/5/33–4.
15. Ibid.
16. Geoffrey Lampe and Don Cupitt to Bernard Palmer, 23 May 1975, CUL MS Add. 9349/3/5/20.
17. Geoffrey Lampe and Don Cupitt to various correspondents, 12 May 1975, CUL MS Add. 9349/3/5/35.
18. Geoffrey Lampe and Don Cupitt to various correspondents, April/May 1975, CUL MS Add. 9349/3/5/32.
19. Kenneth Woollcombe to Geoffrey Lampe, 2 May 1975, CUL MS Add. 9349/3/5/2.
20. Geoffrey Lampe to Kenneth Woollcombe, 26 May 1975, CUL MS Add. 9349/3/5/21, fol. 1.
21. Ibid., fol. 3.
22. Ibid., fol. 4.
23. Ibid., fol. 5.
24. Ibid., fol. 6.
25. Ibid., fol. 7.
26. Ibid., fol. 8.
27. Ibid., fols 9–10.
28. Lampe reported that Dominican friars in the West Indies (perhaps referring to the island of Grenada which is part of the English Dominican province) never exorcised 'because the people are addicted to the occult' (ibid. fol. 9).
29. Ibid.
30. Kenneth Woollcombe to Geoffrey Lampe, 28 May 1975, CUL MS Add. 9349/3/5/22, fol. 1.
31. Ibid., fol. 2.
32. Alan Webster to Geoffrey Lampe, 19 May 1975, CUL MS Add. 9349/3/5/14.
33. Michael Wilson to Geoffrey Lampe, 19 May 1975, CUL MS Add. 9349/3/5/12–13.
34. M. Wilson, 'Exorcism: a clinical/pastoral practice which raises serious questions', *The Expository Times* 86 (10 July 1975), pp. 292–5.

35. Ibid., p. 293.
36. Ibid., p. 292.
37. Ibid., p. 293.
38. Ibid., p. 295.
39. Robert Runcie to Geoffrey Lampe, 2 May 1975, CUL MS Add. 9349/3/5/39.
40. Hugh Montefiore to Geoffrey Lampe, 19 May 1975, CUL MS Add. 9349/3/5/15.
41. Newspaper cutting from *The Times*, 20 May 1975, CUL MS Add. 9349/3/5/16.
42. Douglas Feaver to Geoffrey Lampe, 22 May 1975, CUL MS Add. 9349/3/5/18.
43. John Richards to Geoffrey Lampe, 9 July 1975, CUL MS Add. 9349/3/5/25.
44. According to his obituary in *The Times*, 16 November 1985, p. 10 col. G.
45. Maurice Wiles to Geoffrey Lampe, 6 May 1975, CUL MS Add. 9349/3/5/44.
46. Peter Baelz to Geoffrey Lampe, 7 May 1975, CUL MS Add. 9349/3/5/46.
47. John Macquarrie to Geoffrey Lampe, 4 May 1975, CUL MS Add. 9349/3/5/48.
48. Petitpierre (1976), pp. 43–4.
49. Ibid., p. 45.
50. *Report of Proceedings* (London: Church Information Office, 1975), vol. 6:1, p. 361.
51. *The Alternative Service Book* (Oxford: Oxford University Press, 1980), p. 230.
52. Holeton (1998), pp. 302–3.
53. N. Milner, 'Giving the Devil His Due Process: Exorcism in the Church of England', *Journal of Contemporary Religion* 15 (2000), pp. 247–72, at p. 251.
54. A. Johnson, 'Minister "touched women" at exorcism', *The Guardian*, 5 December 1994.
55. Milner (2000), pp. 252–3.
56. Ibid., p. 254.
57. J. La Fontaine, 'Satanism and Satanic Mythology', in W. De Blécourt, R. Hutton and J. La Fontaine (eds), *Witchcraft and Magic in Europe: The Twentieth Century* (London: Athlone, 1999), pp. 81–140, at pp. 115–38; D. Frankfurter, *Evil Incarnate: Rumors of Satanic Conspiracy and Satanic Abuse in History* (Princeton, NJ: Princeton University Press, 2008), pp. 2–3.
58. Milner (2000), p. 260.
59. Waters (2015a), pp. 114–15.
60. Collins (2009), p. 183.
61. Ibid., pp. 112–14.
62. Ibid., p. 115. Smith (2016), p. 41 notes that some clergy with a charismatic background became diocesan exorcists.
63. Collins (2009), p. 116.
64. Ibid.

65. Ibid., p. 117.
66. Ibid., p. 118.
67. Ibid., pp. 90–1.
68. Ibid., p. 91.
69. Ibid., pp. 93–4.
70. Ibid., pp. 96–7.
71. Ibid., p. 94.
72. Ibid., pp. 94–5.
73. B. Brandon, *The Healing Ministry – Developments since the Publication of A Time to Heal*, GS Misc 835 (London: Church House Publications, 2006), pp. 1–2.
74. D. Walker, *The Ministry of Deliverance* (London: Darton, Longman and Todd, 1997), p. 2.
75. Ibid., p. 7.
76. Ibid., p. 41.
77. Ibid., pp. 45–6.
78. Ibid., p. 9.
79. M. Israel, *Exorcism: The Removal of Evil Influences* (London: SPCK, 1997), p. 1.
80. Ibid., p. 8.
81. Ibid., pp. 98–9.
82. Ibid., p. 100.
83. Collins (2009), p. 184.
84. *ATTH*, p. viii.
85. Ibid., pp. 169–71.
86. Ibid., pp. 171–2.
87. Ibid., pp. 172–4.
88. Ibid., p. 178.
89. Ibid., p. 167.
90. Ibid., p. 168.
91. Ibid., pp. 179–80.
92. Ibid., p. 168–9.
93. Ibid., p. 174.
94. Ibid., pp. 175–7.
95. Ibid., p. 173.
96. Ibid., pp. 177–8.
97. Ibid., p. 179.
98. Ibid., p. 178.
99. Ibid., p. 180.
100. Perry (1987), pp. 120–39.
101. R. Deadman, J. Fletcher, J. Hudson and S. Oliver (eds), *Pastoral Prayers: A Resource for Pastoral Occasions* (London: Continuum, 1996), pp. 12–14.
102. Ibid., p. 9.
103. *Common Worship: Pastoral Services* (London: Church House Publishing, 2000), p. 94. For the 'Prayers for Protection and Peace' see pp. 95–9.

104. Perry (1987), pp. 115–16.
105. *ATTH Handbook*, pp. 36–7.
106. It is also unclear why *Common Worship* requires an exorcist to be a priest rather than a deacon; the Roman Catholic church has required exorcists to be priests only since 1917 (Young (2016a), p. 194).
107. Milner (2000), p. 248.
108. Ibid., p. 249.
109. Smith (2016), p. 121.
110. S. Hunt, 'All Things Bright and Beautiful: the rise of the Anglican charismatic church', *Journal of Empirical Theology* 13 (2000), pp. 16–34, at p. 21.
111. Milner (2000), p. 259.
112. Ibid., pp. 260–1.
113. Ibid., p. 261.
114. Ibid., p. 265.
115. Ibid., p. 269.

CHAPTER 6   ANGLICAN EXORCISM IN THE TWENTY-FIRST CENTURY

1. G. Dow, *Deliverance: Sharing Experience in the Ministry of Deliverance* (Lancaster: Sovereign World, 2003), p. 12.
2. Ibid., p. 58.
3. H. Montefiore, *The Paranormal: A Bishop Investigates* (Leicester: Upfront Publishing, 2002), p. 111.
4. Ibid., p. 113.
5. Ibid., p. 117.
6. Ibid., p. 128.
7. Ibid., pp. 130–1.
8. Gardiner (2015), pp. 30–2.
9. Ibid., p. 75 (ancestral spirits); p. 121 (physical ejection of spirits).
10. Ibid., p. 122.
11. *Report of Proceedings*, vol. 36:2 (London: Church House Publishing, 2005), p. 53.
12. Ibid., pp. 72–3.
13. For the full text of the guidelines see 'The House of Bishops' Guidelines for Good Practice in the Deliverance Ministry 1975 (revised 2012)', churchofengland.org/media/1734117/guidelines%20on%20deliverance%20ministry.pdf, accessed 9 August 2017.
14. B. Brandon, 'Symptoms of Spiritual Crisis and the Therapeusis of Healing', rcpsych.ac.uk/pdf/Symptoms%20of%20spiritual%20crisis.%20Beatrice%20Brandon.pdf, accessed 7 August 2017.
15. 'Diocese of Canterbury: Guidelines for the Ministry of Deliverance', canterburydiocese.org/media/forms/deliverance/guidelinesforthe ministryofdeliverance.pdf, accessed 14 August 2017.

16. 'The Diocese of Exeter: Bishop's Guidelines for Ordained Ministry: Section 6 – Funerals and Other Pastoral Offices', exeter.anglican.org/wp-content/uploads/2014/10/funerals-and-other-pastoral-offices.pdf, accessed 14 August 2017.

17. R. Inwood, 'Ad Clerum – Healing and Deliverance Ministry', southwell.anglican.org/wp-content/uploads/2014/07/Deliverance-jul14.pdf, accessed 14 August 2017.

18. P. Ashworth, 'Deliver us from evil', *Church Times*, 17 February 2017, pp. 21–2.

19. J. Woolmer, 'An undramatic ministry, usually', *Church Times*, 17 February 2017, p. 23.

20. J. Woolmer, *Healing and Deliverance* (London: Monarch, 1999), p. 35.

21. Hill (2007), p. 178.

22. Ibid., pp. 21–2.

23. D. B. Stevick, 'Canon Law', in S. Sykes, J. Booty and J. Knight (eds), *The Study of Anglicanism*, 2nd edn (London: SPCK, 1998), pp. 218–45, at p. 221.

24. Perry (1987), p. 118.

25. 'Guidelines for the professional conduct of the clergy (Revised Edition) 2015', churchofengland.org/about-us/structure/general-synod/about-general-synod/convocations/guidelines-for-the-professional-conduct-of-the-clergy/guidelines.aspx, accessed 27 July 2017.

26. On the Clergy Discipline Measure see Hill (2007), pp. 187–8.

27. Ibid., p. 316.

28. Ibid., pp. 345–6.

29. Richards (1974), pp. 170–1.

30. Gardiner (2015), p. 119.

31. *Promoting a Safe Church: Policy for Safeguarding Adults in the Church of England*, GS Misc 837 (London: Church House, 2006), p. 13.

32. Ibid., p. 39.

33. *ATTH Handbook*, p. 27.

34. Ibid., pp. 36–7.

35. B. Brandon, 'Symptoms of Spiritual Crisis and the Therapeusis of Healing', rcpsych.ac.uk/pdf/Symptoms%20of%20spiritual%20crisis.%20Beatrice%20Brandon.pdf, accessed 7 August 2017.

36. Smith (2016), p. 185.

37. Gardiner (2015), p. 52.

38. Ibid., p. 129.

39. There are exceptions; according to Richards (1974), p. 189 one of his parishioners encountered a man 'with an evil face' wearing a cloak while walking in the woods and sent him running away with the sign of the cross.

40. On demonological 'inversion' see S. Clark, 'Inversion, Misrule and the Meaning of Witchcraft', *Past and Present* 87 (1980), pp. 98–127. It should be noted that belief in witchcraft as a cult never took hold in England.

41. Richards (1974), p. 38.
42. R. Hutton, *Pagan Britain* (New Haven, CT: Yale University Press, 2013), pp. 331–3.
43. See ibid., pp. 77–80, 120–1.
44. Richards (1974), pp. 95–6.
45. B. Brandon, 'Symptoms of Spiritual Crisis and the Therapeusis of Healing', rcpsych.ac.uk/pdf/Symptoms%20of%20spiritual%20crisis.%20Beatrice%20Brandon.pdf, accessed 7 August 2017.
46. It should be noted that this does not mean that the discipline of parapsychology itself, understood as the objective *investigation* of parapsychological claims, is pseudo-science.
47. Milner (2000), p. 250.
48. J. Davies, *Exorcism from a Catholic Perspective* (London: Catholic Truth Society, 2009).
49. Young (2016a), pp. 233–4.
50. Perry (1987), p. 118.
51. G. Leavey, 'The Appreciation of the Spiritual in Mental Illness: A Quantitative Study of Beliefs Among Clergy in the UK', *Transcultural Psychiatry* 47 (2010), pp. 571–90, at pp. 573–4.
52. Ibid., p. 577.
53. Ibid.
54. Ibid., p. 580.
55. Ibid., p. 581.
56. Ibid., pp. 584–5.
57. Ibid., p. 585.
58. Ibid., p. 586.
59. Ibid., p. 587.
60. Ibid., p. 584.
61. Ibid., p. 586.
62. Waters (2015a), pp. 100–1.
63. Ibid., pp. 104–5.
64. 'The Merrily Watkins novels', philrickman.co.uk/merrily, accessed 20 November 2017.
65. R. Coles, 'Defence Against the Dark Arts', in J. Harrison (ed.), *Harry Potter: A History of Magic* (London: Bloomsbury, 2017), pp. 166–8, at p. 168.
66. Gardiner (2015), pp. 144–5.

Bibliography

MANUSCRIPTS

Cambridge University Library (CUL)
  Add. 9349
Lambeth Palace Library (LPL)
  3575
  Benson 116
  BM 15–BM 18
  Coggan 6
  F. Temple 54
  Fisher 119
  Fisher 135
  Lang 156
  Tait 234
  Tait 270

PRINTED SOURCES

Alexander, M., *To Anger the Devil: An Account of the Work of Exorcist Extraordinary the Reverend Dr Donald Omand* (St Helier: Neville Spearman, 1978).

Almond, P. (ed.), *Demonic Possession and Exorcism in Early Modern England* (Cambridge: Cambridge University Press, 2004).

The Alternative Service Book (Oxford: Oxford University Press, 1980).

Anderson, A., *An Introduction to Pentecostalism: Global Charismatic Christianity* (Cambridge: Cambridge University Press, 2004).

Andrews, J., 'Napier, Richard', in *ODNB*, vol. 40, pp. 181–3.

Ayris, P., 'Canon Law Studies', in P. Ayris and D. Selwyn (eds), *Thomas Cranmer: Churchman and Scholar* (Woodbridge: Boydell, 1993), pp. 316–24.

Barry, J., *Witchcraft and Demonology in South-West England, 1640–1789* (London: Palgrave MacMillan, 2012).

Blagrave, J., *Blagraves Astrological Practice of Physick* (London, 1671).

——, *The Evil Spirit Cast-Out* (London, 1691).

Bourne, H., *Antiquitates vulgares* (Newcastle, 1725).

Bowd, S., 'John Dee and the Seven in Lancashire: Possession, Exorcism, and Apocalypse in Elizabethan England', *Northern History* 47 (2010), pp. 233–46.

Brandon, B. (ed.), *The Healing Ministry – Developments since the Publication of A Time to Heal*, GS Misc 835 (London: Church House Publications, 2006).

Brandon, B. and Gunstone, J. (eds), *A Time to Heal: A Report for the House of Bishops on the Healing Ministry*, GS 1378 (London: Church House Publishing, 2000).

—— (eds), *A Time to Heal: The Development of Good Practice in the Healing Ministry: A Handbook*, GS Misc 607 (London: Church House Publishing, 2000).

Bray, G. L., *The Anglican Canons, 1529–1947* (Woodbridge: Boydell, 1998).

Brown, T., *The Fate of the Dead: A Study of Folk Eschatology in the West Country after the Reformation* (London: Folklore Society, 1979).

Brownlow, F. W., *Shakespeare, Harsnett and the Devils of Denham* (Newark, NJ: University of Delaware Press, 1993).

Byrne, G., *Modern Spiritualism and the Church of England, 1850–1939* (Woodbridge: Boydell and Brewer, 2010).

Caciola, N. M., *Afterlives: The Return of the Dead in the Middle Ages* (Cornell University Press, 2016).

Cambers, A., 'Demonic Possession, Literacy and "Superstition" in Early Modern England', *Past and Present* 202 (2009), pp. 3–35.

Cameron, E., *Enchanted Europe: Superstition, Reason, and Religion, 1250–1750* (Oxford: Oxford University Press, 2010).

Chanter, J. F., 'Parson Joe and his Book', *Devon and Cornwall Notes and Queries* 8 (1914–15), pp. 87–8.

The Church's Ministry of Healing: Report of the Archbishops' Commission (London: The Church Information Board, 1958).

Clark, S., 'Inversion, Misrule and the Meaning of Witchcraft', *Past and Present* 87 (1980), pp. 98–127.

Clarke, R., *A Natural History of Ghosts: 500 Years of Hunting for Proof*, 2nd edn (London: Penguin, 2013).

Coles, R., 'Defence Against the Dark Arts', in J. Harrison (ed.), *Harry Potter: A History of Magic* (London: Bloomsbury, 2017), pp. 166–8.

Collins, J. M., *Exorcism and Deliverance Ministry in the Twentieth Century: An Analysis of the Practice and Theology of Exorcism in Modern Western Christianity* (Bletchley: Paternoster, 2009).

Collinson, P., *From Cranmer to Sancroft* (London: Continuum, 2006).

Common Worship: Pastoral Services (London: Church House Publishing, 2000).

Cranfield, N. W. S., 'Bancroft, Richard', in *ODNB*, vol. 3, pp. 647–55.

Davies, J., *Exorcism from a Catholic Perspective* (London: Catholic Truth Society, 2009).

Davies, O., 'Methodism, the Clergy, and the Popular Belief in Witchcraft and Magic', *History* 82 (1997), pp. 252–65.

———, *Witchcraft, Magic and Culture 1736–1951* (Manchester: Manchester University Press, 1999).

———, *Popular Magic: Cunning-Folk in English History*, 2nd edn (London: Continuum, 2007a).

———, *The Haunted: A Social History of Ghosts* (London: Palgrave MacMillan, 2007b).

———, 'Magic in Common and Legal Perspectives', in D. J. Collins (ed.), *The Cambridge History of Magic and Witchcraft in the West: From Antiquity to the Present* (Cambridge: Cambridge University Press, 2015), pp. 521–46.

Davies, R., *Bishop Nathaniel Spinckes and the Non-Juring Church* (London: Royal Stuart Society, 2007).

Davis, C. H. (ed.), *The English Church Canons of 1604* (London: H. Sweet, 1869).

De Blécourt, W., 'The witch, her victim, the unwitcher and the researcher: the continued existence of traditional witchcraft', in W. de Blécourt, R. Hutton and J. de la Fontaine (eds), *Witchcraft and Magic in Europe: The Twentieth Century* (London: Athlone Press, 1999), pp. 141–219.

Deacon, T., *A Compleat Collection of Devotions* (London, 1734), 2 vols.

———, *A Full, True and Comprehensive View of Christianity* (London, 1748).

Deadman, R., Fletcher, J., Hudson, J. and Oliver, S. (eds), *Pastoral Prayers: A Resource for Pastoral Occasions* (London: Continuum, 1996).

Dee, J. (ed. E. Fenton), *The Diaries of John Dee* (London: Day Books, 1998).

Dow, G., *Deliverance: Sharing Experience in the Ministry of Deliverance* (Lancaster: Sovereign World, 2003).

Duffy, E., *The Stripping of the Altars: Traditional Religion in England, 1400–1580* (New Haven, CT: Yale University Press, 1992).

Easterbrook, J., *An Appeal to the Public Respecting George Lukins* (Bristol, 1788).

Ebon, M., *Exorcism Past and Present* (London: Cassell, 1975).

Ellis, B., *Raising the Devil: Satanism, New Religions, and the Media* (Lexington, KY: University Press of Kentucky, 2000).

Elmer, P., '"Saints or Sorcerers": Quakerism, Demonology and the Decline of Witchcraft in Seventeenth-Century England', in J. Barry, M. Hester and G. Roberts (eds), *Witchcraft in Early Modern Europe: Studies in Culture and Belief* (Cambridge: Cambridge University Press, 1996), pp. 145–82.

———, *Witchcraft, Witch-Hunting and Politics in Early Modern England* (Oxford: Oxford University Press, 2016).

Elton, G. R., *Policy and Police: The Enforcement of the Reformation in the Age of Thomas Cromwell* (Cambridge: Cambridge University Press, 1972).

The First and Second Prayer Books of Edward VI, ed. E. C. S. Gibson (London: J. M. Dent, 1910).

F[isher], J., *The Copy of a Letter Describing the Wonderful Woorke of God in Delivering a Mayden within the City of Chester* (London, 1565).

Frankfurter, D., *Evil Incarnate: Rumors of Satanic Conspiracy and Satanic Abuse in History* (Princeton, NJ: Princeton University Press, 2008).

——, 'Where the Spirits Dwell: Possession, Christianization and Saints' Shrines in Late Antiquity', *Harvard Theological Review* 103 (2010), pp. 27–46.

Freeman, T. S., 'Demons, Deviance and Defiance: John Darrell and the Politics of Exorcism in late Elizabethan England', in P. Lake and M. Questier (eds), *Conformity and Orthodoxy in the English Church, c. 1560–1660* (Woodbridge: Boydell, 2000), pp. 34–63.

——, 'Darrell, John', in *ODNB*, vol. 15, pp. 166–7.

——, 'Foxe, John', in *ODNB*, vol. 20, pp. 695–709.

Gardiner, K., *The Reluctant Exorcist: A Biblical Approach in an Age of Scepticism*, 2nd edn (Watford: Instant Apostle, 2015).

Gibson, M., *Possession, Puritanism and Print: Darrell, Harsnett, Shakespeare and the Elizabethan Exorcism Controversy* (London: Pickering and Chatto, 2006).

Glanvill, J., *Saducismus triumphatus* (London, 1681).

Goddu, A., 'The Failure of Exorcism in the Middle Ages', in Zimmerman, A. (ed.), *Soziale Ordnungen im Selbstverständnis des Mittelalters*, Miscellanea Mediaevalia 12/2 (Berlin: Walter de Gruyter, 1980), pp. 540–57.

Hacking, R. D., *Such a Long Journey: A Biography of Gilbert Shaw, Priest* (London: Mowbray, 1988).

——, 'Shaw, Gilbert Shuldham', in *ODNB*, vol. 50, pp. 97–8.

Hall, J. (ed. J. Pratt), *The Works of the Right Reverend Father in God Joseph Hall, D.D.* (London, 1808), 10 vols.

——, (ed. P. Wynter), *The Works of the Right Reverend Joseph Hall, D.D.* (Oxford: Oxford University Press, 1863), 10 vols.

Hamblin, D. J., 'Those Mad, Merry Vicars of England', *Life* 58:4 (29 January 1965), pp. 76–83.

Hammond, G., *John Wesley in America: Restoring Primitive Christianity* (Oxford: Oxford University Press, 2014).

Hargreaves, J. A., 'Treacy, Eric', in *ODNB*, vol. 55, pp. 243–5.

Harmes, M., 'The Devil and Bishops in Post-Reformation England', in M. Harmes and V. Bladen (eds), *Supernatural and Secular Power in Early Modern England* (Farnham: Ashgate, 2015), pp. 185–206.

Harsnett, S., *A Discouery of the Fraudulent Practises of Iohn Darrel* (London, 1599).

Hastings, A., *A History of English Christianity, 1920–2000*, 4th edn (London: SCM Press, 2001).

Hempton, D., *The Religion of the People: Methodism and Popular Religion c. 1750–1900* (London: Routledge, 1996).

Hill, M., *Ecclesiastical Law*, 3rd edn (Oxford: Oxford University Press, 2007).

Hinde, W., *A Faithfull Remonstrance of the Holy Life and Happy Death of Iohn Bruen of Bruen-Stapleford, in the County of Chester, Esquire* (London, 1641).

Hole, C., *English Folklore* (London: Batsford, 1940).

Holeton, D. R., 'Initiation', in S. Sykes, J. Booty and J. Knight (eds), *The Study of Anglicanism*, 2nd edn (London: SPCK, 1998), pp. 293–307.

Hunt, S., 'All Things Bright and Beautiful: the rise of the Anglican charismatic church', *Journal of Empirical Theology* 13 (2000), pp. 16–34.

Hutton, R., *The Triumph of the Moon: A History of Modern Pagan Witchcraft* (Oxford: Oxford University Press, 1999).

——, *Pagan Britain* (New Haven, CT: Yale University Press, 2013).

Israel, M., *Exorcism: The Removal of Evil Influences* (London: SPCK, 1997).

Jewel, J. (ed. J. Ayre), *The Works of John Jewel* (Cambridge: Parker Society, 1848), 4 vols.

Johnstone, N., *The Devil and Demonism in Early Modern England* (Cambridge: Cambridge University Press, 2006).

J[ollie], T., *A Vindication of the Surey Demoniack* (London, 1698).

Jones, W., *A Course of Lectures on the Figurative Language of the Holy Scripture* (London: SPCK, 1864).

La Fontaine, J., 'Satanism and Satanic Mythology', in W. De Blécourt, R. Hutton and J. La Fontaine (eds), *Witchcraft and Magic in Europe: The Twentieth Century* (London: Athlone, 1999), pp. 81–140.

Leather, E. M., *The Folk-lore of Herefordshire* (Hereford: Jakeman and Carver, 1912).

Leavey, G., 'The Appreciation of the Spiritual in Mental Illness: A Quantitative Study of Beliefs Among Clergy in the UK', *Transcultural Psychiatry* 47 (2010), pp. 571–90.

Levack, B. P., *The Devil Within: Possession and Exorcism in the Christian West* (New Haven, CT: Yale University Press, 2013).

Linklater, J., 'Bell, book and stethoscope', *Spectator* 7662 (2 May 1975), p. 546.

MacDonald, M., *Mystical Bedlam: Madness, Anxiety and Healing in Seventeenth-Century England* (Cambridge: Cambridge University Press, 1981).

——, (ed.), *Witchcraft and Hysteria in Elizabethan London: Edward Jorden and the Mary Glover Case* (London: Routledge, 1991).

Maddocks, M. (ed.), *The Christian Ministry of Deliverance and Healing: A Report from the York Group* (York, 1974).

Malia, L., 'A Fresh Look at a Remarkable Document: Exorcism: The Report of a Commission Convened by the Bishop of Exeter', *Anglican Theological Review* 83 (2001), pp. 65–88.

Mandelbrote, S., 'Hutchinson, John', in *ODNB*, vol. 29, pp. 14–15.

Marshall, P., *Beliefs and the Dead in Early Modern England* (Oxford: Oxford University Press, 2002).

Maxwell-Stuart, P. G., 'King James's Experience of Witches, and the English Witchcraft Act of 1604', in J. Newton and J. Bath (eds), *Witchcraft and the Act of 1604* (Leiden: Brill, 2008), pp. 31–46.

——, *The British Witch: The Biography* (Stroud: Amberley, 2014).

Milner, N., 'Giving the Devil His Due Process: Exorcism in the Church of England', *Journal of Contemporary Religion* 15 (2000), pp. 247–72.

Monod, P. K., *Solomon's Secret Arts: The Occult in the Age of Enlightenment* (New Haven, CT: Yale University Press, 2013).

Montefiore, H., *The Paranormal: A Bishop Investigates* (Leicester: Upfront Publishing, 2002).

Morel, A.-F., 'Church Consecration in England 1549–1715: An Unestablished Ceremony', in M. Delbeke and M. Schraven (eds), *Foundation, Dedication and Consecration in Early Modern Europe* (Leiden: Brill, 2012).

Neil-Smith, C., *The Exorcist and the Possessed: The Truth about Exorcism* (St Ives: James Pike, 1974).

Newton, S., 'The Forgotten History of St Botwulf (Botolph)', *Proceedings of the Suffolk Institute of Archaeology and History* 43 (2016), pp. 521–50.

Nicholls, W., *A Supplement to the Commentary on the Book of Common Prayer* (London, 1711).

Nicolotti, A., *Esorcismo Cristiano e Possessione Diabolica tra II e III Secolo* (Turnhout: Brepols, 2011).

Nienkirchen, C. W., *A. B. Simpson and the Pentecostal Movement: A Study in Continuity, Crisis, and Change* (Eugene, OR: Wipf and Stock, 2010).

Oldridge, D., *The Devil in Tudor and Stuart England*, 2nd edn (Stroud: History Press, 2010).

Omand, D., *Experiences of a Present Day Exorcist* (London: Kimber, 1970).

Oppenheim, J., *The Other World: Spiritualism and Psychical Research in England, 1850–1914* (Cambridge: Cambridge University Press, 1986).

Parry, G., *The Arch-Conjurer of England: John Dee* (New Haven, CT: Yale University Press, 2011).

Pederson, R. J., *Unity in Diversity: English Puritans and the Puritan Reformation, 1603–1689* (Leiden: Brill, 2014).

Perry, M. (ed.), *Deliverance: Psychic Disturbances and Occult Involvement* (London: SPCK, 1987).

Petitpierre, R. (ed.), *Exorcism: The Report of a Committee convened by the Bishop of Exeter* (London: SPCK, 1972).

———, *Exorcising Devils* (London: Hale, 1976).

Poole, R. (ed.), *The Lancashire Witches: Histories and Stories* (Manchester: Manchester University Press, 2002).

Porter, R., 'Witchcraft and Magic in Enlightenment, Romantic and Liberal Thought', in M. Gijswit-Hofstra and R. Porter (eds), *Witchcraft and Magic in Europe: The Eighteenth and Nineteenth Centuries* (London: Athlone Press, 1999), pp. 191–254.

Promoting a Safe Church: Policy for Safeguarding Adults in the Church of England, GS Misc 837 (London: Church House, 2006).

Report of Proceedings (London: Church Information Office, 1970–present), 27 vols.

'The Response to the Appeal. From Prelates, Pundits and Persons of Distinction', *Borderland* 1 (July 1893), pp. 10–11.

Richards, J., *But Deliver Us From Evil: An Introduction to the Demonic Dimension of Pastoral Care* (London: Darton, Longman and Todd, 1974).

Roberts, R. J. and Watson, A. G. (eds), *John Dee's Library Catalogue* (London: Bibliographical Society, 1990).

Robinson, H. (ed.) *The Zurich Letters* (Cambridge: Parker Society, 1842–45), 2 vols.

Robinson, J., *Divine Healing: The Holiness-Pentecostal Transition Years, 1890–1906* (Eugene, OR: Pickwick, 2013).

——, *Divine Healing: The Years of Expansion, 1906–1930* (Eugene, OR: Pickwick, 2014).

Sands, K. R., *Demon Possession in Elizabethan England* (Westport, CT: Praeger, 2004).

Scot, R., *The Discovery of Witchcraft*, 2nd edn (London, 1665).

Sharpe, J., *The Bewitching of Anne Gunter: A Horrible and True Story of Deception, Witchcraft, Murder, and the King of England* (London: Routledge, 2000).

Sire, H. J. A., *Father Martin D'Arcy: Philosopher of Christian Love* (Leominster: Gracewing, 1997).

Sluhovsky, M., *Believe Not Every Spirit: Possession, Mysticism, and Discernment in Early Modern Catholicism* (Chicago, IL: University of Chicago Press, 2007).

Smith, G. R., *The Church Militant: Spiritual Warfare in the Anglican Charismatic Renewal* (Eugene, OR: Pickwick, 2016).

Sorensen, E., *Possession and Exorcism in the New Testament and Early Christianity* (Tübingen: Mohr Siebeck, 2002).

Stevick, D. B., 'Canon Law', in S. Sykes, J. Booty and J. Knight (eds), *The Study of Anglicanism*, 2nd edn (London: SPCK, 1998), pp. 218–45.

Summers, M., *Witchcraft and Black Magic* (Rider and Co: London, 1946).

Sweet, R., *Antiquaries: The Discovery of the Past in Eighteenth-Century Britain* (London: Hambledon and London, 2004).

Taylor, J. (ed. R. Heber and C. P. Eden), *The Whole Works of the Right Rev. Jeremy Taylor, D. D.* (London: Longman, Brown, Green and Longmans, 1847–54), 10 vols.

Telford, J., *The Life of the Rev. Charles Wesley, M.A.* (London: Methodist Book Room, 1900).

Thomas, K., *Religion and the Decline of Magic: Studies in Popular Beliefs in Sixteenth- and Seventeenth-Century England*, 4th edn (London: Penguin, 1991).

Thurston, H. (ed. J. H. Crehan), *Ghosts and Poltergeists* (London: Burns and Oates, 1953).

Trench, R. C., *Notes on the Miracles of Our Lord* (London: John W. Parker, 1846).

——, *Notes on the Miracles of Our Lord*, 5th edn (London: John W. Parker, 1856).

Twelftree, G. H., *In the Name of Jesus: Exorcism among the Early Christians* (Grand Rapids, MN: Baker Academic, 2007).

Venn, J., *Biographical History of Gonville and Caius College 1349–1897* (Cambridge: Cambridge University Press, 1897–1972), 4 vols.

Walker, A. G., 'The Devil You Think You Know: Demonology and the Charismatic Movement', in T. Smail, A. G. Walker and N. G. Wright (eds), *Charismatic Renewal: The Search for a Theology* (London: SPCK, 1995), pp. 86–105.

Walker, D., *The Ministry of Deliverance* (London: Darton, Longman and Todd, 1997).

Waters, T., 'Maleficent Witchcraft in Britain since 1900', *History Workshop Journal* 80 (2015a), pp. 99–122.

——, 'Magic and the British Middle Classes, 1750–1900', *Journal of British Studies* 54 (2015b), pp. 632–53.

Webling, A., *The Two Brothers* (Leicester: Edmund Ward, 1948).

Webster, R., '"Did God Do That?": Common and Separating Factors of Eighteenth-Century Methodism and Contemporary Pentecostal and Charismatic Renewal' in R. Webster (ed.), *Perfecting Perfection: Essays in Honour of Henry D. Rack* (Cambridge: James Clarke and Co., 2016), pp. 208–32.

Wesley, J. (ed. N. Curnock), *The Journal of the Rev. John Wesley, A.M.* (London: Charles H. Kelly, 1909–16), 8 vols.

Westwood, J. and Simpson, J., *The Lore of the Land: A Guide to England's Legends, from Spring-Heeled Jack to the Witches of Warboys* (London: Penguin, 2005).

Wiles, M., 'Lampe, Geoffrey William Hugo', in *ODNB*, vol. 32, pp. 347–8.

Williams, C., *The Treatment of Insanity by Exorcism* (London: Ambrose, 1908).

Williams, O., 'Exorcising Madness in Late Elizabethan England: "The Seduction of Arthington" and the Criminal Culpability of Demoniacs', *Journal of British Studies* 47 (2008), pp. 30–52.

Williamson, F., *Social Relations and Urban Space: Norwich, 1600–1700* (Woodbridge: Boydell, 2014).

Wilson, M., 'Exorcism: a clinical/pastoral practice which raises serious questions', *The Expository Times* 86 (10 July 1975), pp. 292–5.

Woolley, R. M., *Exorcism and the Healing of the Sick* (London: SPCK, 1932).

Woolmer, J., *Healing and Deliverance* (London: Monarch, 1999).

Young, F., 'Catholic Exorcism in Early Modern England: Polemic, Propaganda and Folklore', *Recusant History* 29 (2009), pp. 487–507.

——, *English Catholics and the Supernatural, 1553–1829* (Farnham: Ashgate, 2013).

——, *A History of Exorcism in Catholic Christianity* (London: Palgrave MacMillan, 2016a).

——, 'Bishop William Poynter and Exorcism in Regency England', *British Catholic History* 33 (2016b), pp. 278–97.

——, *Magic as a Political Crime in Medieval and Early Modern England: A History of Sorcery and Treason* (London: I.B.Tauris, 2017).

NEWSPAPERS

Church Times
2 March 1917
8 May 1970
17 February 2017

The Guardian
5 December 1994

The Times
26 March 1975
27 March 1975
16 November 1985

TELEVISION DOCUMENTARY

The Power of the Witch: Real or Imaginary? (1971), youtube.com/watch?v=wi9pZEhNQvQ.

WEB SOURCES

Brandon, B., 'Symptoms of Spiritual Crisis and the Therapeusis of Healing', rcpsych.ac.uk/pdf/Symptoms%20of%20spiritual%20crisis.%20Beatrice%20Brandon.pdf.

'Diocese of Canterbury: Guidelines for the Ministry of Deliverance', canterburydiocese.org/media/forms/deliverance/guidelinesfortheministryofdeliverance.pdf.

'The Diocese of Exeter: Bishop's Guidelines for Ordained Ministry: Section 6 – Funerals and Other Pastoral Offices', exeter.anglican.org/wp-content/uploads/2014/10/funerals-and-other-pastoral-offices.pdf.

'Guidelines for the professional conduct of the clergy (Revised Edition) 2015', churchofengland.org/about-us/structure/general-synod/about-general-synod/convocations/guidelines-for-the-professional-conduct-of-the-clergy/guidelines.aspx.

'The House of Bishops' Guidelines for Good Practice in the Deliverance Ministry 1975 (revised 2012)', churchofengland.org/media/1734117/guidelines%20on%20deliverance%20ministry.pdf.

Inwood, R., 'Ad Clerum – Healing and Deliverance Ministry', southwell.anglican.org/wp-content/uploads/2014/07/Deliverance-jul14.pdf.

'The Merrily Watkins novels', philrickman.co.uk/merrily.

Index

Lightning Source UK Ltd.
Milton Keynes UK
UKHW022219071221
395227UK00007B/450

9 780567 692931